300 Best Aviation Web Sites
and 100 More Worth Bookmarking

More Aviation Titles from McGraw-Hill

The Illustrated Buyer's Guide to Used Airplanes, Fourth Edition
Bill Clarke

Airplane Ownership
Ronald J. Wanttaja

Aviation Computing Systems
Mal Gormley

The Aviation Fact Book
Daryl E. Murphy

Beyond the Checkride:
What Your Flight Instructor Never Taught You
Howard J. Fried

Flight Instructor's Pocket Companion
John F. Welch

Airplane Maintenance & Repair:
A Manual for Owners, Builders, Technicians and Pilots
Douglas S. Carmody

The $100 Hamburger:
A Guide to Pilot's Favorite Fly-In Restaurants
John F. Purner

300 BEST AVIATION WEB SITES

AND 100 MORE WORTH BOOKMARKING

By John A. Merry

McGraw-Hill

New York San Francisco Washington D.C. Auckland Botogá
Caracas Lisbon Madrid Mexico City Milan
Montreal New Delhi San Juan Singapore
Sydney Tokyo Toronto

Merry, John A.
    300 best avioation web sites: and 100 more bookmarking/by
    John A. Merry.
    p. cm
    Includes index.
    ISBN 0-07-134835-2
    1. Aeronautics—Computer network resources Directories.   2. Websites
    Directories. Title.
    TL563.5.M47 1999
    025.06'3877—dc21   99-29312
                                                                              CIP

McGraw-Hill

A Division of The McGraw·Hill Companies

    2 3 4 5 6 7 8 9 0 DOC/DOC 9 0 4 3 2 1 0 9

ISBN 0-07-134835-2

*The sponsoring editor for this book was Shelley Carr, the editing supervisor was
Frank Kotowski, Jr., and the production supervisior was Pamela A. Pelton.
Cover art and book design by Marla Meredith.*

It was set in Berkely.

Printed and bound by R. R. Donnelley and Sons Co.

McGraw-Hill books are available at special quantity discounts to use as pre-
miums and sales promotions, or for use in corporate traing programs. For
more information, please write to the Director of Special Sales, McGraw-Hill,
11 West 19th Street, New York, NY 10011. Or contact your local bookstore.

  This book is printed on recycled, acid-free paper containing
a minimum of 50% recycled, de-inked fiber.

The information provided and otherwise found in works mentioned here is
not valid for navigation or for use in flight. Always consult the relevant publications for current and correct information.

All brand names and product names used in this book are trademarks, registered trademarks, or trade names of their respective holders.

*Dedicated to Jerry and Susan. Their love of
fun, flying, and friends brightens the lives
of everyone they know.*

Contents

Army Aviation Directory

Aviation Business Center

Aviation Organizations and Associations

Pilot Resources

Flight Training and Flight Schools

Aviation Online Magazines and News

CONTENTS

Aviation Entertainment

Aviation Employment

Combing the Web for worthwhile aviation sites may leave you cringing at the clock. The limitless selection can easily be overwhelming, not to mention time consuming. Even fishing with your favorite search engine oftentimes reels in every site except the one you want. Enter *300 Best Aviation Web Sites . . . and 100 More Worth Bookmarking*.

This book is the second edition to its predecessor *200 Best Aviation Web Sites*. Besides the addition of 100 more fully reviewed sites, *300 Best Aviation Web Sites* now includes e-mail addresses, updated reviews to the last edition's sites, and two new categories: Flight Training & Flight Schools and Airlines.

The following pages represent over 5,000 hours of browsing and reviewing. Here you'll find award-winning sites ranging from aviation news to pilot resources, hand-picked by pilots for pilots. The book's purpose, of course, is to help you avoid a tedious cyber-hunt enroute to aviation's better Web sites. And, rest assured that the choosing was performed in a completely unbiased way. Nothing listed here appeared as a result of paid advertising or other favorable treatment. If we thought the site to be worthy of your time, we've included it.

Review Rating Criteria

As with most reviews, the author's subjectivity ultimately becomes the predominant rating criteria. However, knowing that wouldn't fly with most aviation enthusiasts, I've established a few more tangible guidelines against which *300 Best Aviation Web Sites* were judged:

Content: Did I uncover practical data and substance or a cesspool of typos and blurry plane pics?

Layout/Design: Was I bored to tearful yawns or mystically enthralled with site aesthetics?

Functionality: Is site navigation a frustrating maze of futility or a wondrous example of efficiency?

Overall Audience: Does the site offer benefits to twelve people or a million and twelve?

Scale:

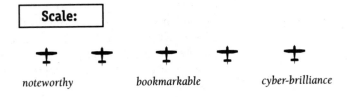

noteworthy *bookmarkable* *cyber-brilliance*

While each site's address and content has been checked (and rechecked), please bear in mind that addresses and page info may change or evaporate completely with time. It's simply the nature of the beast.

To keep up with aviation's dynamic sites, however, you are invited to check into *300 Best Aviation Web Sites'* Online Updates page for the latest in additions, deletions, and address (URL) changes. Stop in by pointing your browser to:

http://www.300bestaviation.com/bookupdates

Each of the 300 sites found in the book, as well as the 100 bookmarkable listings, will be continuously monitored for changes and reported to you via the Online Updates page. Whether you're having trouble accessing a site, or just want a list of site modifications, give the page an occasional visit. It may save you some frustration.

Whether you're new to the Web or surfer savvy, I can't stress enough the importance of using the most current version of your browser (see definition below). Today, Web design gurus pour over HTML code and graphics hoping to serve up a cutting edge experience for you—the aviation surfer. But, if you're flying under the hood with a rusty old browser, you probably won't see the visual treats or hear the roar of a biplane. In short, you'll miss out. My advice is to stay current by downloading the newest version on occasion. How do you know when a new version is out? Keep in touch with your browser's home page (http://www.netscape.com, http://www.explorer.com, etc.) or visit a browser news site like Browser Watch (http://browserwatch.internet.com). Then, simply download the newest version for free. Similarly, "plug-ins" (see definition below) and helper applications change too. Be sure to have the latest and greatest or prepare to forgo the true multimedia experience.

Although the following may be old news for seasoned surfers, new Internet users may appreciate a quick intro on Web browsing basics. If you fall into the rookie category, welcome to the Web.

First, some terminology:

Browser—A software program used to view and navigate Web pages and other information. The most popular browsers include Netscape Navigator and Microsoft Explorer. We recommend using the latest versions of either of these two browsers, as most Web sites are formatted specifically for them.

URL—A Uniform Resource Locator (URL), also referred to as a Web site address, points to a specific bit of information on the Internet. For example, "http://www.200bestaviation.com" is a URL.

Bookmarks/Favorites—Most browsers offer a convenient way of storing and organizing your favorite Web sites in the form of a "bookmark" or "favorites" index. Adding a site to a bookmark/favorites list saves you the effort of retyping the site's URL during future visits.

Plug-In—As you access some sites in this book, you may notice the need for "plug-ins," or helper applications, to run video or audio features on the site. When using the latest versions of Netscape Navigator or Microsoft Explorer, you'll discover most plug-ins are already installed. However, if you find you're lacking a specific plug-in, chances are you'll be able to download it free. Most Web sites will provide a link back to the plug-in download site.

Second, armed with the above knowledge you're ready to begin browsing. Simply type in the site address into your browser's location/address box and press "enter." Be sure to pay particular attention to any special characters or uppercase letters in the URL. To access each site, you'll need to type the address *exactly* as it appears in this book.

Third, be patient. Unforeseen forces sometimes determine your success at bringing up a site. It may be temporarily down. The actual communication lines may be jammed with too many users during peak times. Or, the site simply has withered away. Our advice? Try retyping the address another day, and move on to a site that does work.

So go on now, type, click, and bookmark.

Airlines

Airliners.Net

http://www.airliners.net

e-mail: admin@airliners.net

BRIEFING:

So you enjoy airliner photos? Try over 15,000 with Airliners.Net.

Fee or Free: Free. Just remember to register (also free). You'll see a personalized front page, newly added photos since your last visit, and e-mail notification of changes.

The Jumbo 747 overseeing your browsing options gives you perfect symbolism. Airliners.Net's photographic database and entertaining feature selections are enormous—almost exceeding gross take-off weight. My browser got a bit bogged down, but loading time is worth it. Really. Once you're into and out of ground effect the spectacular view takes shape.

Your first visual references begin with page design and organization. From the graphically spectacular main menu, site options are thoroughly summarized. Instant photo search capabilities, with basic or advanced option, uses simple category selectors and pull-down lists from which to choose. Side text menus even line the page perimeter with unlimited airliner factoids and picture options.

Next, begin sampling the nice variety of pages. Aircraft stats & history, aviation forum & live aviation chat are a good start. Move even further into the Lighter Side (funny aviation pictures with commentary), and a great aviation store for more airliner extras.

Lastly, the real behemoth may be found in Airliners.Net's inexhaustible database of over 15,000 photos. Yes 15,000. Give your search criteria or choose from many pre-defined sections: Our Best Shots, Classic Airliners, Military Aircraft, Special Paint Schemes, Accidents, Airport Overviews, Flight Decks, Air to Air, Aircraft Cabins, and more. Many more.

Swissair

http://www.swissair.com
e-mail: online form

BRIEFING:

This brilliant dissemination of Swissair info is ripe for a bookmark.

First a few of my Swiss favorites: chocolate, watches, skiing, and now Web perfection in the form of Swissair's cyber presence. Web-wise Swissair has incorporated all of my page design favorites juxtaposed with a team of navigational essentials. Text links, site map, and pull-down "pick" boxes join forces with a summarized menu of commonly used functions to tantalize world travelers with Internet bliss.

Content-wise, Swissair's travel guide is especially worthy of note. With its city tips and thoughtful destination data bank you become distinctly aware that Swissair is a prominent world carrier for a reason. Read on about places like: Amsterdam, Athens, Boston, Budapest, Hamburg, Lisbon, Osaka, Vienna, Zurich, and others. Even topics such as: Swiss tourism, exchange rates, railways, special interests (golf, youth, and families), and airport maps reward the viewer with useful and detailed insight.

Of course if you're more in the mood to skip the fluff, just go straight to Booking by Flights (thoughtful instruction provided if you need it), schedule information, arrival/departure information, or Qualiflyer personal account data.

So easy. So thorough. So convenient. So Swiss.

Free or Fee: Free.

Frontier Airlines

http://www.flyfrontier.com

e-mail: info@flyfrontier.com

BRIEFING:

Destination?
The new
Frontier.

Cyberspace—the new frontier for Frontier. Don't be confused. I'm not exploring the historical tribute to the Frontier of old—the airline that ceased operations in 1986 following its acquisition by Newark-based People Express. I'm inviting you to dabble online into today's Frontier Airlines, which lifted off again in 1995.

With its Denver hub Frontier Airlines shuttles folks east and west via wildlife-laden 737s and a clickable mouse. The latter's a bit less expensive, but its information is rich. A simple left-margin menu tells the story at a glance: hometown hospitality and straightforward style. Your simple selection guides you through the site's pages of: Going Places (a great clickable map used to check Frontier flight schedules and routes by date); News (plenty of press release-style company news listed by descriptive title); Talk to Us (many listed phone numbers—including those to make reservations, mailing address, and e-mail address); Guest Book; About Frontier; and Just for Fun (Frontier aircraft wallpaper to download—complete with simple instructions).

Remember, no online booking is available yet (as of review time). Don't worry, you won't even notice with such a smorgasbord of quality clicking at every turn.

Fee or Free: Free.

Hawaiian Airlines

http://www.hawaiianair.com

e-mail: webmaster@hawaiianair.com

RATING

BRIEFING:

A taste of tropical pleasures awaits the online browser here.

Yes I became tempted immediately. As soon as I reviewed the opening page's current Honolulu weather conditions (75.9°F), I was just about to book online. Reviewing a site like Hawaiian Airlines is probably not the best idea during a bitter cold winter morning. My weather woes aside, Hawaiian Airlines' site will warm anyone's online experience year-round.

Simplicity rules the Web wonders of the "Wings of the Islands." On loading, your first stop succinctly provides you with viewing itinerary options. "Reservations" prompts you through a series of well illustrated stops (the route map clearly breaks down the options and whets your appetite to get away). "Schedules" provides flight info for the six beautiful islands of Oahu, Hawaii, Kauai, Maui, Molokai, and Lanai. "Destination" info refreshes your memory of the pleasures of tropical bliss. "Services" makes known Hawaiian's stellar in-air and on-the-ground services.

Another convenient nicety is the listing of all pertinent company contact info at the bottom: corporate address, mailing address, phone, fax, e-mail, and special reservations phone numbers (if online booking's not for you).

Be sure to sign up for CyberPilot to get auto e-mail deliveries of new HawaiianMiles offers and other discounts. What more incentive do you need? Aloha!

Fee or Free: Free.

Midwest Express Airlines

http://www.midwestexpress.com

e-mail: none provided

BRIEFING:

A gutsy little
airline that
continues to
win awards in
"real life" and
now online.

No they're not a globally minded airline powerhouse. But, you'd never know it from their respectable Web site offerings. With flavor and flair Midwest Express Airlines makes its mark online with a surfer-friendly site. This Milwaukee-hub airline packs a resourceful punch with a barrage of electronic pages. Ease your seat back and join me for a recap.

Midwest Express carefully makes use of all your favorite navigation essentials: fancy buttons, simple text menus, quick searching, thorough site map, "top of page" returns, and embedded description links. But site mechanics alone does not earn mastery. The real mastery found here may be in the site's comprehensive info offerings. Get flight info (routes, schedules, destination info, fare quotes, vacation packages, and more); learn about the company; and check into frequent flyer info (current programs and promotions, member account info, enrollment, redeeming miles, and more). Or, be reassured with thorough description of outstanding services (dining, industry awards, maintenance & safety, aircraft statistics, seat map, and more).

Clever little extras pop up everywhere, like a fun Java map of cities when searching timetables. Click on the origin city, which will turn green. All dots representing cities served by your chosen departure point will turn blue. Just select a blue dot (city) to continue. Will the Web's multimedia magic never cease?

Fee or Free: Free.

Air France

http://www.airfrance.fr/en/
e-mail: online form

RATING

Finally a breath of fresh cyber-air, Air France's mega-site depository includes much more than the standard airline essentials. Yes, within its cool, European Web shell beats a more entertaining array of variety.

First, a confirmation on what you'd expect. Digesting schedules, booking, frequent flyer info, travel services, destinations, and Paris hub info fill the better part of a day. But, the beauty (besides subtly striking page design) lies in the extras. For example, you rarely find such a fascinating historical journey of an airline. And, Air France's will exceed your expectations. Turn the pages through 60 years of history, featuring an evolving fleet and emerging passenger service.

An equally entertaining feature not normally found in airline sites is a festivals directory based upon your travel dates. Browse through over 600 festivals, cultural events, and exhibitions in over 50 countries. Find event details on: world music, classical music, dance, jazz, rock & pop, theatre, exhibits, film, and parades. It's perfect for planning extra activities during your upcoming Air France trip.

Finally, don't miss the awe of an in-depth look at Concorde—the myth and reality.

Fee or Free: Free.

Continental Airlines On-Line

http://www.flycontinental.com
e-mail: online form

RATING

+ + +

BRIEFING:

Heavily "menu-ized," continental-size compilation of company offerings.

Nearing the point of over-organization, Continental's site gives you more menu options per square inch than any of its competitors. Their daily updated, Internet interface sports: top and bottom pull-down menus; "quick click" topic menus in the body; and icon-oriented button menus (also mirrored for top and bottom page use). Even the button-type menus have "flyover" sub-menus. So, if you find yourself lost at Continental Airlines On-Line, you probably shouldn't be handling a mouse in the first place. There's just no way to lose your way.

Deals fill the screen on start-up, as do a mega-site load of Continental info and options. If you're like me, and you prefer mini summaries before you click, try the site index. It's excellent. Then, get off the ground with resources like: real time flight information ("up to the moment" they assure), ticket purchasing online, OnePass frequent flyer promotions, products and services descriptions, Continental Magazine tease, Continental vacations packages, SkyMall catalog shopping, inflight services, and a healthy list of travel resources.

Oh, and don't leave without at least a click into the Destination Guide. It's pretty thorough.

Fee or Free: Free.

SkyWest

http://www.skywest.com

e-mail: info@skywest.com

BRIEFING:

High profile regional commuter arrives on the Web scene in style.

Over 800 daily flights to 65 cities in 13 western states and Canada. Now, you may add to the stats thousands of monthly "hits" to their SkyWest Web stopover. Popularity and name recognition are not strangers to SkyWest, even online. A key player as a regional connection airline for Delta and United, SkyWest dazzles Web travelers too with a site worthy of respect from the airline mega-site crowd.

Design is stellar, if not cutting-edge; menus and frames work with dexterity together; graphics, photos, and maps are easy to read; and helpful contact information is always within a click or two.

Whether browsing as a customer or more on a corporate level, SkyWest serves up equal portions of "five-plane" organization and quality information. For example, dipping into the customer-oriented pot of options, you'll find: flight reservations (links to Delta or United Online reservations), frequent flyer program info, route map, airport layout maps (Los Angeles, Portland, Seattle-Tacoma, San Francisco, and Salt Lake City), aircraft information (photos, QuickTime VR tours, technical info, seating charts, etc,), air cargo info, and customer service.

Fee or Free: Free.

Alaska Airlines/Horizon Air

http://www.alaska-air.com

e-mail: online form

BRIEFING:

Fully functional airline site with full service flair.

Functional, practical, and proficient seem to best describe not only the Alaska/Horizon Air Web site, but the entire operation in general. The company has obviously maintained its focus on efficiency and service with its dual airline (one company) online interface.

A simple, yet well-designed main page flashes your site choices in a no-nonsense manner. Quite frankly this site's built for speed. Mach II type speed. Top and bottom menu bars keep you comfortably focused while main body info fills the middle.

Currently serving cities in Alaska, Arizona, California, Idaho, Montana, Nevada, Oregon, Washington, Canada, and Mexico, Alaska Airline/Horizon Air satisfies your curiosity in travel info and trip planning with Web prowess. Flight schedules, downloadable timetable, online reservations, and flight status info will probably be your most popular choices. But, a huge section on mileage plan info may pique your curiosity. There's also a helpful trip planner, filled with info on travel resources, destinations, route map, and Q&A.

Yes, even this lower profile, big hearted company proudly pushes its own Web specials, e-mail announcement service, vacation packages, and mile deals. Click in and be pleasantly surprised.

Fee or Free: Free.

Northwest Airlines WorldWeb (NWA)

http://www.nwa.com

e-mail: online form

RATING

BRIEFING:

Northwest serves up a visual feast coupled with flawless navigation.

NWA's organization, style, and overall Web brilliance follows suit with a long list of online airline award winners. The site is structurally perfect, visually stunning, and thoroughly useful. NWA's WorldWeb encompasses everything the Web is supposed to do: inform, sell, and entertain.

Before I launch into the treasure chest of content, NWA's navigation demands some praise. While I've found most airline sites to be fairly clever with navigational elements, I must say that NWA's WorldWeb is flawless. Main content is divided into five major areas. Section menus will dim upon use. Or, track your site position by following upper left tabs. As you navigate, new tables will appear—highlighting the page you are on and illustrating the path used to get there. Clicking on a tab will return you to that page.

Oh, and there are many pages that warrant a second look. A TravelCenter makes the passenger's life easy with online reservations, future schedules, destination info, travel tips, and more. Products & Services teaches about on-board service info, gift shopping, etc. And, Vacation Packages tempt your thirst for really getting out and about.

Certainly there's much more. Read about everything site-wide in handy, summarized capsules.

Fee or Free: Free.

Trans World Airlines (TWA)

http://www.twa.com
e-mail: online form

RATING

+ + + + +

BRIEFING:

TWA—
Thoroughly
Wondrous
Airline site.

TWA: the mammoth of years past and the new vision that soars today shines in digitized delight online at twa.com. Such a Goliath among airlines, TWA could have opted for mega-site photos and larger-than-life graphics. Thankfully the reigns were taken by folks who aim to satisfy the browsing public. Photos, graphics, and menus retain perfectly understated balance. So, I won't need to summon the bandwidth police. In fact, load time with my average speed modem was surprisingly fast.

The contents you ask? A well-organized wealth of informational opulence awaits you. Through omni-present top and bottom menus you'll break into: schedules and reservations, frequent traveler information, info about TWA, getaway vacations, hot deals, airport information, travel agents area, passenger services, cargo services, and an outline of site contents.

Fee or Free: Free.

Air Canada

http://www.aircanada.ca/home.html

e-mail: online form

RATING

BRIEFING:

Yes, Air Canada excels with its flashy flair for flight info. But look deeper for some nice extras.

Yet again, when your aviation cyber searching turns up the hum drum, look to high-end airline sites to jazz up the viewing. And, Air Canada's cyber presence doesn't disappoint. Rather, this mega-airline stopover gleams with a shiny exterior. Whether you're French-fluent or English only, the cyber world of Air Canada is instantly at hand. Just point and click.

Wrapped up in a better-than-average package, the traditional airline elements line the pages. Schedules & reservations (cyber ticket office), traveler services (cool travel planning assistant, in-flight special services, in-flight entertainment, etc.), Aeroplan mileage info, vacation packages, and more make planning and preparation with Air Canada simple.

Traversing a bit off the main flight path, though, a few sparkling site specialties are worthy of note. First, a "what's new" teaser section will pique your curiosity with many tantalizing topics: from expansion of electronic ticketing to Aeroplan specials to e-mail special offers. Even check your Aeroplan balance online. Second, a schedule checking area makes planning your trip a snap—especially with thorough instructions and helpful hints. Finally, my personal favorite: the marvelously designed Skyriders Club page has fantastic online activities, coloring books, stories, and more for kids.

Fee or Free: Free.

America West Airlines

http://www.americanwest.com

e-mail: online form

BRIEFING:

Now boarding: efficient online reservations and deals, deals, deals.

Wheeling and dealing online, America West Airlines shows off its power for promotion with a site packed to the rafters with specials, vacation packages, double FlightFund mile deals, and more. Just scan the Highlights. The list of offers becomes so lengthy it's "scrollable." Handy summaries of each whet your penny pinching appetite, and text links fly you to more complete details.

Once your heart rate recedes from promotion overload, mouse over to the left-margin laundry list of site clickables. Online reservations, products & services, corporate information, vacation packages, travel agent-only info, and a site map tree provide a well rounded introductory itinerary.

Along with easy to read content, page mechanics fall into the exceptional variety. Main menu icons, text link back-ups, and concise summaries steer you properly and avoid the "wild goose chase" approach. Graphics and photos must be lean and mean because loading time is happily quick. The handy site map gives you an easy overhead view of everything. And, there's a load to digest.

Fee or Free: Free.

Virgin Atlantic

http://www.fly.virgin.com

e-mail: us.customer.service@fly.virgin.com

BRIEFING:

Living up to its name for style and service, Virgin's Web site doesn't disappoint.

Custom-tailored to region, your Virgin Atlantic online flight starts out smooth and ends even better. Pick your departure region—U.K. & N. Europe, Japan, Southern Africa, U.S.A., Australia, etc.—and move into a host of attractive options. Schedules and booking, services, news (in the form of company press releases), frequent flyer info, Meeting Place, and site search get you started.

More adventurous types will find themselves heading straight for the Vacations area. European vacation packages are many. Just scan the options of packages, lodgings, Steppin' Out Service, pricing, Virgin in London, and special offers.

Once you've selected a package and packed your bags, browse through their service classes: economy, premium economy, and upper class. Get the details and descriptions for each—even if you're just checking in on the treats of upper class. Hey, economy's just fine too. Find out here.

Fee or Free: Free.

American Airlines

http://www.aa.com

e-mail: webmaster@aa.com

RATING

BRIEFING:

Find booking, travel info, specials, and overall perfection here.

Only the truly Web-competent understand the merging of high-end design with day-to-day practicality. AA.com's Web presentation is so flawless you don't even realize its functionality. It's just naturally flowing. For example, the intro page spews organizational perfection with a full list of categorized sections. Each area then has its own pull-down sub-menu. The best part? Know what you're getting into ahead of time with brief summaries. Even if you get confused, which you won't, members and guests need only visit a well scripted help area, overflowing with tips and login instruction.

A sneak peek of clickable options include: news at American Airlines, travel planning (fare, gates & times, reservations, schedules) Aadvantage program info, programs & services (too many to list), and corporate info (job opportunities, etc.). Of course, like the others, AA.com promotes its specials. And yes, there's a long list of them. From "Today's Specials" through "Specials Information," this area alone prompts a bookmark.

The key to AA.com's site is becoming an Aadvantage member. With membership you'll gain access to the heart of the site's wealth: booking flights, making reservations, and managing your Aadvantage account. Sure, on a guest-only basis there's plenty to see and do. But, become a member for catch-all online participation.

Fee or Free: Free.

Southwest Airlines

http://www.southwest.com

e-mail: none provided

RATING

BRIEFING:

How novel: an airline with a bit of a sense of humor. Fun and practicality prevail here. It's a great way to fly.

In the spirit of fancy, fun-loving flair, the Southwest Airlines Home Gate sports an electronic ticket counter—sans the airport chatter and babies wailing. Even a clickable Herb Kelleher picture graces the "back wall."

All snickering aside, the visual counter interface is not only fun, it's easy to use. Steering away from multiple sub-menus and pull-down lists, the "counter" points you in the direction of a few major site resources. More comes in the form of text links below. Get travel facts, schedules, fares, and reservations by clicking the wall-mounted phone. Or just check schedules, destinations, and frequent flyer program info via counter displays and maps. A special offer banner leads you to Rapid Rewards, and a News bin holds the latest company press releases. If you're so inclined, a handy Resumes in-box is self explanatory for employment seekers.

Although the "ticket counter" method of navigation is simplistically whimsical, practicality prevails with an alphabetized table of contents. Get a summarized description and clickable links to everything site-wide. From a gallery of video and print ads to city information to shopping with SkyMall, over 50 different site areas are a click away.

Fee or Free: Free.

United Airlines

http://www.ual.com

e-mail: online form

Not one to be outdone by others who spin airline Webs, United checks in with a well designed (if award-winning) company presence. They've made excellent use of navigational niceties essential with sites this large. I found myself relying on convenient pull-down topic boxes, but a site map, site search, and link menus also guide your way.

Sure every traveler's whim is answered here. Whether it's reservations and planning, info at the airport, a tour of "in the air" services, Mileage Plus info (FAQs, summary, special offers, partners and program info), or even United's laundry list of services, chances are your questions will be answered online. The Upon Arrival area gleams with a wealth of informational riches for national, as well as international, travelers. Get a handy peek into: city guides, currency, visa/customs, embassies, foreign languages, baggage info, and weather.

If you're like me, you've made the decision to circumvent travel agents long ago and book flights directly online. Today's access to real-time fares and availability info is everywhere. And, of course, United is no exception. If you plan to book with United online, you'll need to register first. Then, you'll be on your way. Registering also entitles you to United's E-Fares.

Fee or Free: Free. Registration required if booking online.

British Airways (BA)

http://www.british-airways.com

e-mail: bafeedback@agency.com

RATING

BRIEFING:

Serving up more than just tea and crumpets, BA's online world is entrancing and useful.

You've got to have some pretty high-powered equipment to service the kind of artistry and volume found at British Airways online. They've obviously invested a bit into design talent as well. For someone like me who spends hours rummaging through hideously designed pages, a layout with real graphic design shines like an airport beacon in the fog. Photo usage, page presentation, database queries, and the like dance in perfect harmony site-wide.

The whole company's represented here one way or another. You get to choose how detailed or simplistic your BA site experience will be. Go quickly to four main topics: Flights (schedules & booking), Executive Club, On Holiday, or Worldwide (pick a BA Web site closer to home). Delve into a world of extraneous, yet interesting BA info. For, example, special offers, scrolling news and promotions (lots!), company info, great travel Q&As, and more fill your screen.

My favorite site stopover by far involves a tour through personalized travel miniguides. Whether it's Amsterdam, Zurich, or any of the 99 destinations in between, create your own custom-tailored travel guide based on your data input. Select dining, accommodations, language, price range, and sight-seeing preferences. A richly informative miniguide just spits out!

Fee or Free: Free.

Delta Air Lines SkyLinks

http://www.deltaairlines.com

e-mail: online form

RATING

BRIEFING:

Looking for
perfection
online? Delta's
just the ticket.

If it's possible to reach visual and organizational perfection in today's ever-changing Web world then Delta's done it. Although load time suffers slightly, you'll be happily clicking along nevertheless within the artfully designed realm of SkyLinks. Menus, Java scripts, pull-down boxes, help solicitations, and summarized text links form this virtual wonderland. Beauty, brains, and online booking—now that's euphoria.

If you're just browsing, not booking, you could spend forever reading and clicking through every resourceful page. Every nook and cranny offers some special or info tidbit on which to feast. Read through Delta Vacations for the latest in a multitude of vacation packages (including air, car, and hotel). Check out airport layouts to get a leg up on connections and parking. Look through Delta's destination maps. Or, find out when Aunt Tootie gets in by checking arrival/departure info. Of course, if you want to skip the glitz and info, jump straight to Reservations, Check Fares, and Buy Online. Oh, and if you're into SkyMiles, one click gets you into the pages to check your current balance. How close are you to earning free travel?

Fee or Free: Free.

US Airways

http://www.usair.com

e-mail: online form

RATING

BRIEFING:

An Envoy-class approach to airline Web presentation.

Mirroring their style in the air, US Airways shines online too with its catch-all TravelWorks info resource. Clever, clean, and concise, the site gives you the corporate looking professionalism you'd expect from US Airways. Loading is fast, options are clear, and menus are everywhere.

Your travel choices are many, but not so many that a day of clicking is consumed. Certainly the essentials are at the ready: online reservations booking, schedule viewing, company info, and Dividend Miles stuff. But, as expected you get a bit more with US Airways. Travel news keeps you current on company news and specials. Car and hotel booking is also conveniently clickable. And, extensive passenger info makes research a snap. Read about premium travel, consumer tips (good!), aircraft diagrams, airport maps, baggage requirements, and even the current movie guide for Overture (US Airways inflight entertainment system).

Another favorite most will appreciate may be found in Special Fare Opportunities. Get up-to-the-minute postings on special offers, special rates, group rates, shuttle fares, and E-savers (special discounted fares via e-mail).

Fee or Free: Free.

Airlines of the Web (AOW)

http://flyaow.com

e-mail: online form

BRIEFING:

Fancy airline-
only interface
combines info,
resources, and
reservations.

Brought to you by the capable folks at Internet Travel Network (ITN), which in itself is award-winning, Airlines of the Web is an ITN sub-site with loads of airline-online info. Just step into the well-thought-out terminal. Clickable sources for a variety of topics are all within mouse range. But don't worry, the intimidating volume of info behind the scenes is easily accessible with AOW's handsome interface.

Offering way more than just airline information, AOW seeks to become your primary center for reservations, frequent flyer info, and tips for airline travel. While visiting, however, I gravitated more to the seemingly limitless selection of airlines (actually about 500 world-wide) and the "Hangar's" directory.

To uncover your airline(s) of choice, start by selecting a region. Africa, Asia, Australia, Caribbean, Europe, Middle East, North America, or South America. Once a region is selected, your airline links unfold—be prepared for a long list. Some links provide handy notes that clue you in as to if the site is official, unofficial, and its language.

Tired of traversing airline sites? Skip to the aircraft specifications (over 100 aircraft detailed), manufacturers, virtual airlines, former airlines, and more.

Fee or Free: Free.

Cathay Pacific

http://www.cathaypacific.com
e-mail: online form

RATING

BRIEFING:

World-class world carrier knows what it means to be World Wide Web savvy.

I'd say service to 48 cities on five continents thrusts Cathay Pacific into "major carrier" airspace. As such, you'd expect a grand online adventure to whisk you and your mouse away to distant lands. Well, pack your bags before you log on because Cathay Pacific's Web wonders will sweep you up into its network of travel possibilities.

As sure as the world is round, Cathay Pacific casts a brilliant light on true Web style and artistry. The best part? Most who browse the pages won't even realize the stellar design and layout. They'll just happily click through each page with ease and satisfaction not realizing the underlying brilliance. For example, pages are uncluttered to the point of simple. Pull-down menus get you just about anywhere site-wide. And, all graphics, illustrations, and photos have been tastefully chosen with quick downloading in mind.

Content-wise, all of your air travel expectations will be met with the standard fare of: flight info, frequent flyer propaganda, cyber offers, destination info, aircraft seating and in-flight services, and more.

Fee or Free: Free.

AirTimes

http://www.airtimes.com

e-mail: psloan@airtimes.com

RATING
++

BRIEFING:

A thorough look
into the airline
world—past and
present.

Although its subtitle alludes to history, this airline-specific site pleasantly surprises with breaking news as well as historical highlights. You won't be "wowed" with design by anyone's standards, but the fantastic depth of info shines anyway. The archaic laundry list of hyperlinks almost seems apropos. A few "new" tags and links back to the top of the list comprise the only attempt at organization.

You may want to stick around for content, however. Updated weekly, you'll tap into current industry news as well as archived press releases. A smattering of online annual reports also peeks into the more recent trends and ramblings among the big jet pros. Then, reminisce with articles on airline history. Read about Transamerica Airlines Corporation (text and graphics from 1932). Or, delve into a detailed photo history of California's largest intrastate carrier—Pacific Southwest Airlines.

Get comfy here with a favorite beverage. The captain has turned of the "fasten seat belts" sign.

Fee or Free: Free.

Bookmarkable Listings

Airways Magazine
http://www.airwaysmag.com
e-mail: airways@nidlink.com
Current airline news, commercial air transport-related gifts, and printed magazine subscriptions available online.

Online Airline Phone Numbers Directory
http://www.citytravel.com/airphone.htm
e-mail: webmaster@citytravel.com
Long list of toll-free airline phone numbers sorted by name.

Airline Information On-Line
http://www.iecc.com/airline/
e-mail: airinfo@iecc.com
Answers to frequently asked questions about airline schedules, fares, reservations, and online travel agents.

Qantas Airways
http://www.qantas.com
e-mail: online form
Get online info for schedules, fares, holiday specials, and inflight shopping.

KLM Royal Dutch Airlines
http://en.nederland.klm.com
e-mail: online form
Book directly online, read about flight services, or get frequent flyer info.

Midway Airlines
http://www.midwayair.com
e-mail: comments@midwayair.com
Find flight schedules, special offers, aircraft info and destination highlights from this East Coast carrier.

Japan Airlines
http://www.jal.co.jp
e-mail: webmaster@jal.co.jp
Read a complete reference guide for international passengers as well as Japanese tourist information.

Singapore Airlines
http://www.singapore.com
e-mail: online form
This giant site features schedules & route map, company alliances, products & services, and other travel resources.

AirTran Airlines
http://www.airtran.com
e-mail: online form
Schedules, reservations, specials, and e-fares begin your AirTran online adventure.

American Trans Air
http://www.ata.com
e-mail: webmaster@ata.com
Lots of vacation packages, special fares, and general flight info is ripe for the clicking.

Canadian Airlines
http://www.cdnair.ca
e-mail: online form
Multilingual corporate info offering for reservations, time tables, destination profiles, and specials.

Pan Am World Airways
http://www.panam.org
e-mail: webadmin@panam.org
Historical perspective of Pan Am's aircraft, employees, and company.

Airjet Airline World News
http://AirlineBiz.com
e-mail: admin@AirlineBiz.com
Airline news, links, and gallery with free e-mail subscription service.

Aviation Directories

The Aviation Directory

http://www.aeroseek.com

e-mail: contact@aeroseek.com

RATING
✝ ✝ ✝

BRIEFING:

Good, solid aviation directory shines with substance, not style.

Billed as the Internet's "aviation only" search engine, The Aviation Directory screams mediocrity except for one sparkling savior: variety.

Yes, there are actually many aviation-only directories—all pretty good, some really good. But quantity, quality, and variety are the differentiating factors. Put aside this directory's garden variety design and open your mind to its labyrinth of categories. Nice, thoughtfully specific topics guide your direct course to: air carriers, aircraft acquisition, aircraft operation, aircraft specific (sites dedicated to specific aircraft), classifieds, databases, general aviation & sport aviation, images, publications, safety, and more.

Okay. I almost hear you asking, "yeah, but what about quantity in each category?" And, the answer is: sufficient, but not overwhelming. At review time about 2,000 site links graced The Aviation Directory's pages.

Top 5% sites (loosely described as "cool"), a nifty keyword search, and more round out your page options.

Fee or Free: Free.

FlightSearch

http://www.flightsearch.com

e-mail: comments@flightsearch.com

RATING

+++

BRIEFING:

Shining like a rotating beacon in fog, FlightSearch gives worthy pointers to aviation sites. But, you'll be impressed with the extras.

With FlightSearch your aviation Web location needs are met. But, its flair for extras keeps you coming back.

A nice, easy-to-use search box steers you toward their store of linked offerings. From adventures to airport restaurants to services, it's all here. Aircraft, airlines, getaways & resorts, and more contain a respectable variety of sites, but reach over to the right-hand menu and get a bit more for your browsing time. In the News stirs up a few current event articles from a variety of sources (CNN, ABC News, etc.). Read about stuff like: Lunar Missions and Airport Hacking by Teens. Then, introduce your kids to a friendly Web site created specifically for them, called PlaneKids. Or skip to FlightLink, which directs you to an interesting enterprise of aviation related free banner ad listing.

Finally, at the heart of FlightSearch's "Extras" menu, National Listing serves up a tasty array of nationwide flight instructor listings. This vast database catalogs instructors by name, city, state, type of instruction, or area code. Judging by the quantity of listing instructors, they're gaining some nationwide interest.

Fee or Free: Free.

FlyByWeb

http://www.flybyweb.com

e-mail: tschaeff@qcaccess.net

Tucked away near Davenport, Indiana, a couple of guys (one's a pilot, one's a Web guru) are spinning a pretty resourceful aviation web. FlyByWeb is the resulting product from "countless hours of research for the benefit of aviation enthusiasts everywhere." There's no question this compilation of categorized links did take some time. It also goes without saying that it certainly is a benefit to browsing aviators.

The simple, yet mildly appealing design is anchored by a heavily filled left-margin frame. Your menu options are many, so settle in with nourishment at the ready—you may be here awhile. Get to your aviation destination quickly with categories that are alphabetized and organized into sub-topics for fast searching. Keywords are highlighted in red, where applicable, to help expedite your search.

Although each category lacks volumes of listings, you will uncover variety and quality. Use the left menu bar to begin displaying your selections in the target (right) window. Find the good stuff in: airports, airlines, accident reports, aircraft sales, associations, employment, flight training, fun links, parts, professional services, software, and more.

Fee or Free: Free.

OpenAirNet

http://www.openairnet.com

e-mail: flymaster@openairnet.com

RATING

BRIEFING:

Good place to start for an aviation link search or finding a fun place to fly near you.

Whether searching for a Web destination or a favored fly-in, your resourceful friends at OpenAirNet have your best interests in mind. They do the searching (as do fellow flyers) and list the findings online. Specifically, you're invited to search the concise list of great aviation links. They've narrowed the Web's wonders to a grouping of categorized site stopovers: latest aviation news, miscellaneous aviation searching, weather, career, aviation goods, books & videos, photography, FAA, and aerobatics.

Equally concise, yet operationally perfect is OpenAirNet's use of simple design and flawless organization. Thankfully, they employ generous "white space," mostly text, a few photos, and easy site search engines. Just see for yourself. You'll quickly zip to a list of: fun places to fly by city and/or state; aviation events by city and/or state; or business, clubs, and associations by city and/or state. Adding an entry is free, so the site is sure to blossom quickly.

The only drawback? The Fun Places to Fly area needs to fill up a bit. Some states offer only a smattering of entries. Although growing, this great site depends on you. Hey, add an entry, it's free.

Fee or Free: Free.

Aeroguide

http://www.aeroguide.com

e-mail: info@aeroguide.com

RATING

† † †

BRIEFING:

Simple aviation directory taps into some stellar sites with ease.

Fee or Free: Free. Tap into Aeroguide for info on free Web pages for qualified organizations.

In my humble opinion, there just can't be too many aviation directories that give you a nice summary of page contents before you click. Sure this is a more time intensive way of setting up a directory-type site, but time conscious surfers appreciate it. What's better, Aeroguide combines its thoughtful link summaries with simply perfect page presentation.

The options aren't many at first. FBO listings, aviation books (via Amazon.com), free listing information, and aviation links might seem too simplistic for a directory. But, therein lies the beauty. So often missing the point, other mega directories confuse and disorient the casual aviation surfer. Aeroguide breaks through the thick fog and identifies quality aviation sites of interest to us pilot types. Once into the link lists, your options increase because there are quite a few sites to visit. Clickable FBOs seem to cover the country, from Adirondack Regional Airport to the Aero Centre in Kansas City to Winston Field FBO Services in Snyder, Texas. Similarly, the long list of other aviation links comes fast and furious. Aviation, manufacturer, and weather links fill your screen with quick word-only links and considerate before-you-click summaries.

Rising Up Aviation Resources

http://www.risingup.com

e-mail: online form

BRIEFING:

Yes the directory's good, but the extras keep you coming back.

Like a hot mountain thermal, Rising Up Aviation Resources lifts the link list directory into a new dimension. Sure the aviation links are here, carefully categorized and subcategorized into a list of clickable summary descriptions. Flawless by directory standards, it's fast, accurate, informative before you click, and maneuverable. But, the extras push Rising Up into the elite hangar of award winners. Why? Because it employs that award-winning team of: ease of use, speed, and clean layout. Add in some extras that aren't always found at directory sites, and you've got yourself a bookmark addition. Quick top-story, aviation-specific news links take their place on the start-up screen, as do discussion forums, airplane performance specs, FARs online, and practice FAA tests.

Rising Up's main reason for success, comprehensive directory info, earns accolades for its many levels of sub-topics and essential summary descriptions of each site—a must for the time conscious browser. Current main topics which are further broken down include: aircraft related, airlines and carriers, associations, education and training, government, military, pilot resources, sport aviation, and more. Searching, top site lists, random link picks, and adding a link are equally informative.

Fee or Free: Free.

4Aircraft.com

http://www.4aircraft.com

e-mail: info@4internet.com

```
RATING
+ + +
```

BRIEFING:

4Aircraft.com joins a host of other topic specific Web guides from the people at 4Internet.com.

A specialty Web guide from the 4Internet.com Network, 4Aircraft.com is exactly what its name implies—a jumping off point to aircraft-related sites. While its supersonic loading speed will surprise you, its related aviation sister sites will delight you. When you're through scanning the aircraft-specific stuff, stroll over to the equally enriching sites of: 4Airinfo.com, 4Airline.com, 4Charter.com, 4Destinations.com, 4Pilots.com, and 4Travel2.com.

With sparkling clean page presentation, you're aircraft-related options become crystal clear. For example, links you may find under "vendors" include: Corporate Aircraft Turnkey Services, Aircraft Are Us, Wayfarer Aviation, Van Bortel Aviation, and more. Under "publications & associations" expect to find stuff like: National Business Aviation Association, Scramble Magazine, Aircraft Owners & Pilots Association, Sport Aviation, and more. "Information & services" promotes sites such as: Garret Aviation, NOAA's Aircraft Operations Center, Duncan Aviation, and more. You get the idea. Lots of links can be found for aircraft-inquiring minds.

Fee or Free: Free.

Aerospace Mall

http://www.aerospacemall.com

e-mail: online form

RATING
+++

BRIEFING:

Aerospace Mall opens its cyber doors to linked resources and information.

Different from a real-life mega mall, Aerospace Mall makes shopping for aviation-related information easy— and you don't even need to find a parking spot. Although buying and selling is not the focus of this mall, information exchange is. The mall directory gets you to your topic of choice quickly with no crowds or waiting.

Although some superfluous stuff floats around in the mall, of real interest is the industry news and the mall directory. Sure, if you're looking at significant ground time, you can browse through the corporate profile, a free hit counter, games, and more. But, the good stuff, the meat of the mall, is in information.

Stop into the directory for pointers to: aircraft, airlines, industry news, services, space, and suppliers (links to the vast Aerospace supplier network).

Fee or Free: Free.

Smilin' Jack

http://www.smilinjack.com

e-mail: jackirwin@smilinjack.com

RATING
✝ ✝ ✝

BRIEFING:

A quality
aviation/airline
directory that
keeps you
"smilin'."

Thoughtfully void of giant pictures and silly graphics, this sleek aviation directory creates minimal drag and maximum lift. As noted on the page itself, it was designed for easy loading and navigation. A simple menu guides you into efficiently organized content for: airlines (a huge list of airline links), fun flying (hyperlinks to popular sites), servers (more links—mostly directory sites), airports (comprehensive list of major international stuff), shopping, home pages (miscellaneous smattering of favorites), and weather (over 31 sites make you weather wise).

By the way, in case your inquisitive mind really wants to delve into the background of Smilin' Jack, here's the scoop: he was a newspaper cartoon character created by Zack Mosley that ran from 1933 through 1973.

Fee or Free: Free.

Aviation Internet Resources

http://AIR-online.com

e-mail: online form

RATING

BRIEFING:

Aviation subject searching doesn't get much better than this—really!

Tired of wading through unproductive online searches that cut into flying time? Well, roll your clicker into this breath of fresh air for to-the-point info. The folks at Aviation Internet Resources invite you to simply enter some pointed keywords for aviation-only database searches.

The efficiently designed index page employs conveniently clickable topics for: airlines, airports, photographs, message forum, aviation multimedia files, aviation news sources, daily link news, and more.

If you're a traveler (hey, you are an aviation enthusiast...), I urge you to sample the Internet Travel Network online reservations system—it's well done and free! Take a trip through the online demo to discover: a secure online reservations system, low fare search mechanism, traveler's profile feature, and more.

Fee or Free: Free.

Captain Bob's Pro Pilot Page

http://www.propilot.com

e-mail: bob@propilot.com

```
RATING
┼┼┼┼
```

BRIEFING:

A simple, easy-going collection of aviation stuff for your viewing and listening pleasure.

Captain Bob's Pro Pilot Page isn't about giant, slow loading plane pics. Nor is it particularly fancy with modem-stalling graphics. It is, however, a solid, simple resource for pilots and aviation enthusiasts. Period.

Captain Bob (a California captain for Skywest Airlines), with his cyber enthusiasm, has amassed a nice collection of aviation-related links and resources. The best parts? The page doesn't take forever to load, it's free of memberships, and all the hyperlinks seem to work without fail.

When you can catch your breath from all those giant, time-wasting aviation sites, check in here for: hordes of aviation links, airline/airport-specific sites, weather resources, a pilot bulletin board that's full of entries, an interesting commentary on regional airline careers, background on Captain Bob, lots of live video cams of Doc's FAR Forum, and more.

My personal favorite: the live links to DFW Air Traffic Control and Chicago Air Traffic Control. To tune in, though, you will need a RealAudio player or equivalent. Most newer browser versions have one built right in.

Fee or Free: Free.

DeltaWeb Airshow Guide

http://www.deltaweb.co.uk/asgcal

e-mail: webmaster@deltaweb.demon.cu.uk

RATING

✝ ✝

BRIEFING:

Conscientiously updated worldwide guide to airshows.

As noted in the Guide's text descriptions, airshows by their very nature are apt to change—sometimes radically—at the last minute. DeltaWeb's Airshow Guide does a great job combining current updates with well oiled page organization.

The calendar is arranged by region (as of review time regions include the UK, North America and Europe, and the rest of the world) and further subdivided into months. Simply find your region and pick a month. Airshows will be listed in date order with location, short descriptions, and contact info. For example, a June airshow listing might read: "Saturday 7, Scott AFB, Illinois. HQ Air Mobility Command Base Open House and Airshow USAF 50th and Salute to the Berlin Airlift, Thunderbirds and Golden Nights. Tel: USA 618-256-1663."

Navigation throughout is painless. From each page additional months for the same region are readily available via your clicking fingertips. Conversely, other regions for a chosen month are standing by simply with a click of the regional icon.

Fee or Free: Free.

The American & Canadian Aviation Directory Online

http://www.infomart.net/av

e-mail: acadir@infomart.net

RATING

✝✝✝

BRIEFING:

Complete American and Canadian aviation site directory that lists, searches, and categorizes without charging a penny.

Bursting at its cyber-seams, the American & Canadian Aviation Directory is a one-stop resource with over 32,000 aviation companies listed. Conveniently available via a custom site searching tool, this aviation-only smorgasbord launches you into online aviation with only a couple of clicks.

Once you've maneuvered around the site's miscellaneous banners, your search form should begin to come into view. Simply enter any or all pertinent query data—from category to telephone number—and search. The directory does the rest. After it chunks through a fairly complete database on the other end of your modem, up pops your results. Category curious? Here are the highlights (with a lot of other stuff in between): aircraft charter/non-scheduled air transportation; aircraft dealers and brokers—retail; airports, flying fields, and airport terminal services; flight training, airports and aircraft maintenance, aircraft finance, aircraft storage; and more.

Itching to get your own aviation site noticed? Add your own Web site address and company details here—it's free. Hey, when did you last read the words "free" and "aviation" in the same sentence? That's what I thought. Take advantage!

Fee or Free: Free.

AirNemo

http://www.geocities.com/CapeCanaveral/4285

e-mail: airnemo@geocities.com

RATING

+ + +

BRIEFING:

An airline-info diamond in the rough that's hard to find using traditional search engines. You'll be glad I did the digging.

It's never late. Departures are always on time—24 hours a day. You won't even need to sprint to the gate. Just grab a mouse and settle into a first-class seat. Destination? AirNemo—The Best Links to Airline Sites. Dedicated to the air transportation industry, AirNemo boasts a knowledgeable site author behind the scenes who works for an international airline in Brussels, Belgium. As such, you might have guessed French descriptions are conveniently standing by if English won't do.

Stylishly unobtrusive graphics and icons dominate the visual horizon, while excellent organization makes for frustration-free navigation. Look for convenient site codes like "new" flags, "official/unofficial" designations, and more. And, tying the pages together with invisible packing tape is a nice omni-present, bottom-page frame menu.

At first glance, you may think that airline links and stats make up the entire site contents. While it's true, you'll find commercial aircraft characteristics about the B747-400, A340-200, and MD-95, and others, I urge you to dig deeper. The corporate aircraft characteristics, acronyms, conversion tables, links, sites, and codes are fascinating. Even if you disregard all of the above recommendations, do tap into the weekly Air Bulletin. It's simply a well done online gem for aviation, air travel, and related issues.

Fee or Free: Free.

Aviator's Reference Guide

http://www.phd.nl/aviation

e-mail: aviators.reference.guide@earthcorp.com

BRIEFING:

Unprecedented aviation searching tool devoted to an earth-shattering list of reference links.

It's such a simple aviation searching breakthrough. Yet, the Aviator's Reference Guide seems to be the pioneer. What is this simple, yet overlooked aviation Web wonder? It's an omni-present menu bar at the top of your screen used to quickly move between aviation topics of interest. Once you've chosen and clicked into an aviation reference link, such as N-registered Aircraft or The Airman's Information Manual, the reference topic menu stays with you wherever you go.

Always at hand, the unobtrusive bar menu takes up almost no screen space, but speeds searching time 100-fold. Done working with the Airport Data by Name/Code Query? Move on to, say, Aviation Headline News by clicking the pull-down, quick-link list of topics. If needed, "back" or "forward" options are also at the ready.

Okay, the searching tool is cool, but does the Aviator's Reference Guide contain the juicy aviation data you're always craving? You be the judge. Tap into: Airport Web Sites, The FARs, Meteorology Guide, Weather Abbreviations, Pilot Air News, Professional Pilots Rumor Network, Airline Directory by Country, Pilot Supplies, and way more topics than I have room to list.

Fee or Free: Free.

VirtualAirlines.com

http://www.virtualairlines.com

e-mail: none provided

RATING
++

BRIEFING:

**A handy hub
dedicated to the
fanciful world of
virtual airlines.**

New and needed as a central virtual airline hub, VirtualAirlines.com boldly presents its "gateway to the virtual airline world." With the virtual airline (VA) industry evolving into a complex maze of airlines and offerings, VirtualAirlines.com's gateway makes the search for VA-related companies and news an easy one.

The popular business of running a virtual airline involves flying routes, following procedures, promotion, and more. Without the expertly organized guide of VirtualAirlines.com, the pilots, operators, and passengers would find themselves hopelessly lost.

Brushing under the tarmac a few description typos, the site expertly organizes and informs its stopover surfers with brevity and style. Aesthetics, in the form of well-used graphics and layout add to the experience. But, at the core, the airline menu ultimately gets you to a huge list of VA airline links. Other clickable options are: VA News, Organizations, Team One, Discussion, and more.

Visit VirtualAirlines.com. There's no waiting. The terminal parking's free. And, the flights are always on time.

Fee or Free: Free.

SpaceZone

http://www.spacezone.com

e-mail: member@spacezone.com

RATING

+ + + + +

BRIEFING:

A masterful mix of multimedia gizmos and futuristic design for space-age enthusiasts.

Almost as infinite as its subject, the SpaceZone site touches down upon an unending collection of goodies. News, events, history, and education certainly create a solid core. But, the true site mission revolves around a multimedia mix of unearthly content and out-of-this-world presentation. Contained within an electrifying display of design, fun gadgetry includes live NASA audio/video and coverage of space-related news, events, missions, and more. The true gravity of this site's excellence takes hold with topics like MIR Space Station news, NASA Television updates, and Hall of Exhibits. Get the latest headlines or view the most recent series of video. For an uninterrupted experience, though, be prepared with your multimedia browser plug-ins of: VDOLive Player, RealAudio, and QuickTime (or their equivalents). Not plug-in savvy? Don't scrub the launch. SpaceZone conveniently offers the downloading links— remember they're free.

Once you're up on the most recent reports and rendezvouses, go back a few light years into a complete look at space history. With stunning visual images and rare NASA footage, SpaceZone captures the excitement of exploration. Get space privy with astronaut biographies, space history timeline, mission footage & photographs, personal accounts, and planetary probes.

Fee or Free: Free.

This heavenly compilation is enough to make you weightless with space-driven ecstasy. If the page design doesn't launch you, the content will.

Russian Aviation Page

http://aeroweb.lucia.it/~agretch/RAP.html

e-mail: agretch@aeroweb.lucia.it

Getting globally gregarious, I've accidentally stumbled across one of the world's most exhaustive informational sites on the Web today. The Russian Aviation Page is utterly bottomless in depth and pleasantly surprising in breadth.

Faster than a MiG-21 flyby, a flurry of well designed aviation info bursts onto your screen from the moment you type the address. Even if Russian aviation stats and features aren't high on your bookmark list, I nevertheless encourage a visit. There's news, Russian aviation FAQs, museum review, digital movies, image archive, monthly Russian aviation trivia, and countless links.

Although page contents are carefully arranged and presented with award-winning style, there's almost too much to digest in one modem visit. Plan accordingly. Multiple menus, helpful search engines, and "new/ update" tags offer the best assistance as you maneuver through this Russian wonder.

Skimming the Soviet surface, some must-see features include: chronology (development of the aviation industry in Russia and Soviet Union: 1916–1946), Soviet version of Top Gun, Soviet Superfortress—the Tu-4 Story, and the many downloadable movies.

Intrigued by Soviet sites? Researching Russian aviation? Stow away on a Tu-142 and join other enthusiasts here.

WWW.NOTAM.COM

http://www.notam.com

e-mail: webmaster@notam.com

RATING

BRIEFING:

Interested in hang-gliding, commercial aviation, and general aviation? Here's your one-stop shop.

OK, it's a little bit all over the map. Smooth out your sectional and plan a course through this diversified directory. Tap into airports, airlines, classified ads, career, flight sim, general aviation, news, supplies, weather, and more. Then, stray from the straight and narrow with ultralights, microlights, hang-gliding, and para-gliding.

For those looking for more one-on-one connections, your clickable choices include: a huge variety of newsgroups, penpals, resume connection, corporate aviation, resume exchange, discussion forums, chat room, and post office.

Kick your feet up and explore here—there's something for everyone.

Fee or Free: Free.

AERO.COM—Future of Aviation

http://aero.com

e-mail: none provided

RATING
✝ ✝ ✝ ✝

BRIEFING:

Have patience while loading— a worldwide reference resource of magazines, newspapers, and newsletters are worth the standby time.

Yes, you'll have to wait a few seconds for the main menu to load—but it's worth it. This nice little directory of links features a couple of extras you wouldn't normally find: ballooning, parachutes, and a helicoptorial, for instance. Step into On-line Reading for an eye-opening list of magazines, newspapers, and newsletters. The AERO.COM Departments Directory features a fairly comprehensive topic list of: art/photography, experts page, research center, flight planning, flying shoppe, museums, news, organizations, and more.

You can also tap into the FAA Online for *NorCAL, SoCAL, Hi Desert Airman, Pacific Island Flyer,* and The Aviation Yellow Pages.

Fee or Free: Free. Get on their mailing list for updates.

TOTAVIA–Aviation Search Engine

http://www.totavia.com

e-mail: admin@totavia.com

RATING
+++

BRIEFING:

Nifty little directory site is a Canadian aviation catch-all.

Canadian? Cool. Brought to you by the folks up north, TOTAVIA gives you a compact site of variety. You'll run into stuff like: aviation news, C-number search, new aviation mall (a few items as of review time), photos, and weather. Highlights include: Canadian airshows online, as well as links to U.S. & U.K. events and airshows; aviation forums and online chatting; and a huge photo archive comprised of individual collections.

Compensation for the dizzying array of choices comes in the form of handy navigation. A great search engine, links with descriptions, and pull-down menus help unleash the overwhelming volumes of Canadian aviation info.

Fee or Free: Free.

The Air Affair

http://www.airaffair.com

e-mail: wingnut@airaffair.com

RATING

╪ ╪ ╪

BRIEFING:

An online directory that gives you stunning efficiency by people who know what they're doing.

It's always refreshing to find an aviation site that truly has your interests in mind. The Air Affair does have the news, photos, links, and event listings that most "e-zines" have. But once you begin maneuvering through the selections, you notice the distinct difference of complete organization and speed. Put another way, VORs work fine most of the time, but it's nice to just punch the GPS a few times and get to your destination with ultimate ease. The Air Affair features: designed to be browser independent (nice); lack of frivolous graphics (not necessarily a beautiful piece of Web art—but it's fast); thoughtful searching engines for fuel prices; local flight training locator; and well-thought-out page navigational aids.

Bookmark this site for the ultimate in: events, aviation fuel prices, aviation library, flying destinations, flight training locator, other aviation Web sites, Ask Propellerhead, and photo gallery.

Fee or Free: Free.

Landings

http://www.landings.com

e-mail: landings@landings.com

BRIEFING:

Award-winning directory/ database for every aviation subject imaginable.

Dubbed "aviation's busiest cyber-hub," Landings guides you into a huge, expertly maintained collection of info goodies. Sophisticated search engines move you through FAA and Canadian regulations, AIM, the pilot/ controller glossary, service difficulty reports, airworthiness alerts, NTSB briefs, N-numbers, the FAA Airman Database, airman knowledge test info, and more. There are good links all over the place. Directory subjects include: aerobatics/flying, aircraft sales, aircraft-service/ parts, manufacturers, airlines, airports, aviation BBSs, aviation images, aviation news groups, avionics, companies, flight schools/FBOs, flight planning, general aviation, GPS/technologies, hang-gliding/paragliding, helicopters/gyrocopters, homebuilding, military, museums/history, publications, soaring, travel tours, and worldwide weather links that would leave goose bumps on a meteorologist.

The best part of this enormous informational grab bag is at-a-glance navigation. You'll find the concise "front page" offers news and quick-click menu categories. Check in here often. They maintain and update regularly.

Fee or Free: Free, but do sign the log book for special offers and invites.

The Aviation Home Page

http://www.avhome.com

e-mail: garret@avhome.com

RATING
+ + + + +

BRIEFING:

One click and you'll see why it's an award-winning aviation directory. Intelligently organized categories are completely searchable. It easily speeds you to your destination.

Just when you thought there were enough aviation directories... surprise! Here's another one. But, this award-winning site is simple and searchable. Completely redesigned and current, the Aviation Home Page gives you a nice summary BEFORE you click on subjects. Great idea—I wish more directories made it this easy. Sift through: airlines and airports; clubs, organizations, and companies; academies, universities, flight schools, and FOBs; federal and military resources; newspapers, magazines, events, and museums; flight simulation; art, photography, and poetry; weather, meteorology, and satellite images; others & miscellany; and more!

Before departure be sure to look into their Select Sites that focus on the better aviation sites. Just select a category and find your favorite.

Fee or Free: Free.

AirNav

http://www.airnav.com

e-mail: pas@airnav.com

RATING

✦ ✦ ✦ ✦

BRIEFING:

A virtual smorgasbord of free airport, navigational fix, and fuel data.

OK. Enough flying frivolity. Let's get down to some serious navigational aids. AirNav pulls critical flight planning data out of cumbersome FAA publications and displays it on a virtual silver platter. Free and at your fingertips, you'll breeze through current facts, figures, and frequencies. Click on Airport Info for an amazing array of searchable airport data (way more than what you would find in the Airport and Facilities Directory). Navaid Info gets into the nitty-gritty about radio navigation (VORs, NDBs, TACAN, marker beacons, etc.). Fix Info provides enroute fixes, airway intersections, and waypoints ("From AAAMY to ZZAPP"). Then, figure in your pit stops with the Fuel Stop Planner.

It's a well-organized site, to begin your well-organized flight planning.

NOTE: It's important to remember that info contained here is NOT valid for navigation or for use in flight. It is simply provided as a tool. Use data at your own risk.

Fee or Free: Free.

E-Flight Center

http://e-flight.com

e-mail: editors@e-flight.com

```
RATING
+ + +
```

BRIEFING:

Originally flight simulation-related. A new look, however, reveals good commercial and private aviation news and info.

At first glance, E-Flight might seem a tad scattered—there's a lot of stuff dedicated to news, reports, and articles. Commercial and private aviation news, in the form of features and current events, abounds too. But before scanning your bookmark list, grab your mouse and stay awhile. The current events are worth reading; the latest and greatest aircraft are profiled; there's vast amounts of airport info; and yes, a pilot's discussion lounge. Under the Flight Sim area you'll find excellent, in-depth reviews on simulator add-ons and related products (example screen shots give you a heads-up on product quality). The World section gives you an international list of aviation's interesting sites—most with descriptions.

Step into the E-Flight Center with coffee in hand, a mouse on the pad, and flight simulator questions in mind. Have a nice flight.

Fee or Free: Free. You'll need to initiate the password procedure to contribute in the pilot's lounge.

Cyberflight

http://www.access.digex.net/~ooblick/cyberflight.html

e-mail: ooblick@access.digex.net

RATING
✈ ✈ ✈

BRIEFING:

A Maryland-based, East Coast directory site that's in complete disarray. The redeeming quality? It's roll-out-of-your-chair funny.

Where to start describing Cyberflight... Um, it's an autobiographical diary of perilous cross-country expeditions and a hodgepodge of links (some even non-aviation related). Toss into the cyber-blender a little sarcasm mixed with rambling commentary, and you've got an amazingly entertaining online place to visit. Don't forget to check out the embedded photos—they're a riot as well.

Once you cut through numerous solicitations for "lots of money" (donations, I guess), you'll learn where to fly to food; find "cool" airports; find what's new at Cyberflight; learn to fly; shop; learn about aviation weather; and stumble across a host of miscellaneous stuff in Various & Sundry.

Although there's actually some good info here, it's a great place to visit for some old-fashioned hysterical high jinks.

Fee or Free: Free.

R/C Web Directory
Master List of All Sites

http://www.towerhobbies.com/rcwmaster.html

e-mail: info@towerhobbies.com

RATING

BRIEFING:

Not pretty, but you'll find pages and pages and pages of remote control aircraft links. Not sure where to find radio-controlled (r/c) info? Start here.

During your initial visit, you'll just have to trust me that every radio-controlled aircraft link is here. This "old-style" laundry list of links does have everything—it's just painful to sift through it all. Frequent visitors may want to rely on the "new" tags for the most recent additions.

Loosely organized by headings, you'll find r/c links to: aircraft info and files; airplane-oriented sites; sailplane-oriented sites; helicopter-oriented sites; r/c clubs and organizations (broken down by state/country); r/c manufacturers & suppliers; r/c magazines; and miscellaneous sites.

Have your favorite beverage and snack standing by, you'll be here awhile if you're into r/c stuff. It's just a mind-boggling, grocery list of r/c that would cause an enthusiast to hyperventilate.

FYI: Although mostly r/c aircraft, you'll need to sidestep a few boats, cars, trucks, and other inferior vehicle categories.

Fee or Free: Free.

Charlie Alpha's Home Page

http://www.hiway.co.uk/aviation/aviation.html

e-mail: chris@inform.hiway.co.uk

RATING
†† ††

BRIEFING:

Bravo to Charlie Alpha for his diligence in promoting UK/ Europe flying. It's quite simply the UK's home base home page.

I recommend a stopover here for jumbled, all-over-the-place, punctuation-less brilliance. Granted, its limited scope emphasizes general aviation in the UK. A few things, at the time of review, were a little lean on info (give him time). But sidestepping the landmines unearths some glimmering gems. For example, you'll find *Pilot* magazine's link here (mostly UK, but some articles pertain to all pilots); events; associations; Charlie's Chat (online forum); great conversion tables (demystifies pressure, speed, temperature, time, volume, weight, and others); weather info; aviation humor; a growing list of UK pilot e-mail addresses; a long list of UK aviation trade pages; and lots of quality links. If you are interested in UK/Europe flying, there's enough knowledge, resources, and perspectives here to burn the better part of a day.

Fee or Free: Free.

AeroLink

http://www.aerolink.com

e-mail: info@aerolink.com

RATING

BRIEFING:

An award-winning global info-source that overflows with clickable mastery.

Fashionably designed and desperately needed, AeroLink really shines with its well-oiled search engine machinery. Peer into its linked offerings, and you'll get goose bumps over its simple, yet practical efficiency.

Four menu options provide clickable doorways into this aviation "link farm:" Links, QuickSearch, Add One, and About AeroLink.com. (First-timers may want to check into About AeroLink.com before jumping into the list of hyperlinks.) Major search categories in which you'll find yourself pleasantly inundated include: academia, air carrier-cargo, air carrier charter, aircraft operators, airports, aircraft maintenance, associations, general/sport aviation, military/defense, piloting, publications, rotary wing, safety, weather, and many more.

Next, step into the specific subcategory. Yes, the refined searching is endlessly exhaustive. Finally, for adventurous surfers who happen to have their own aviation-related home page, Add One does just what it says—easily.

I know. You're thinking no site can be this good. Well, just type in the address and thank me later.

Fee or Free: Free.

Aero Web:
Aviation Enthusiast's Corner

http://aeroweb.brooklyn.cuny.edu
e-mail: air-info@brooklyn.cuny.edu

Meander through the contents and you'll uncover this site's reason for being: variety. Although it's pleasant graphically, you'll really appreciate the nice smattering of useful information. Maintained by the hardworking volunteers at Brooklyn College, categories include: a museum index by location; an aircraft locator by type and manufacturer (here you'll find a long list of aircraft with some combination of descriptions, performance, specs, and museum display location); an air show location and performance index; air shows by month; aviation history features; aviation records; some local New York stuff; and more.

Even while skipping among Aero Web's offerings, you'll never lose your place—thanks to handy page menu headers. So, let loose and have some fun here. True enthusiasts will learn something.

Fee or Free: Free.

Women in Aviation
Resource Center

http://www.aircruise.com/wia
e-mail: hmh@women-in-aviation.com

RATING
✝ ✝ ✝

BRIEFING:

This female-only forum opens the door into a world of women-in-aviation info.

With similar veracity as Amelia Earhart, the Women in Aviation site sheds important light on resources that might have appeared dim. This site firmly establishes an educational link to seemingly hard-to-find resources, such as: books, education and training, mailing lists, museums, networking online, organizations, publications, upcoming events, videotapes, women-in-aviation in business, and more.

Cleanly arranged and quick to access, this cyber-forum makes networking convenient. There's a list of women-in-aviation contacts, complete with titles and e-mail accounts. Or, participate in open discussions with the site's online forum. Whether you're here to browse or choose interactive involvement, straightforward directions and descriptions abound.

Fee or Free: Free.

Bookmarkable Listings

FBO-Aviation
http://www.fbo-aviation.com
e-mail: jda@ecmis.net
Many FBO Web site links, as well as a more complete link directory to other aviation topics.

Aircraft World
http://www.aircraftworld.com
e-mail: info@aircraftworld.com
Aviation link directory serves up a variety of categories.

Alex's Helicopter Home Page
http://www.geocities.com/CapeCanaveral/3838
e-mail: amartins@abordo.com.br
Model and full-size helicopter information and resources.

Air Cargo Online
http://www.cargo-online.com
e-mail: webmaster@cargo-online.com
Central cargo database of available air charter capacity worldwide.

R/C Airplanes NET
http://www.rcairplanes.com
e-mail: none provided
Specific areas of info concerning radio-controlled airplanes based upon user requests.

The Flying High Page
http://www.zoncom.com/flyinghigh.html
e-mail: none provided
Personal Web site offering categorized links and miscellaneous Chicago-based info.

Air Cargo Newsgroup Home Page
http://www.mta-ic.com
e-mail: moderators@mta-ic.com
A Web site hub for the Air Cargo Newsgroup: misc.transport.air-industry.cargo.

Seaox Air-Medical Page
http://www.seaox.com
e-mail: webmaster@seaox.com
Air medical links, graphics, and industry info.

The Pilot Pitstop
http://www.mindspring.com/~anna716/index.html
e-mail: thepilotpitstop@mindspring.com
Miscellaneous, non-categorized list of aviation links.

Israeli Airpark
http://www.airpark.org.il
e-mail: none provided
Articles, information, and links for the worldwide
aviation community.

AviationNet
http://www.aeps.com/aeps/avnethm.html
e-mail: aeps@aeps.com
Industry resource center offering news, link directory,
schools, and more.

Calin's Aviation Index
http://www.calinsai.com
e-mail: mail@calinsai.com
A central source of aviation contacts and news.

Airshow.com
http://www.airshow.com
e-mail: none provided
Collection of current air show schedules, performers,
and related information.

Airship and Blimp Resources
http://www.hotairship.com
e-mail: roland@hotairship.com
A volunteer effort to provide airship information to
newcomers and veteran aeronauts.

Aileron's Place
http://www.akula.com/~aileron
e-mail: aileron@akula.com
A personal collection of aviation and flight simulator links.

Antique Aircraft Enthusiasts
http://www.wingsofhistory.org
e-mail: webmaster@wingsofhistory.org
Link resource for antique aircraft, including museums, organizations, and directory sites.

Army Aviation Directory
http://www.jiga-watt.com/AVNDirectory/
e-mail: stef@mosquitonet.com
Voluntary database used to locate former Army aviation personnel.

Aviation Business Center
http://www.airsport.com
e-mail: webmaster@airsport.com
Links to businesses supplying products, services, and information to the aviation community.

Aviation Organizations & Associations

WASP-WWII

http://www.wasp-wwii.org

e-mail: webmaster@wasp-wwii.org

RATING

BRIEFING:

The rich history of Women Airforce Service Pilots during World War II is a fascinating read.

Over 50 years ago exactly 1,857 young women pilots came from all over the U.S. to become Women Airforce Service Pilots (WASP) during World War II. WASP-WWII online brings the rich WASP history to light to honor their contributions. Yes, this well designed Web tribute has the photos and history. But, if that's all you see you've missed the point. A huge compiling of stories and records, audio and words, tell quite a gripping story.

Circumvent the unnerving array of banners, Web rings, and ad links on start-up to begin the journey. Once inside the clutter turns to compiled history, nicely organized. The official menu for WASP invites you to experience: Scrapbook (pictures and stories), Tributes, Resources (articles, lesson plans, and papers about the WASP), WASP Chat, Songs (audio clips and lyrics sung by WASP), Audio (speeches on the WASP), Planes, Records (official scanned documents), WASP Forum, Contacts, and more.

Keeping the interest up for the casual Web wanderer is WASP's attention to detail (minimal typos) and great writing among the many snippets, articles, reports, and historical perspectives. Old-time photos are captivatingly enlightening.

For a real thrill, download the video for a brief history of the WASP.

Fee or Free: Free.

National Warplane Museum

http://www.warplane.org

e-mail: elmira@warplane.org

RATING

BRIEFING:

The V-77
Stinson? Alive
and well thank
you, via this
online museum.

Physically located at Elmira-Corning Regional Airport, New York, and on virtual tour via cyberspace, the National Warplane Museum site is captivating. Graphically motivated, behind-the-scenes buffs have obviously zeroed in on exceptional design. Better still, this mix of visual treats doesn't make a mockery of your modem. Loading is fairly efficient, multiple types of menus are always at hand, and the "cockpit" aircraft searching feature is fun.

Sure there's the usual on tap, like: Museum's Mission, Sorties (where the Museum's planes have been and where they are moving around to), Enlistment Form for Members and Volunteers, News, Pilot Interviews & Stories, Links to other sites, and more. But where you're going to want to spend some time is the online plane collection. Just find your favorite in the pop-up window and enjoy. From an F-14 Tomcat to an L-3 Grasshopper, it's all here via mouse and modem.

Fee or Free: Free.

Aviation History On-Line Museum

http://www.aviation-history.com

e-mail: lpdwyer@aol.com

RATING

BRIEFING:

Tour this online
museum for a
cyber-stopover
into the archives
of aviation
history.

Aviation enthusiasts young and old will revel in the
online convenience of this interactive museum tour. No
dusty textbooks here. Just pixel-quality pictures and
lots of insightful description. Those with a fancy for
flying will quickly become enamored with a nice
collection of historic aircraft.

Neatly indexed by manufacturer and country, a quick
click launches you into a concise aircraft summary—
with an option for the full text version. Although the
punctuation-challenged descriptions run amok, the
facts and stories are still fascinating. The hand-picked
index of aircraft includes more than a few of my favorites: P-26 Peashooter, Mosquito, P6 Sea Master, Spitfire,
P-47 Thunderbolt, B-24 Liberator, P-40 Warhawk, and
The Concorde. Yes, even the Corcorde. Hey, it's still a
history-making phenomenon.

Once you've saturated your curious mind with aero
wonders, there is still more to study. Mouse over to the
left-margin buttons for: Aircraft Engines, The Early
Years, Construction Technology, Theory of Flight,
Aviation Magazine, Airmen, and more.

Fee or Free: Free.

Helicopter History Site

http://www.helis.com

e-mail: online form

RATING

┼ ┼

BRIEFING:

Though not a scholarly resource, this rotor wonder offers some fun pictorial history.

Whirling in a virtual fog of shaky English translation and painful layout, The Helicopter History Site emerges unscathed as an award winner nonetheless. Carefully navigating through the random ad banners and slow-to-load pictures, you'll stumble across a surprising collection of helicopter history. Your first tip is to gather ample amounts of patience and understanding.

Setting aside for the moment any hope of design or typo-free description, navigating within the site is actually easy. Thanks to a main menu content index by timeline or company and handy continuation links, maneuverability resembles that of a Bell 430. Stepping through the decades of manufacturers, models, and inventors, the historical tour holds your hand through many decades. Although descriptions are brief, the pictorial reviews are good, showing a nice "helio-progression." From Leonardo Da Vinci's Helical Air Screw to the Bell/Boeing 901 Osprey (V-22), if you're a helio-buff raise your level of history knowledge here.

Fee or Free: Free.

TheHistoryNet Archives— Aviation and Technology

http://www.thehistorynet.com/THNarchives/AviationTechnology
e-mail: online form

RATING

✛ ✛ ✛ ✛

BRIEFING:

Gather around the monitor for some good, old-fashioned aviation tales.

Stemming from the first-rate excellence of TheHistoryNet, the Aviation and Technology Archives promise a well-documented review into the history of aviation.

Unlike the drab presentation often associated with historical reference, TheHistoryNet's insights come alive with color and style. Obviously well-researched, the writing is flowing and interesting—a key ingredient in successful informational ventures. Photos and illustrations are many, but none so large that modem time is compromised. Each article even offers a one-page summary with a link to the full text.

For a history site covering more than just aviation, the depth of aero articles is impressive. I saturated my brain with features like: "Airmail's First Day"; "The Guggenheims, Aviation Visionaries"; "Kalamazoo 'Air Zoo'"; "Luftwaffe Ace Gunther Rall Remembers"; and "Stealth Secrets of the F-117 Nighthawk."

When you've finally reached the end of the archived Aviation and Technology list (60+ entries), a convenient left-margin index invites you to explore other historical topics. Although these have nothing to do with aviation, the invitation still stands.

Fee or Free: Free.

US Air Force Museum

http://www.wpafb.af.mil/museum

e-mail: champpa.rr@usafa.af.mil

BRIEFING:

Stop by for Air
Force specs
o'plenty—you'll
be bombarded
with bombers
and inundated
with insight.

It's a good thing that superb site navigation, in the form of a left-margin menu, takes you by the hand. Without its directional beacon you'd be lost in a virtual sea of bombers, trainers, and fighters. The sheer volume of images and history falls into the unbelievable category. Plan for extensive viewing if you're an Air Force admirer.

While I'm certainly not trying to diminish the importance of the actual museum in Dayton, Ohio, this promo site is quite a spectacle in itself. In my opinion, one of the best starting points for a mega-site like this, is to take some virtual tours. My favorites are the Korean Conflict, Presidential Aircraft, and R&D Hangar. Then, start browsing through the multitudes of aircraft and special galleries. Modern Flight, Early Years, Air Power, Space Flight, and others present fantastic capsules of memories. From History to Engines & Weapons, there's more than a couple days worth of viewing here alone.

Fee or Free: Free.

National Air & Space Museum (NASM)

http://www.nasm.si.edu

e-mail: web@www.nasm.edu

RATING

BRIEFING:

The Wright
Brothers would
be proud to take
this cyber-
museum tour.
Although the
online museum
is fascinating in
pixel version,
don't let it quell
your thirst for
seeing the real
thing.

It's simple and informative—the way a world-class museum otta be. The Smithsonian Institute's online National Air & Space Museum gives you a virtual look at aviation and space history. Click through museum maps and exhibits, educational programs, NASM news and events, NASM resources, or just general information about the museum itself. A convenient, clickable museum map points you in the direction of your favorite exhibits. From Milestones of Flight to Rocketry & Space Flight, you'll scan through online gallery greatness.

Have a specific question or winged fancy? Just jump into the powerful search engine. Search the Smithsonian Web by typing your phrase(s) or keyword(s). It's history at your fingertips.

Fee or Free: Free.

San Diego Aerospace Museum

http://www.AerospaceMuseum.org

e-mail: none provided

RATING

✝✝✝

BRIEFING:

Dazzling aviation history through a futuristic Web site tour.

Wow! High resolution pictures, well-written history, and perfect organization catapult the online edition of San Diego's Aerospace Museum into a must-see site. Aviation enthusiasts and historians are in for an exhibit tour encompassing the Dawn of Powered Flight through the Space Age.

True, online is a nautical mile from the real thing, but begin your journey here. There's hordes of fascinating info. Delve into the Montgolfier Brothers' Hot Air Balloon of 1783 (the first manned vehicle in recorded history to break the bonds of gravity), or read about your favorites: Lindbergh, Earhart, Gagarin, Armstrong, and more. Museum hours, fees, phone number, location, collection listing, and special event services are just a click away also. If you're just revisiting, quickly find new additions in: What's New at the Museum, Education Programs, and Library/Archives.

Recommendation? See the online version, then be dazzled by the real-life stuff.

Fee or Free: Free to view, fee for in-person museum tour.

The Air Capital

http://www2.southwind.net/~wknapp/air_cap

e-mail: chrome@feist.com

RATING

†††

BRIEFING:

Enjoy masterful navigation through the early years of The Air Capital.

You're thinking that aviation history means textbooks, microfiche, and Great Granddad's yellowing photos. Well, don't reach for your library card just yet. Explore the breakthrough aviation beginnings in Wichita, Kansas (The Air Capital) right here at the Aviation History of Wichita's home page.

Deftly navigating the early aircraft years (1911-1929), this site offers wonderfully written accounts and informative historical facts. The mostly text-based history does include some fun photos and graphical representations. A series of chapters chronicles Wichita's flying fancy: "The Beginning of a Love Affair"; "Flying by the Seat of Your Pants"; "Wichita's Father of Aviation"; "Building Planes and All That Jazz"; "Travel Air—A Major Success"; "Trouble in Paradise"; "Cessna Sets Out Alone"; "Stearman Returns"; "Wichita—The Air Capital"; and "The Rest as They Say is History."

It's the perfect place to relive the lives of aviation greats like Clyde Cessna, Eugene Ely, Earl Rowland, Walter Beech, and more. Your thirst for aviation knowledge ends here—it's an oasis.

Fee or Free: Free.

Aviation Institute

http://cid.unomaha.edu/~unoai/aviation.html

e-mail: unoai@cwis.unomaha

RATING

+ + +

BRIEFING:

Recruiting tool for UNO's Aviation Institute with an eye toward useful info for non-aviation-education seekers.

This higher learning site soars with knowledge not only relating to aviation, but effective self-promotion as well. Gliding effortlessly through the Aviation Institute's pages, you'll realize that all of its wisdom, visually appealing style, and useful information coagulates into a nicely packaged recruiting presentation. If you're in the market for lofty education—great—begin your search here at University of Nebraska at Omaha's Aviation Institute. Take a sneak peek into course lecture notes, programs and projects offered, careers in aviation, key reasons to enroll, Institute background info, etc. Explore undergrad and graduate programs, flight training, or an aviation minor.

Non-education-bound browsers will find the info here useful as well. An aviation links area brings you information on organizations, online magazines & news, airlines, businesses & manufacturers, weather, employment, resources, and more. Oh, and be sure to check out the Aviation Institute-sponsored Journal of Air Transportation World Wide. It's packed with articles and online dialog from many experts.

Fee or Free: Free.

A Virtual Museum Describing the Invention of the Airplane

http://hawaii.cogsci.uiuc.edu/invent/airplanes.html
e-mail: bradshaw@cogsci.uiuc.edu

RATING

BRIEFING:

A cyber-museum for aviation invention enthusiasts.

You don't have to keep your voice down or worry about knocking anything over in this museum—it's virtual. Its beneficial contents, however, are tangible and inviting. Fun graphics and sporadic quotes make learning via computer an online adventure. Step into the museum for: The Tale of the Airplane: A Puritan Fairy Tale; The Design and Test Strategy of Invention; Doing it Wright; The Dark Unhappy Ending; and The Bibliography (a list of relevant readings for those who wish to learn more). Also on cyber-tap are special features like 3-D models of early aircraft, photo & movie gallery, inventors gallery, plane database, and more.

No, it doesn't substitute for a live walk around of The Spruce Goose or The Wright Glider. But, the enjoyment and learning potential is as real as can be in this virtual wonder.

Fee or Free: Free.

Amelia Earhart

http://www.ionet.net/~jellenc/ae_intro.html

e-mail: jellenc@ionet.net

BRIEFING:

A brilliantly orchestrated Web tribute to America's most famous aviatrix, Amelia Mary Earhart.

Delving into the wonderfully ambitious world of Amelia Earhart, this cyber-tribute justifies every one of the awards it has garnished. Expertly written, illustrated, and presented, this online tour of Ameila's courage takes the browser through: The Early Years, The Celebrity, and The Last Flight. The fascinating text is easy to read and insightful. Clickable photos are scattered throughout, as well as clickable icons that take you into each chapter.

Included with Amelia's story are a few extras. Scan through unconfirmed themes as to her mysterious disappearance. Or, browse info regarding the Earhart Project—an investigation launched in 1988 by The International Group for Historic Aircraft Recovery (TIGHAR) to conclusively solve the mystery of Amelia's disappearance.

For those wanting to continue the education, tap into the site's film links to Flight for Freedom, Amelia Earhart, and Amelia Earhart: The Final Flight. Other related links include: Discovery Gallery, Tall Cool Woman, The Sky's the Limit, Famous Women in Aviation, People's Sound Page, Mystery of Amelia Earhart, Howland Island, and The Ninety-Nines.

Fee or Free: Free.

TIGHAR

http://www.tighar.org

e-mail: TIGHAR@aol.com

RATING

++++

BRIEFING:

Fascinating historical research masterfully displayed by the world's leading aviation archaeological foundation.

Pulled from the deepest, darkest caverns of the Web's cyber-cellars, TIGHAR (The International Group for Historic Aircraft Recovery) has, itself, been discovered. Not familiar with this diamond-in-the-rough? The nonprofit organization happens to be the world's leading aviation archaeological foundation. Their goals of finding, saving, and preserving rare and historic aircraft are artfully displayed here—online.

Fascinating history presented through well-written and descriptive pictures are at your disposal. Read through a thought-provoking investigation into the disappearance of Amelia Earhart in The Earhart Project. Learn about the disappearance of Nungesser and Coli aboard l'oiseau Blanc in Project Midnight Ghost, and probe into rumors that WWII German aircraft still survive in underground bunkers in Operation Sepulchre.

Also available: historic preservation articles, other resources, and a look into the TIGHAR Tracks Journal.

Fee or Free: Free to view. Regular, student, and corporate TIGHAR memberships available.

Dryden Research Aircraft Photo Gallery

http://www.dfrc.nasa.gov/gallery/photo/photoServer.html

e-mail: Robert.Binkley@dfrc.nasa.gov

RATING

BRIEFING:

Researching research aircraft? Or, just need a couple of fun copyright-free photos? Here's your site.

A dizzying array of digitized delights are housed here at the Dryden Research Aircraft Archive home page (physically located at the NASA Dryden Flight Research Center at Edwards, California). With over 1,200 images, the archive offers a huge selection of research aviation photos dating back to 1940. No copyright protection is asserted for any of the photos unless noted.

Site info is grouped by: photo, movie, graphics, audio, FAQ, and many other aircraft image archives.

From the B-47 Stratojet to the F-14 Tomcat—it's all a keystroke away.

Fee or Free: Free.

Center for Advanced Aviation System Development (CAASD)

http://www.caasd.org

e-mail: infoadmin@bell.mitre.org

RATING
+ +

BRIEFING:

An FAA-funded, not-for-profit organization researching important aviation topics.

Just when you thought this dry, governmentally funded yawn machine could put you easily to sleep, I urge you to shake off the drowsiness and look deeper into its fascinating core of hot topics and research areas. Their goal: "operating in the public interest to resolve global aviation issues through research." Wait. Before you move to your bookmark list, click through its five categories: about CAASD, reaching CAASD, accomplishments, research areas, and hot topics.

I found myself leaning more toward the research areas and hot topics. I think you'll discover some thorough, insightful information (including charts) relating to: air traffic control, global communications, navigation (excellent!), surveillance management, architecture, airports, Free Flight, user request evaluation tools, and automated surveillance.

The content will pleasantly surprise—just slip past the "plain Jane" shell.

Fee or Free: Free.

The Ninety-Nines
International Organization of Women Pilots

http://www.ninety-nines.org

e-mail: webmaster@ninety-nines.org

RATING

BRIEFING:

Cyber-headquarters for the women-only Ninety-Nines.

Originally funded in 1929 by ninety-nine licensed women pilots, the Ninety-Nines organization catapults its promotion of flight fellowship with this thoroughly informative online presence. Although its crude design and lackluster site navigation offer a minor downside, the benefits are well worth the visit.

A bookmarkable must for all female aviation enthusiasts, The Ninety-Nines pages provide unending resources. In addition to organization and membership info, other topics include: The Ninety-Nines in Aviation History, Women in Aviation History, Forest of Friendship, 1929 Invitation, Women Pilots Today, Hear a Little History, The Ninety-Nines Museum of Women Pilots, Learn to Fly, Future Women Pilot Program, Scholarships, Grants & Awards, Calendar of Events, Aerospace Education, Air Races, Airmarking, and more.

Fee or Free: Free unless you join.

Women in Aviation International (WAI)

http://www.wiai.org

e-mail: wai@infinet.com

```
RATING
+ + +
```

BRIEFING:

Expanding the lofty horizons of active women pilots and wanna-bes.

Piloting a national and international cyber-course, the Women in Aviation International pages hone in on needed resources for aviation's women enthusiasts. Female site-seekers may be disappointed at first with WAI's lackluster design. But, once you begin clicking into its content, you'll feel better.

Tapping into WAI Events gives you dates, times, and places of WAI-specific events. WAI News offers topical press releases. Education gets into the good stuff with profitable scholarship info. Your Career takes you to a current aviation job list with descriptions. And, yes, there's Online Shopping available for WAI necessities. Membership info, conference dates, *A4W Magazine* (a few editorial gems to peruse), guestbook, and Web links are also at your clicking fingertips.

With their self-proclamation, "Women in Aviation is dedicated to the encouragement and advancement of women in all aviation career fields of interests," WAI and its site are great first steps for aviation-interested ladies.

Fee or Free: Free to view, fee-oriented membership.

The National Transportation Safety Board (NTSB)

http://www.ntsb.gov

e-mail: none provided

RATING

BRIEFING:

An online look into the darker side of aviation—the accidents.

Although you may not expect it, a subtle array of graphical gadgetry takes flight here. But obviously, subjects with which the NTSB deals don't lend themselves to frivolity. Uncover the site's dry contents and you'll realize why its investigation wisdom becomes instantly worthwhile. Why? Because learning from the mistakes of other aviators is relatively painless.

If you're curious, you'll find tidbits of miscellany, like: about the NTSB recommendations and accomplishments, publications, news & events, job opportunities, search, and related sites.

Hopefully, though, your real investigative interests will guide you to the insights and descriptions of over 41,000 aviation accidents—there's even a handy database search capability! Or, clicking into aviation accident statistics reveals tables from the annual aviation accident press release, passenger fatality accident tables, and most recent monthly statistics. And, when you're ready to learn more, lists of accident reports and studies may be ordered.

If an accident should happen to you, info on NTSB reporting is easily found online.

Fee or Free: Free.

National Aeronautics and Space Administration (NASA)

http://www.nasa.gov/

e-mail: comments@www.hq.nasa.gov

RATING

+ + + + +

BRIEFING:

Blast off into this bookmark-bound space voyage—it's quite a ride.

Building award-winning Web sites for aerospace surfers isn't rocket science. Then again, compared to the thousands of rejected sites I've hastily passed up, maybe it is.

As if the online mission control team were holding your hand through each page and topic, site navigation is effortless. Brilliant description-oriented links combine with fancy quick-click icons to launch you into un-earthly euphoria. Uncluttered page layouts give you fascinating info, helpful pictures, and plenty of easy-reading "white space."

Skipping directly into the Office of Aeronautics & Space Transportation Technology area, you'll climb into juicy research topics like: high speed travel, general aviation revitalization, next generation design tools & experimental aircraft, current events, library, commercial technology, and more. For other NASA favorites click into: Today@NASA (breaking news and project details); Q&A (great collection of thought-provoking questions and thorough answers); Gallery (video, audio, and still images); and Space Science (planetary exploration, astronomy, & research into the origins of life).

Fee or Free: Free.

Air Force Link

http://www.af.mil

e-mail: none provided

RATING

BRIEFING:

Official U.S. Air Force site proudly serves its online viewers with regimented excellence.

A model of Web perfection, the Air Force Link easily busts through my scale's five-plane ceiling. Criteria I've set aside for site organization, content, graphics, and intended audience are masterfully adhered to with style and purpose.

The opening menu gives you a hint as to the Web wonders you'll find lurking inside. Loading speed and appropriate presentation are perfectly balanced. But, before you get too dazzled, slip into the complete site map navigation page—arranged in graphical "tree" format or text-only map. Going a step further into navigational bliss, a site searching tool is also located on the page. With the Air Force Link's resources, you just can't get lost.

Content-wise, a fantastic array of goodies begins with News, Careers, Library, Sites, Images, AF Link Jr (great Air Force stuff directed at kids), Spotlight, and Top Story. Specifically, Air Force Career subcategories include: civilian, enlisted, officer, and retiree—all come complete with pay charts. And, the Images page serves up an enormous list of high-resolution pictures—a search tool just for photos makes browsing easy.

The Air Force Link successfully defends its surfers against the ghastly mess so often found in aviation Web offerings. Click in and see for yourself.

Fee or Free: Free.

National Air Traffic Controllers Association (NATCA)

http://www.natcavoice.org

Staff@natcavoice.org

RATING
+ + + + +

BRIEFING:

National Air
Traffic
Controllers
Association
members have a
bit more to say
than just,
"traffic at your
eleven o'clock
position."

Curious about the voice behind that terse air traffic controller instruction? Get a better fix on that scratchy radio enigma with the cyber-version of The NATCA Voice. An info-packed forum for the National Air Traffic Controllers Association (NATCA), The Voice shouts its political opinions and speaks to important aviation legislation issues.

This no-nonsense forum brings you well-written articles and hard-hitting insight into the NATCA. Your first pleasant experience begins with site navigation that's almost as good as their flight following. You will find a Java-based clickable index, along with omni-present main menus. Once you do delve into a topic of choice, you'll exchange the cloud deck of confusion with good information and politically charged commentary.

The main page takes you quickly into NATCA, labor, or aviation. After that you're invited to tap into: The NATCA Voice Shop (items to support your "voice" and union), Web links, public BBS & chat, and swap meet. Looking for something particular? Just search the NATCA Ring. Hey, with the folks at the National Air Traffic Controllers Association, you'll easily find your Web site destination. It's what they do.

Fee or Free: Free.

Cessna Pilots Association (CPA)

http://www.cessna.org

e-mail: info@cessna.org

RATING

BRIEFING:

Compilation of Cessna-specific, technical insight mainly geared to the CPA member.

It's no surprise that one of the world's most popular flying machines has its own association. Better still, the Cessna Pilots Association now provides its members and nonmembers this outstanding online technical information center.

Mainly a gentle nudge into CPA membership, the site does a good job of describing each available Cessna-specific resource before you click. *CPA Magazine* talks about the monthly publication—devoting 100% to solid technical data about maintaining and operating Cessnas. Tech Notes and Handouts store a series of helpful documents ranging from FAQs concerning Cessna problems to sources of discount parts. Cessna owners will also appreciate the Technical Hot-Line, Technical Library, Cessna Buyer's Guides, Systems & Procedures Courses, and Group Aircraft Insurance Program.

Updates are handled regularly with a thorough info expansion in the members-only area with: an online version of the latest issue of *CPA Magazine*, access to CPA's entire library of Tech Notes, and online discussions of Cessna-related issues.

Fee or Free: Free, but the good stuff requires membership in CPA.

Of course, as with all organized organizations, online membership is clickably convenient. If you're a Cessna owner, it's a "no-brainer."

International Miniature Aircraft Association (IMAA)

http://www.fly-imaa.org

e-mail: VICEPRESDUKE@worldnet.att.net

RATING
✝✝

BRIEFING:

Large scale, radio-controlled cyber-center for fellow enthusiasts.

You can almost hear that high pitch engine whine before you reach the IMAA's pages. Those in the know, however, have become familiar with the more beefy sounds emanating from these larger-than-life, radio-controlled beauties. The next time you look up and see a Red Baron Super Stearman, a Byron Staggerwing, or a P51D, its pilot might just be on the ground with you.

Nourishing the large scale radio-controlled craze, The IMAA offers its online "hub" as a great central info resource. Here you'll pick up the course for local listings of chapters by district, as well as individual district news and photo coverage. A fantastic site index quickly breaks down the goodies: How to Join IMAA, How to Sanction an IMAA Event ("Rally of the Giants" for example), *High Flight Magazine* and Article Archives (IMAA's official printed publication), IMAA Events Calendar, Announcements, and Flight Gear Accessories.

If time is limited, do make a touch-and-go into the photo coverage and reports from the last Rally of the Giants. These cherished large scale aircraft are amazing to behold—even digitally. And, if you're an enthusiast don't miss IMAA classifieds. Take advantage of free personal classifieds, or scan through the commercial ad listings.

Fee or Free: Free unless you join IMAA.

The IMAA site. It's a huge miniature aircraft haven. Grab the controls and stay awhile.

Helicopter Association International (HAI)

http://www.rotor.com

e-mail: WEBMANAGER@rotor.com

RATING

BRIEFING:

Your online chopper choice, courtesy of The Helicopter Association International.

Fee or Free: Free parts searching for all! Parts listing for HAI non-members is free for a limited time.

Non-fixed wing fans need only arrive at this cyber-pad and clear some room on the bookmark list. You'll be back again.

Although the HAI site's in kind of a design spiral, sprawling volumes of worthwhile content more than compensate. Neatly arranged in columnar, text-based hyperlinks, rotor surfers will revel in clickable delight. Heliport searching is simply a matter of entering a city, state, or heliport. The Events Calendar & Heli-expo info give you a heads up on shows near you. And, the HELicopter Parts Search (HELPS) database teams parts listers and parts searchers effortlessly, for free!

Packed into the HAI site is a content load that would make an Aerospatiale Lamb 315B buckle. Click for industry news and archived info updated daily, online publications, chat rooms, bulletins, hot spots, education, conferences and jobs, e-mail list services, regulatory issues, aircraft for sale/lease, and way more than I have room to list.

Among my site favorites is the Cornerstone feature. This computerized civilian/military registry identifies standouts in the helicopter industry. Read through biographical data and scan pictures of thousands of helicopter professionals. It's a great way to track down a friend or colleague.

AirLifeLine

http://www.airlifeline.org

e-mail: staff@airlifeline.org

RATING

++

BRIEFING:

Find the online cyber-scoop for those in and around medical missions.

Just as the World Wide Web offers up a 24-hour labyrinth of resources, AirLifeLine proudly stands by with its own important network. As outlined in its online presence, AirLifeLine is a "nonprofit charitable organization of private pilots who donate their time, skills, aircraft, and fuel to fly medical missions."

The site clearly identifies organization goals and a myriad of FAQs with a simple contents list. Take a quick jump into: Services We Offer, Who May Use AirLifeLine, How Can You Help, AirLifeLine Volunteer Pilots, and Mission Requests. You'll quickly notice AirLifeLine skips the fancy GIFs and graphical fanfare associated with most of today's Web sites. The obvious concentration leans toward organization info—both for potential pilots and those needing medical transport. For example, private pilots may learn more about volunteering by clicking into AirLifeLine and the Private Pilot. Here, you'll browse careful text-based details about the missions—who qualifies, how they are requested, and how each is accepted. Pilot's Liability, Requirements for Joining, and Membership Application Details are also at the ready.

Curious about signing up? Read the letters to AirLifeLine. You simply can't help but be inspired to fire up your trusty flying machine and make a difference.

Fee or Free: Free.

Fly-In.org

http://www.fly-in.org

e-mail: webmaster@eaa.org

RATING

BRIEFING:

Oshkosh online—officially brought to you by the Experimental Aircraft Association (EAA).

Wittman Regional Airport in Oshkosh, Wisconsin. Perhaps you've heard of it. Every year a few aviation enthusiasts stop by for a week and mingle with airplanes and fellow aviators. Actually, the event numbers speak more clearly to its worldwide appeal: over 850,000 attendees, 12,000 airplanes, 2,800 show aircraft, 700 exhibitors, and 500 forums. Numbers like these require hordes of promotion. Enter Fly-In.org.

Peek through this virtual window of Fly-In.org to get the complete skinny on this year's Experimental Aircraft Association AirVenture Oshkosh Convention. Although most of the site info during my review alluded to the upcoming event at the time, you'll get the same scoop for the next show and a thorough recap of the last one. Click your way through AirVenture Pictures, AirShow Gallery, daily news articles and press releases, and much more.

Probably during your visit, you'll spend the most time boning up on the upcoming Oshkosh info. An organized display prompts you easily through the photos and descriptions of: Oshkosh arrival procedures, tentative schedule of performers, exhibitors, day-by-day info, where to stay, transportation, monthly updates, forums, and admission rates.

Fee or Free: Free.

American Institute of Aeronautics and Astronautics (AIAA)

http://www.aiaa.org

e-mail: webmaster@aiaa.org

RATING

+ + +

BRIEFING:

The AIAA creates the epitome of Web excellence for aerospace resources.

Fee or Free: Free.

Consistent with its professional nature and world-recognized resources, The AIAA blasts off into cyberspace with over 65 years of excellence. Technically touching on aerospace support services, the AIAA site closes in upon the perfect online template for resource sites. In every category I hold dear (content, layout, functionality, and audience), this aviation presence dominates.

First, join me in a functionality analysis. The introductory page loads quickly and gives the aerospace enthusiasts the entire site summary at a glance. Click either the illustrated icon or the text link—in both cases you arrive at, and transition through, your destination frustration-free. Second, layout steals a page from some Web expert's manual. You'll wander through appropriately illustrated icons and perfectly proportioned text pages. Bandwidth-hogging pictures are nonexistent and descriptions sparkle with clarity. Third, the overall intended audience not only includes AIAA members, but ALL enthusiasts involved in the arts, sciences, and technology of aerospace.

Finally, content should be reason enough for a bookmark. Stretch your mouse hand, and follow me into: career planning and placement services (mainly for members), AIAA Bulletin (industry news, services, events, employment services, and more), conferences & professional development, technical activities, publications, customer service, and more.

World Flight 1997

http://www.worldflight.org

e-mail: none provided

RATING

BRIEFING:

Soaring
chronicles of the
re-creation of
Amelia Earhart's
1937 world
flight.

Of course World Flight 1997 has come and gone. The re-creation and completion of Amelia Earhart's 1937 World Flight is a thing of the past. My hope, though, is that this online time capsule will stick around awhile. The daily chronicles of Linda Finch's heroic flight are of the timeless variety.

Originally introduced as an interactive way for students to follow along with Ms. Finch's daily journey, World Flight 1997's site now becomes a cyber-shrine to this fantastic flight. Learn more with a look into crew bios, aviation facts (trip facts, photos, plane, engines, and history), flight map, and weather reports along the way. With limited time, you may want to jump directly to the pilot's log. This firsthand account of the journey is captivating. You'll find unedited honesty!

Mixed in with the interactive content and expertly chronicled journey, the site's design soars triumphantly as well. The intro page uses an illustrated cockpit to showcase the site's clickable contents. Continuing on to selected topics will also reveal clever illustrations and visual navigational aids.

Fee or Free: Free.

Blue Angels

http://www.blueangels.navy.mil

e-mail: bawebmaster@ncts.navy.mil

RATING
+ + +

BRIEFING:

A dizzying
aerobatic
spectacle in real
life and online.

Blasting onto the scene in a spectacular blue streak, the Navy's Blue Angels page simple dazzles. With expected style and skill, this Navy promo team demonstrates Web prowess as well. The site's perfect blend of synchronized navigation, speed, and flashiness almost rivals that of their in-air shows. Layout, clickable menu graphics, and well-chosen photos begin the online adventure. Then, informative text tells the rest of the story. Get the initial briefing by clicking into the squadron history, covering aircraft types, missions, and objectives. Next, a look into biographies, officers, and the enlisted team focuses on the professionals behind the glitz—demonstration pilots, C-130 pilots, support officers, and maintenance & support team.

By far my favorite site feature is the proud display of photos and movies in the gallery. You'll be bombarded with maneuvers, jets, and formations—enough to keep you busy for awhile.

Fee or Free: Free.

USAF Thunderbirds

http://aeroweb.brooklyn.cuny.edu/events/perform/tb/tb.html

e-mail: air-info@brooklyn.cuny.edu

```
RATING
++
```

BRIEFING:

A fast, sleek, and thoroughly entertaining site almost mirroring the real life stuff.

Also graceful in the online skies, the Thunderbirds display perfect pageantry and digitized delights. And, as you would expect, uniformity and solid organization provide the glue to hold it all together.

A bit light on photos, the site focuses more on history, technique, and people behind the scenes. The well-written descriptions offer a fresh perspective and more insight anyway. Fascinating Thunderbird info can be quickly found by clicking into these articles: the Thunderbird Legend Lives On, Thunderbird History, The F-16 Fighting Falcon, Pratt & Whitney F100-PW-220 Turbofan Engine, Pilots Display American Airpower, Maintainers Keep Thunderbirds Airborne, Support Critical Piece of Thunderbird Puzzle, and Quotes.

As you'd expect in this promo site, the current air show schedule is conveniently clickable. Courtesy of the Aviation Enthusiast Corner (also an award-winning site in this book), you'll be hyperlinked to a long list of shows—complete with date, show title, and city. Further links provide actual location, contact, and performers.

Fee or Free: Free.

National Business Aircraft Association (NBAA)

http://www.nbaa.org

e-mail: info@nbaa.org

RATING

BRIEFING:

An organized organization with a resourceful site committed to NBAA membership.

Almost needing a suit and tie to view, NBAA's site exudes professionalism, style, and a hard sell toward membership. The nonmember area offers inexhaustible info on products and services. Clickable subjects include: Welcome; NBAA Membership (get the sign-up details here); Seminars and Conventions (dates & times); Selected Publications Online; Political Issues (info on aviation policy at the state and congressional levels); Products & Services; The NBAA History; and Travel Sense (business travel productivity software).

Existing NBAA member? Just fill out the application form and move into the member-only area. Tap into: flights & maintenance operations, NBAA Air Mall, political & tax issues, site-wide search, and Ask the NBAA Staff.

Fee or Free: Some info is free for nonmembers. Join the NBAA and get into more good stuff.

Aviation Safety Connection (ASC)

http://www.aviation.org

e-mail: webmaster@aviation.org

RATING

✝ ✝ ✝ ✝

BRIEFING:

Nonprofit site furthering air safety through discussion groups.

With an honest, thorough approach, the ASC jumps into the cockpit with all of us and guides us through important topics like: cockpit command responsibilities, human error factors, and behavior patterns. There's a pilot lounge, bulletin board, ready room discussion forum, a library, and review of accident reports.

The emphasis here is on fundamental safety issues. The ASC uses accident and incident case histories to fine-tune the decision-making process. Through its online offering, the ASC makes it easy for all of us to learn from the mistakes of others. Conveniently, message and reply forms are strategically placed throughout the site. Forms are available for: The Webmaster, messages, subscriptions (free registration to *Cockpit Leadership*); e-mail to the editor, discussion group area; and the librarian.

Quite simply, ASC makes it easy to be a safer pilot.

Fee or Free: Free.

Aircraft Owners & Pilots Association (AOPA)

http://www.aopa.org

e-mail: aopahq@aopa.org

RATING

BRIEFING:

Yes. It's a recruiting tool. But, if you're interested in joining the world's largest general aviation advocacy organization, you can sign up here.

From magazines to trade shows and fly-ins to their Air Safety Foundation, AOPA isn't used to taking the number two position. Just like everything AOPA does, this site included, skillful organization has propelled this necessary association into the aviation limelight since 1939. This site, developed for membership and club benefits info, makes it easy to see why AOPA ranks among the 100 largest membership organizations in the United States. You'll find current fly-in info, pilot news, an intro into learning to fly, a sample of their printed magazine (*AOPA Pilot*), & yes, membership information (fees, application, etc.)

Existing members may tap into their own section for: 24-hour access to searchable databases, weather info, back issues of *AOPA Pilot*, events, and more.

Fee or Free: Free to view, fee for AOPA membership.

National Aeronautic Association (NAA)

http://www.naa.ycg.org

e-mail: naa@naa.ycg.org

RATING

BRIEFING:

Yet another
worthwhile site
promoting a
worthwhile club.
Have a look—it
may be for you.

Looking to entice new members into aviation and air sports, NAA's site invites you to grab your GPS and explore a "world of aviation" through NAA membership. Sign-up info, mission statement, corporate membership, affiliates, contacts, and a look at "NAA Today" are all here. Fun little tidbits include: aeronautical records, aero clubs, and air sports associations.

Not easily found in most aviation Web site link lists, NAA's special links to air sports include: Academy of Model Aeronautics, Balloon Federation of America, Experimental Aircraft Association, Helicopter Club of America, International Aerobatics Club, Soaring Society of America, United States Hang Gliding Association, U.S. Parachute Association, and the United States Ultralight Association.

Fee or Free: Free
to view, fees for
NAA membership.

MicroWINGS

http://www.microwings.com

e-mail: fltsim@microwings.com

RATING

+ + +

BRIEFING:

Informative online hangout for flight simulator types.

Yes, I've even uncovered an association for flight simulator buffs. Here's a reliable, helpful buddy to extract the maximum simulation exhilaration from your favorite flight software. As demonstrated by this site, MicroWINGS fiercely devotes itself to all types of aerospace simulation.

For real, approved flight training or just a chance to dip into the fantasy slipstream, I've found your land-based cockpit pros. Newly updated as of review time, the site has a zillion products to review in the Global Flight Simulation Online Catalog, product reviews, download files, flight simulator crossword puzzles, events, online chatting, and a strong push towards membership in the International Association for Aerospace Simulations. With membership, though, comes hefty product discounts, a full-color magazine subscription, free software, simulator bulletin board access, and more.

Fee or Free: Free to view, but if you're into simulators get the membership.

Experimental Aircraft Association (EAA)

http://www.eaa.org

e-mail: webmaster@eaa.org

RATING

BRIEFING:

Here's an Oshkosh junkie's fix for the whole year.

Wish the Oshkosh fly-in lasted year-round? Before and after the real thing, join EAA members at the official EAA home page to satiate your hunger for fun flying. This slick, handsomely designed gem just shines with plenty of well-organized topics and news in many clickable areas. Reach into the left-margin list for unlimited resources like: AirVenture Oshkosh, auto fuel program, all kinds of EAA-related services and products, museums, regional fly-ins, and more. Get the skinny on current fly-in info under "The Latest," and check out the hot topics of today summarized on the main page.

Great site and organization for enthusiasts of every age and interest—"pilots, designers, builders, dreamers, and doers."

Fee or Free: Free to view, fee for membership. Yes, there's a members-only section. Worthy info awaits.

International Aerobatic Club (IAC)

http://acro.harvard.edu/IAC/iac_homepg.html

e-mail: gei@cfa.harvard.edu

BRIEFING:

Those having an aversion to staying upright will find no downside with this aeronautic club info.

So, you've had enough of straight and level, and you're looking to get inverted. Sift through the nicely organized pages of the IAC to learn more about aerobatics and membership with the IAC. To join, you'll need to be a member of the Experimental Aircraft Association (IAC is a division of the EAA). There's online application info, phone numbers and addresses for the main office in Oshkosh, and a long list of IAC chapters worldwide (some have Web pages).

As with any well-organized club, internal communications are a necessity. And, you'll find it's no different here. At your disposal are lists for an e-mail distribution and IAC snail mail addresses. (By the way, you don't need to be a member to be on IAC's address list.) Member or not, you'll find aerobatic info galore: articles on IAC and aerobatics, aerobatic links, a communications center, aerobatic images, IAC news (recently updated), as well as lots of links.

It's enough info to make your head and your aircraft spin.

Fee or Free: Free to view, fee to join IAA.

Soaring Society of America (SSA)

http://www.ssa.org

e-mail: gei@cfa.harvard.edu

RATING

BRIEFING:

An online
meeting place
for Soaring
Society members
as well as
nonmembers.

You've seen them in their tiny bullet-shaped cockpits floating on elongated wings. For those that glide, the thrill of soaring is infectious. The remedy is to join other thermal-hungry friends online. The official pages of the Soaring Society of America are found here—giving you a link to all phases of gliding nationally, as well as internationally.

The info contained here is organized nicely, graciously avoiding gratuitous photos. You'll find: info on becoming a pilot, where to fly, contests, records, soaring services, SSA membership info, member locator, government affairs, soaring magazine, and safety info.

Soaring buffs and wanna-bes should look into membership. Judging by this site's organization, you'll be in good hands.

Fee or Free: Free
to view, fee for
membership.

Federal Aviation Administration (FAA)

http://www.faa.gov

e-mail: webmasterFAA@faa.dot.gov

RATING

+ + + + +

BRIEFING:

This information-rich governmental site will dazzle you with efficiency.

All government jokes aside (too many to list here), one can only stare slack-jawed at this wondrously efficient, visually appealing FAA piece of mastery. When the weight of federal bureaucracies begins to creep into your business/professional life, you'll find the light at tunnel's end here.

Granted, there's some administration stuff here that most will care less about. But, slip past it, using a nicely designed "Quick Jump" search engine to breeze through traditional red tape. You'll get your questions answered.

Or, examine some newsworthy current events, a long list of FAA highlights (safety, career opportunities, site info), and a handy summarized list of specific FAA offices.

Fee or Free: Free.

Office of Airline Information

http://www.bts.gov/oai

e-mail: wwwoai@bts.gov

RATING

BRIEFING:

An award-winning governmental (yes, governmental) site from the Bureau of Transportation Statistics (BTS) that's shamefully useful.

Yet again, rather than rearing its ugly head of red tape, your government has chosen a course of surprising functionality and automation. Congratulations to the BTS for assembling this amazingly useful treasure of vital transportation information.

Tap into the BTS's Office of Airline Information and you'll open the statistical file cabinets housing: the FAA Statistical Handbook of Aviation, BTS Transportation Indicators, U.S./International Air Passenger and Freight Stats, and the Sources of Air Carrier Aviation Data. Although some stats may be a few years old, there's a wealth of info here on: airline on-time reports, passenger and freight counts, aircraft accidents, airport activity, general aviation aircraft info, aeronautical production, U.S. civil airmen, and more.

Fee or Free: Free.

World Aeronautics Association (WAA)

http://www.meer.net/users/waa/waaintro.htm

e-mail: waa@meer.net

BRIEFING:

Although the pages may not "wow" you, WAA's record-breaker stuff will.

Fee or Free: Free. All areas are accessible, except "Experimental Test Pilot's Club." Internet memberships are free (you'll get an e-mail newsletter subscription), and associate memberships are available for a nominal fee.

After wading through an otherwise long-winded history and purpose preface, you record-breaker types will get to the heart of the hype. Apparently encouraged by Zeus (I'm not sure why), those interested in aerospace records will find an uplifting online haven here. Of course before you reach the clickable record info, you'll be briefed on WAA membership and association benefits. But, once you wiggle past the opening sales pitch, things get a little more interesting. Pilots with the "right stuff" will get itchy just looking through the Categories and Record Areas (wingspan, speed, glider, fuel, propulsion, weight classes, aircraft categories, altitude, etc.). Also interesting are the WAA World Record Repository, The World Aeronautics Hall of Fame, and the Experimental Test Pilot's Club (requires membership—still under construction at review time). Find out how to set a world record and tap into the forms to document a flight.

While mostly text-based, the pages won't knock your socks off, but eager enthusiasts will find fun just the same.

Air Transport Association (ATA)

http://www.air-transport.org

e-mail: ata@air-transport.org

RATING

✝ ✝ ✝ ✝ ✝

BRIEFING:

When not embroiled in fare wars and cutthroat competition, your favorite commercial carriers come here to join forces, data, and knowledge.

Leveled off and cruising at commercial flight levels, you'll find the ATA's official Web site. This cyber-resource is always on time with 24-hours of ATA info for members, and a smattering of info gems for non-ATA types. Mainly serving its 24 commercial carriers (USAirways, United, Northwest, Southwest, TWA, etc.), ATA's well-organized site features an absence of unnecessary pictures and slow-to-load graphics. A slick opening menu gets you into areas concerning general info, services, and member-only stuff. Don't shy away if you're a nonmember. There's a series of interesting things here for you too. The Airline Handbook launches into the history of aviation, deregulation, airline economics, how aircraft fly, the future of aviation, and more. You'll find industry stats, ATA member stock quotes, calendar (events and shows), and an online aviation dictionary (under construction at review time).

Members can tap into an ATA Calendar, Airworthiness Directives, Memos and Data from the ATA's Engineering Maintenance and Materiel Council, Technical Support System, events, publications, and ATA News.

While we all have opinions on the efficiency of commercial carriers, you'll find ATA's site timely, useful, and convenient.

Fee or Free: Free with restricted membership area. See ATA's pages for details.

Angel Flight

http://www.angelflight.org

e-mail: webmaster@angelflight.org

RATING

+++

BRIEFING:

A nonprofit organization that not only moves you, but it transports those less fortunate with medical problems to a treatment destination.

Don't expect fancy graphics, gratuitous plane pictures or rambling commentary here. The text-only descriptions and Q&A are quite enough to send your hope for the human race soaring. The Angel Flight site promotes and explains the aviation community's volunteer service of getting needy folks to diagnosis or treatment. Angel Flight's association of volunteer pilots and non-pilots join forces to: shuttle cancer patients to chemotherapy and surgery; carry people with kidney problems to obtain dialysis or transplants; and bring those with heart-related problems closer to treatment.

With this informative site, prospective volunteers will find many answers to common membership questions, including: Who belongs to Angel Flight?; Who does Angel Flight transport?; Where do calls come from?; Who pays for the flights?; How do I join?; What happens after I join?; and, What is my liability?

Angel Flight's pages are simply a persuasive call to action. Where do I sign?

Fee or Free: Free.

The Mechanic Home Page

http://www.the-mechanic.com

e-mail: mechanic@the-mechanic.com

RATING

BRIEFING:

A quality resource for the true aviation maintenance pro— breathtakingly bookmarkable.

If you're of the variety who tinkers in the cowling or wrenches on undercarriage, wipe off the grease and reach for a mouse. Settling into The Mechanic Home Page reveals a heart-pounding depository of aircraft maintenance technician info. At the center of this site is the Aircraft Mechanics Fraternal Association (A.M.F.A.)—a craft-oriented, independent aviation union. Cleanly organized with great mechanic info, you'll find everything here is easily accessible. From several linked info pages to downloadable files to Java pull-down menus, every site tool is at the ready. Sift through airline news (broken down by major carrier acronyms); enter or read comments on the bulletin board; read about the A.M.F.A.; download many important FAA files; scan the news archive; read observations from industry pros; tap into employment opportunities; learn from miscellaneous mechanic articles; and view the many hot topics currently displayed on the intro page. The functional design and excellent variety of downloadable resources complete the package of perfection.

If you're remotely involved in the nuts and bolts side of aviation, break out your bookmark.

Fee or Free: Free.

Seaplane Pilots Association

http://www.seaplanes.org

e-mail: webmaster@seaplanes.org

```
RATING
+++
```

BRIEFING:

Have a seaplane fancy? Get your feet and your floats wet here.

Although fairly unusual in the Web world, Seaplane Pilots Association is mostly informational. Yes, that means mostly you'll find water-flying facts.

And, if the lack of junky ads weren't reason enough to visit, Seaplane Pilots Association is efficiently organized too. You'll wonder why all aviation sites haven't copied its source code. Simple page links with nice descriptions get you into more water-flying fancy than one should be allowed in a Web visit.

Clickable contents include: Seaplane Flight School Directory, Flight Training Handbook, Book List, Seaplane News Brief, events, calendar, and Seaplane Airlines/Air Taxi Directory (search by region or airline). Further Informational sections point you in the direction of instruction, links, handbooks, and mailing lists. It's a one-stop, seaplane shop.

Members get "special" Web access to even more info resources for water flying fans, like: Certified Flight Instructor Directory, Seaplane Make & Model Directory, and Articles Database (from Water Flying Magazine & Annual).

Fee or Free: Free for lots of info. But, membership gives you even more online resources.

Bookmarkable Listings

World League of Air Traffic Controllers
http://www.wlatc.com
e-mail: wlatc@wlatc.com
The World League of Air Traffic Controllers' site for news, chat, and contact info.

Vietnam Helicopter Flight Crew Network
http://www.vhfcn.org
e-mail: webmaster@vhfcn.org
A forum for recreational communications among aircrew members who served in Vietnam.

Naval Helicopter Association (NHA)
http://www.inetworld.net/rotorrev/index.htm
e-mail: rotorrev@inetworld.net
Features NHA's *Rotor Review* magazine, as well as Navy, Marine Corp, and Coast Guard helicopters.

Lindbergh Foundation
http://www.mtn.org/lindfdtn
e-mail: lindfdtn@mtn.org
Informational source concerning the Charles A. and Anne Morrow Lindbergh Foundation.

United States Parachute Association (USPA)
http://www.uspa.org
e-mail: none available
Serving the only national skydiving association, the USPA, composed of over 33,000 members.

American Bonanza Society
http://www.bonanza.org
e-mail: online form
Informational site dedicated to the owners of Beechcraft Bonanza, Baron, and TravelAir aircraft.

Air Force Association (AFA)
http://www.afa.org
e-mail: com@afa.org
Nonprofit civilian organization promoting the importance of Air Force resources.

Institute of Navigation (ION)
http://www.ion.org
e-mail: webmaster@ion.org
Informational site promoting the advancement of the art and science of navigation.

Civil Air Patrol
http://www.cap.af.mil
e-mail: webmaster@cap.at.mil
Online services and membership center for the Civil Air Patrol.

AirportNet
http://www.airport.org
e-mail: rnf@spyre.com
Member resources for the American Association of Airport Executives and the International Association of Airport Executives.

Port Columbus Historical Society
http://www.asacomp.com/~lcarrier/pchs.html
e-mail: tkeener@asacomp.com
History on airliners scheduled into Port Columbus since 1929.

390th Memorial Museum Online
http://www.390th.org
e-mail: the390th@aol.com
Memorial museum preserving the proud heritage of the 390th Bombardment Group.

History of the Brazilian Air Force
http://www.mat.ufrgs.br/~rudnei/FAB/english.html
e-mail: rudnei@mat.ufrgs.br
Info, stats, air bases, units, and more relating to the Brazilian Air Force.

Rhinebeck Aerodrome Museum
http://www.oldrhinebeck.org
e-mail: jeff@mainstream.net
Sneak peek into this living museum of antique aviation.

Air Cruise America
http://www.aircruise.com
e-mail: rick@aircruise.com
Nostalgic tour of the DC-3, complete with technical specs, type ratings, and more.

The Spruce Goose
http://www.sprucegoose.org
e-mail: garythompson@sprucegoose.org
Unofficial page delves into the history of the Spruce Goose with photos, historical details, perspectives, and more.

American Airpower Heritage Museum
http://www.avdigest.com/aahm/aahm.html
e-mail: jszalkow@avdigest.com
Official pictorial tour and information relating to the American Airpower Heritage Museum of the Confederate Air Force.

Weather

FlightBrief

http://www.flightbrief.com

e-mail: gflewis@flightbrief.com

RATING

+ + + + +

BRIEFING:

Your flying forecast: always clear and unobstructed with FlightBrief.

The sister site to Weather Concepts (also a five-plane mention in this book), FlightBrief seeks to stir the aviator's passion for precise flying-related weather specifics.

With flawless design and organization, FlightBrief mirrors its Weather Concepts twin with every weather facet, including some added bells and whistles: Get Live Wx, Forecasts, Satellite Maps, Depiction Charts, Radar, Surface Analysis, Winds, and more.

But, FlightBrief pushes past its sister site with an aviation-only focus into flight planning info. Click into an easy-to-use route plan that prompts all the standard info. New to the flying scene? Get clickable help with each item. Even a direct link to fuel planning and airport info (courtesy of Airnav) boosts your information level. A click on Resources even provides detailed descriptions of: airspace diagram, airspace definitions, V-speed definitions, and air traffic control procedures. Now, all FlightBrief needs is online flight plan filing. Yes, you guessed it. It's coming soon (as of review time).

Fee or Free: Fee-based, but aviators will find it worthy of a 14-day trial.

Looking for a further push into subscription? How about three- to eight-minute updates on all Nexrad radar images (self-proclaimed to be the fastest on the Internet)? Hey, give the free 14-day trial a go. You've got nothing to loose and thorough weather knowledge to gain.

Aviation Weather

http://www.aviationweather.com

e-mail: weather@weathersite.com

BRIEFING:

Free weather euphoria. Everything's here but the fancy exterior.

Will weather wonders never cease? Loads of free weather tidbits shower the moderately designed pages of Aviation Weather. No, it's not pretty, but the data's here all right. Annoying ad banners and big-time initial download wait give way to a long list of worthwhile SIGMETS, AIRMETS, forecasts, and specific info.

It's true you can pretty much get similar weather details with any number of sites—some free, some not. But, Aviation Weather does a fine job at collecting a few more essentials all in one place (you'll just need to scroll to locate it). Running down the list of options, we pilots will enjoy: SIGMETS (convective, domestic, and international); AIRMETS; METARS; forecasts (TAF, winds aloft, area forecasts, mountain wave, aviation icing maps, and TWEB routes); and other information in the form of time-temp-wind.

Beginners and those needing a refresher will appreciate a thorough explanation of important aviation weather topics, like: AIRMETS, convective SIGMETS, SIGMETS, international SIGMETS, TAF forecasts, and winds aloft plots.

By the way, should you wish to wander into other weather wonderlands, simply visit the omni-present top menu. You'll be transported to specific weather resources for marine, Canadian, agriculture, and more.

Free or Fee: Free.

Pilot Weather Briefing

http://members.aol.com/rlattery/pilot.htm

e-mail: vortex100@aol.com

RATING

+ + +

BRIEFING:

Aviation weather heavyweights pull together a complete briefing picture.

Rounding up data from a variety of respectable sources, Pilot Weather Briefing disseminates the flying weather picture clearly and thoughtfully. It's obvious much flying time was sacrificed to present such a truly useful weather resource.

Design, organization, and helpful tips are excellent. Menus are anywhere and everywhere. Fancy "lit" or "unlit" buttons tell you when you've arrived at a "data page." And omni-present satellite or radar buttons provide easy access to this valuable data. What's more, a helpful page on tips for using Pilot Weather Briefing takes you by the hand and gives you a prop start.

Surface Weather, Upper Winds, Thunderstorms, Turbulence, Icing, and Other Hazards each launch you into specific maps and analyses. Get 12- and 24-hour surface forecasts, 12- and 24-hour significant weather progs, temperature contours, weather depiction, AIRMETS for IFR, and more. Even find today's (yes today's!) airport flight delays.

Did I mention everything's free? Yes, with the help of some Web friends, Pilot Weather Briefing keeps everything current and cost free.

Fee or Free: Free.

WeatherTAP

http://www.weathertap.com

e-mail: webmaster@weathertap.com

RATING

BRIEFING:

Info-rich weather wonder, giving nearly real-time weather for aviators.

Still fumbling around for weather? Slip on the raincoat, pay a tiny monthly fee and get fast, accurate weather 24 hours. WeatherTAP gives you left-margin "quick buttons" into local weather, NEXRAD radar, national weather, aviation weather DTC DUAT, and some other useful services. Updating every six minutes (the time it takes a NEXRAD radar antenna to make a complete sweep of the sky), WeatherTAP uses the exact images and info that is provided to the FAA's air route traffic control centers.

Of course you'll probably dally most in Aviation Weather. Get current stuff like: National Weather Service plots, composite moisture stability, observed winds and temps, surface prognosis, and live data. Also worthy of your time are a host of text products and a customized route briefing section.

When you're ready to file, move directly into DUAT. The convenient link is always at the ready for the "official" briefing.

Fee or Free:
Nominal fee required.

EarthWatch-Weather on Demand

http://www.earthwatch.com

e-mail: webmaster@earthwatch.com

RATING

+ + +

BRIEFING:

Weather imagery at its finest from industry veterans. Bookmark this one for the 3-D visuals!

Now that's where I want to get my weather—from a company famous for developing patented software that integrates 3-D weather visualization with a global database to create a virtual world. EarthWatch Communications brings you cool weather visuals with cutting-edge imagery. Not convinced? Click any one of the choices on the main menu button bar.

Weather headlines, StormWatch, forecast center, satellite & radar, current conditions, and EarthWatch products lead you into pure weather euphoria. Current conditions move you into an updated series of U.S. weather maps—temperature, wind chill, radar, and satellite. Each are clickable for more of a pinpointed view. Clicking into the satellite & radar area, however, will undoubtedly serve up the most fun. High resolution satellite imagery displays uncanny, cutting-edge visuals. My favorite? Try the U.S. 3-D satellite views. Just click your region: South Central, North Central, Southwest, Northwest, and Southeast. Stunning 3-D cloud layers can be seen in fairly good detail. Or, radar revelers need only click once to switch to the radar image version. It's cleverly cool!

Fee or Free: Free.

World Meteorological Organization (WMO)

http://www.wmo.ch

e-mail: webmaster@wmo.ch

RATING
++

BRIEFING:

World Meteorological Organization serves as a respected jumping off point to featured weather wonders.

The World Meteorological Organization. If it seems regal and authoritative, it is. In fact, WMO is the Geneva-based, 185-member organization within the United Nations providing the scientific voice on the state and behavior of the earth's atmosphere and climate. Sound like a good start for world weather link searching?

Thoughtfully providing an English, Spanish, French, and no-frames version, WMO's online presence acts as a wise weather wonderland. Description of the organization itself is lengthy, with a careful emphasis on each of WMO's "majore programmes." Learn about World Weather Watch, World Climate Programme, Atmospheric Research and Environmental Programme, and more. Of more immediate interest to us aviators however, may be the list of worldly links. The menu of options currently (as of review time) includes: libraries, meteorological sites, information sources, and specialized sites. Moving further into Additional Meteorological Information uncovers an index of Meteorological information pointing to sites with national and international reports, forecasts, weather maps, and satellite images.

Fee or Free: Free.

The Weather Underground

http://www.wunderground.com

e-mail: info@wunderground.com

RATING

+ + + +

BRIEFING:

It's not a complete aviation weather provider, but it's sure a simple synopsis.

Most weather Webmasters tucked away in a dark cubicle somewhere have decided that you'll happily wait for high-byte graphics and giant radar maps to load. I, however, fall into the unhappy category when superfluous graphics and unwanted miscellany rain upon my weather inquiries.

If you're an impatient too, go underground in the Weather Underground. It's amazingly easy on your modem and efficiently organized. Don't believe me? The first screen to load gives you three options to find your weather: 1) type your city and state into a search window; 2) click anywhere on the U.S. map; or 3) find your state's hyperlink and click. It's so fast, I become giddy with weather euphoria.

Once you've arrived at the desired city, a table of current conditions provides: time of report, temperature, humidity, wind, pressure, conditions, sunrise, sunset, and moon phase. Forecasts include descriptions and temperature for your desired city, as well as your state's extended forecast.

Fee or Free: Free.

USA Today—Aviation Weather

http://www.usatoday.com/weather/wpilots0.htm

e-mail: online form

RATING

BRIEFING:

The big-name Web source that conveniently narrows its weather focus for pilots.

It's really your call whether or not you'd like to scan the online news from USA Today. However, I'd like to point you toward their specific weather resource for pilots, aptly named Aviation Weather. Mainly it's a collection of links specific to pilots and weather-related issues. The page does an excellent job describing the appropriate resources and offering a corresponding hyperlink. Unlike most online news sources of this caliber, graphics, pictures, and charts are nonexistent. It's simply a quick way into the weather and related tidbits you need.

At the time of review, the site makes it easy to tap into: Studying Clear Air Turbulence, Lightning Protection, Understanding Density Altitude, Flying Into Hurricanes, Pilots Report Hazards to NASA, NASA's Aviation Human Factors Research, and Online Weather Calculator (converting temperatures and calculating density altitude).

Perhaps a bit more specific to weather, the following topics catapult you into a great collection of associated links: thunderstorms, icing, live weather, ground school, and more.

Fee or Free: Free.

National Weather Service

http://www.nws.noaa.gov

e-mail: w-nws.webmaster@noaa.gov

BRIEFING:

Weather service pros give you a 24-hour option for getting the real scoop on Mother Nature's intentions.

Partially obscured among the countless weather resources found on the National Weather Service's site, you'll find a healthy grouping of aviation products. Get current info from Terminal Aerodrome Forecasts, aviation weather discussions, aviation METAR reports, Terminal Forecasts, and more. Mostly text-based, the available forecasts and observations offer accuracy and speed. You won't be waiting for maps or graphics to load.

Pulling back from the focus on aviation, the National Weather Service site also thoroughly covers weather-related topics in a more general sense. When you've got some extra hangar time, be sure to scan through the Interactive Weather Information Network (warnings, zone, state, forecasts), black and white weather maps, U.S. weather bulletins, tropical cyclone warnings and products, fire weather, and Alaska products.

It may not necessarily be pretty, but all your weather is here from those that know.

Fee or Free: Free.

Aviation Weather Center

http://www.awc-kc.noaa.gov

e-mail: webawc@awc.kc.noaa.gov

RATING

BRIEFING:

Preempt your local weather reporter with forecasts from the source.

Weather info doesn't get much closer to the source than this. Without pomp and pageantry, the National Weather Service and The National Oceanic & Atmospheric Administration serve up the Aviation Weather Center with an information-rich presentation. Be forewarned though, you won't come across colorful maps and pretty graphics. Make sure you're up to speed on coded weather info, and you'll breeze through its text-only forecast reports.

Up to 24,400 feet, U.S. forecasts mainly include warnings of flight hazards, such as turbulence, icing, low clouds, and reduced visibility. Above 24,000 feet the Aviation Weather Center provides warnings of wind sheer, thunderstorms, turbulence, icing, and volcanic ash.

Site navigation is relatively easy with many "return to" links. While it may take awhile to become comfortable sifting through site contents, you'll eventually get to: AIRMETS, Area Aviation Forecasts, Domestic SIGMETS, Terminal Aerodrome Forecasts, TWEB Routes, Winds Aloft Forecasts, and more.

Fee or Free: Free.

The Online Meteorology Guide

http://ww2010.atmos.uiuc.edu/(Gh)/guides/mtr/home.rxml

e-mail: ww2010@atmos.uiuc.edu

RATING

┼┼┼┼

BRIEFING:

Meteorology
introduction
with a flair for
current weather
from your
educated friends
at the University
of Illinois.

Always keeping a watchful eye on the weather and Web wonders, I'm always elated when I uncover a combination of the two as well done as WW2010—The Online Meteorology Guide. Sure you can get current weather here (check out the latest handsome revision), but the real impact stems from a combo of current weather AND instructional modules.

Meteorology instructional modules delve into a variety of fascinating topics using charts, graphics, and easy-to-understand description. Light and Optics introduces how light interacts with atmospheric particles. Clouds & Precipitation introduces cloud classifications and developing precipitation. The Forces and Wind module discusses the forces that influence air flow. And, although this is just a taste of the additional contents, read on about: air masses, fronts, weather forecasting, severe storms, and hurricanes.

Thoughtful navigational features are almost too abundant to list, but it's worth noting some of my favorites: an option between full graphics or text-based site layout, a helper menu explaining the site navigation, color coded highlights for current location, and friendly left-margin menus throughout.

Fee or Free: Free.

CNN-Weathernet

http://www.cnn.com/WEATHER

e-mail: online form

RATING

+ + + +

BRIEFING:

Get well-done weather, 24-hours, with CNN's interactive presence.

Adding to a swelling list of lofty weather sites, CNN's weather page blows onto the cyber-scene with its own worldly prognostication. As is often the case with super-sites of this caliber, visually appealing graphics and orchestrated presentation subtly make you feel warm and cozy.

The main page quickly launches you into your desired four-day forecast. Just type your zip code or select your state from a pick list. If world weather is what you're after, just select a region and click. Up pops a corresponding four-day forecast, complete with highs/lows, precipitation, winds, pressure, and humidity. Current weather news, storm center, allergy report, and Biz Traveler are also standing by.

Curious about the bigger picture? Tap into your regional satellite and radar maps—they're easy to read and fast to load. Or, scan through worldwide weather maps and images. From the Africa satellite image to the Europe forecast map, global weather's here for the clicking.

Although completely non-aviation-related, a current news topic list follows you in the left margin. With a click you'll jump to CNN's current news on sports, travel, world, U.S., local, and more.

Fee or Free: Free.

Weather Concepts

http://www.weatherconcepts.com

e-mail: support@weatherconcepts.com

RATING

┼ ┼ ┼ ┼ ┼

BRIEFING:

Any more great features and this weather wonder could soon replace your local TV weather personality.

Functional design and great organization make Weather Concept's weather site one of your first stops for comprehensive weather. Even if you're new to the online weather scene, the transition is easy with an extensive explanation in each section's help section. Once you're comfortable and have given in to a 14-day free trial, have a look at: Live Wx, forecasts, Quickcast, AvCast, Int'l Wx, satellite maps, radar, winds, depiction, temps, precip, and more.

Pay a nominal monthly fee for basic service (everything but the individual NEXRAD Doppler Radar sites), or delve into full-blown weather euphoria with the enhanced service (an additional, yet still nominal monthly fee). The best part? Extensive aviation-related information with instant access to the identical text briefing used by flight service stations.

With area forecasts, METARs, TAFs, TWEBs, sigments, notams, airmets, winds aloft, and pireps what more could you possibly ask for?

Fee or Free: Fee-based. Tempt yourself with a 14-day free trial.

AccuWeather

http://www.accuweather.com
e-mail: info@accwx.com

This award-winning weather site makes it easy to see why good design, layout, and organization speak volumes in online communication.

From the moment you enter, there's no question that some graphics guru got ahold of these pages. Visual wizardry takes the form of icons, illustrations, and easy-to-see maps. But, more importantly, you'll enjoy future return trips due to careful organization. It's so easy to navigate with the masterful visual references.

From the AccuWeather intro page, you'll be invited to enter your city (zip or city/state). Free for anyone, AccuWeather's basic service includes over 43,000 U.S. five-day forecasts, links to international forecasts, local NEXRAD Doppler Radar, and more. Premium service subscribers will receive real-time access to everything. AccuWeather's products include: weather for virtually any spot on earth, special aviation weather section (including direct fight filing with the FAA), satellite pictures, NEXRAD Doppler Radar, weather maps—current forecasts, temperature band maps, current conditions, weather discussions, and more.

It's an organized look at weather, whether you subscribe or not.

Fee or Free: Free for some weather samples; fee-based for full-blown, real-time weather products.

Aviation Model Forecasts

http://weather.unisys.com/aviation

e-mail: none provided

BRIEFING:

**An educated
predictor of
aviation
weather.**

When talk among pilots turns to weather, things usually get more serious. Abandoning any hint of whimsical buffoonery, the Aviation Model Forecasts site sticks to the topic at hand without cracking so much as a smile. From the get-go you'll plunge into technical weather data and forecasting models. Here you'll tap into colorful contour plots for weather forecasts.

Originating from The Department of Earth and Atmospheric Sciences at Purdue University, the WXP Weather Processor analyzes and displays meteorological data and satellite images. Mostly designed for those on a meteorologist's level of understanding, this site does provide non-meteorologists the ability to view the data in varying degrees of complexity.

The plots are usually updated once every twelve hours and offer a full range of forecasting—from twelve hours to ten days. The index includes: individual plot summaries; general forecast plots; initial analyses; 12-, 24-, 36-, 48-, 60-, and three-day forecasts.

Yes it may take awhile to decipher, but you're looking at some highly reliable forecasting here.

Fee or Free: Free.

The Weather Channel

http://www.weather.com

e-mail: online form

RATING

BRIEFING:

The Weather Channel's masterful weather magicians mix visual delights with practicality.

The Weather Channel site—a great example of what happens when you mix talented designers, high-end software gadgetry, efficient hardware, and a team of marketing pros. Let this group loose on the cyber-world, and you get online brilliance. Although you may not get all the pieces of your aviation weather data here, you will get quick, accurate, searchable weather tidbits, including jetstream info, upper air readings, and national airport overview.

If you're a weather enthusiast with a hankering for facts and trivia, you've found your utopia. Start by typing your zip code or city and "Go!" Instantly you'll get stuff like: current temperature, wind speed/direction, relative humidity, five-day forecasts, barometric pressure, and current conditions.

After you've checked out all of your favorite cities, don your slickers and splash through the other fun items here. Dip into breaking weather, tropical update, international cities forecast, maps, TravelWise, and business services. All of the clickable topics move you into logically presented information with visually captivating graphics—with an option to customize your own page.

With this expert site, there's just no downside—unless the predicted weather keeps you grounded, that is.

Fee or Free: Free.

WeatherNet

http://cirrus.sprl.umich.edu/wxnet/

e-mail: macd@cirrus.spprl.umich.edu

RATING

BRIEFING:

Whether you're ready or not for over 380 weather sites— it's here, it's unbelievable, and it's waiting for you.

Sure weather's important to all of us aviation types. But, what you've got here is weather obsession—in the most positive sense, that is. Luckily, the weather worshipping folks at WeatherNet have assembled easy access to over 380 North American weather sites. Yes, over 380. Get your bookmark list cleaned up and get ready to add. At review time the 380 sites are simply listed in alpha order (a tad unwieldy), but look for better organization coming soon.

Aside from this unprecedented library of weather links, you'll find the usual forecast prompted by your city/ state/zip code/country and more great WeatherNet features. Highlights include: Forecasts (organized by state), Radar and Satellite (cool clickable U.S. map), Weather Cams (local photographic peeks into selected cities and popular resort destinations), Travel Cities Weather, and more.

So, if you've got a few minutes to dabble with Doppler or see through satellites, get out your umbrella—you'll always run into weather here.

Fee or Free: Free.

Intellicast

http://www.intellicast.com

e-mail: producer@intellicast.com

BRIEFING:

Knock-your-socks-off graphics combine with user-friendly organization to form weather magic.

Yes, there seems to be a weather site around every link and search engine, but Intellicast has created a unique and well-organized look at worldwide weather. Marvelous graphics and useful visual delights reign supreme here.

There's hordes of cool maps, weather-related icons, and menus. Get started with a main menu that leads to: USA Weather, World Weather, Traveler, and Ski Reports. New topic-specific weather even includes forecasts for golf, tropical getaways, the great outdoors, and sailing. Searching by city is easy. There's a map of popular cities, as well as a clickable list to get to your favorite city's weather. Once you find your city of choice, you'll become weather savvy with instant info relating to temperatures, forecasts, and a host of images to view. The long list of weather images includes: radar, radar summary, satellite, NEXRAD, and precipitation.

While you're visiting don't forget to check into the monthly almanac, featured site selections, and Ask Dr. Dewpoint. It's fun weather fancy for everyone.

Fee or Free: Free.

Bookmarkable Listings

Singer's Lock
http://www.weather.org
e-mail: oosinger@sure.net
Online book offers a "twentieth century look" at meteorology.

Real-Time Weather Data
http://www.rap.ucar.edu/weather/
e-mail: gthompsn@ncar.ucar.edu
Weather data categorized by satellite, radar, surface, upper-air, aviation, and more.

Charles Boley's Weather
http://www.cwbol.com
e-mail: cwbol@hiwaay.net
Personal collection of described links to current weather maps, radar images, and weather newsgroups.

Atmosphere Calculator
http://members.aol.com/nywx/atmoscal.htm
e-mail: nywx@aol.com
Calculates dewpoint, relative humidity, wind chill, heat index, and more based upon information given.

National Climatic Data Center (NCDC)
http://www.ncdc.noaa.gov
e-mail: webmaster@ncdc.noaa.gov
Online collection of resources from the NCDC—the world's largest active archive of weather data.

Sunrise/Sunset
http://tycho.usno.navy.mil/srss.html
e-mail: online form
Automatically calculates sunrise/sunset, twilight, moonrise/moonset with given longitude and latitude.

Pilot
Resources

PilotAge

http://www.pilotage.com

e-mail: Max@PilotAge.com

```
RATING
+++
```

BRIEFING:

Pilotage:
"a form of
navigation by
visual reference
to landmarks"
and a cool
Southern
California Web
site.

If you or someone you know happens to be a Southern California aviator, I'll expect kudos from you for locating this site. Its combo of reference stuff is rewarding. But, non-Southern Cal pilots need not be discouraged. A satisfying assortment of general info awaits you too.

Put aside any hope of luxurious page layout. Just strap in and hang on. Pay careful attention to underlined/linked words because they'll lead you to more information. Scan the clickable contents. You'll notice each has relatively good descriptions before taxiing, so enjoy without frustration. For the Pilot's Companion section serves up enlightening gems for significant others who want to know what the pilot is doing before, during, and after a flight, and why. Hangar Flying, Forums, and Editorials offer entertainment and interaction with discussions on products, vendors, aircraft, and more. Features, Flying Clubs and Organizations, Weather and Other Aviation Links, Aviation Marketplace, and Aviation Events fill up the rest of your viewing time.

Southern California aviation will revel in specific info on local airports. Get airport/facilities info as well as cool, enroute visual perspective photos of the airport.

Fee or Free: Free.

Virtual Flight Surgeons (VFS)

http://www.virtualfs.com

e-mail: info@virtualfs.com

RATING

BRIEFING:

Thoroughly useful online aeromedical consultants keep you flying wise with real answers to real questions.

Whatever ails you fellow flyers, VFS is standing by with an answer online. Visually organized to perfection, you'll avoid the ER-type panic and settle into professionally thorough aeromedical consultation.

From the get-go your board certified physicians are a mere click and question away. A left-margin menu outlines your choices into three manageable levels: The Resource Center, which is free to all pilots, offers a newsletter on medical topics, FAQs, aeromedical links, a bookstore for medical/aviation reading, and answers to medication and drug questions.

Skipping through the fee-oriented service levels of The Waiting Room and Office Visit, you'll be bombarded with an array of specific aeromedical services, including: private consultations, premium newsletter, FAA liaison service, expert witness testimony, and FAA medical certification issues.

What a fantastic, flowing informational resource. Questions about allergies and medications, hypertension, vision surgery, vision abnormalities, cholesterol, or others? Yes. You'll get an answer. Take advantage for health's sake.

Fee or Free:
Some services are free; others are fee-related but reasonable.

Crewmembers International

http://www.crewmembers.com

e-mail: webmaster@crewmembers.com

RATING

+++

BRIEFING:

An insider's resource center for the high flying crews of airlines, military, and corporate aviation.

Kind of new to the commercial carrier online scene, Crewmembers International scores big with a well conceived resource for airline pilots, flight attendants, military aviators, corporate pilots, and others.

Even if you're not among the important crew list above, you probably know someone who fits the Crewmembers description. The exchange of relevant information here is simply unparalleled Web-wide. With weak page design as the only stumbling block, you'll pull away from the jet way and be on your way with great insight nonetheless. The key? Just rely on a long-winded left-margin list of topics (mirrored at page bottom as well).

Aviation professionals will marvel at the sheer volume of tips, tricks, facts, and rumors found in a host of areas. Crew members are invited to transition through: Crashpads, Airport Cars, Ticket Exchange, Aviation Hazards, Layover Tips, Classifieds, Reunions, Crew Message Boards, Tech Center, Track a Flight, Pilot Lounge Chat, Resume Service, and more.

One handy aside: if appropriate, try the "Find a Friend Board." The novel approach to tracking down fellow aviators seems fun & useful.

Fee or Free: Free.

Aviation Law Corporation

http://www.aviationlawcorp.com

e-mail: phil@aviationlawcorp.com

RATING

╋ ╋ ╋

BRIEFING:

True aviation law info online crushes the myth that all aviation law sites are just smoke and mirrors.

Fee or Free: Free, unless you get yourself into trouble and really need Mr. Kolczynski.

Phillip Kolczynski's law Web presence is surprisingly refreshing for only one reason: loads of free aviation law, hints, tips, and explanation. Yes, the focus is on credentials, experiences, and successes. In short it's an online pitch for clients. And no, Mr. Kolczynski's not a Web page designer. His shtick is aviation law. So, don't go crying over boring, "no-frills" page design.

Every online indication points to "big time" aviation law experience. Just dip into any one of a number of in-depth articles on a variety of topics and make up your own mind. The writing is long, thorough, insightful, and current. Even if you aren't in trouble with the law (or the FAA), take a peek at his variety of informational offerings: Aviation Product Liability, NTSB Investigation Guide, Avoiding FAA Sanctions, Post Air Crash Procedures, FAA vs. Airmen (10 Tips), Victims vs. Defective Products, Aircraft Owner Liability, and more. The experience is there, the topics are real-world, and the recommendations are genuine.

Although the articles are worth a bookmark alone, there's much more. You'll find a relatively current online newsletter covering many important topics, aviation safety report form (with FAQs), info on preparing for trial in federal court, and some favorite aviation poems to lighten things up a bit.

Aviation Law Corporation's award-winning site uses candor and credentials to get your attention. My free advice? Listen to counsel. He's got your best interests in mind.

SureCheck Online

http://www.surecheck.net

e-mail: webmaster@surecheck.net

RATING
✝ ✝

BRIEFING:

Checklists o'plenty await your credit card order. But wait, there's more: news and pilot resource links.

Let's be blunt here. You're going to receive a heavy dose of product pitching with SureCheck. What kind of products? Well, primarily you'll be bombarded with aviation checklists—lots of them—in many varieties. And conveniently, they offer secure ordering online.

If you aren't in the checklist market—your ratty 172 checklist card is just fine thank you—you may still want to read further. SureCheck's well designed site does offer a bit more than just stuff to buy. Updated aviation news stands by on the main page with text links to the main story. Although changeable, read about topics like: Hubble Goes to the Limit in Search of Farthest Galaxies; New Safety Program Unveiled: Safer Skies; Get the Latest Hiring Stats; and one of my favorites, Zane's Corner: Flight Training Question of the Day.

Yes, the site's well designed. The news is good. The product ordering section is handy. But, I must say, the pilot resources—in the form of links—are excellent. They've carefully amassed a healthy, not too unwieldy, list of quality links. Each in their own right deserves a bookmark, and many are already award-winners, listed in this book. Click into SureCheck's Pick of the Week, weather info, best source for new pilots, aviation directories, publications, airlines, organizations, manufacturers, and more.

Fee or Free: Free.

RentalPlanes.com

http://www.rent-a-plane.com

e-mail: webmaster@RentalPlanes.com

RATING

BRIEFING:

A huge fleet of rental planes are merely awaiting your command to "clear prop" and go.

True, there's a large contingent of non-owners out there (myself included) who play the rental game. Gladly it's not as awful as renting cars, but I'll welcome any aids to make the process easier. And RentalPlanes.com is just such an aid.

Just as a fully IFR-equipped Cessna 172 has the tools for guidance, RentalPlanes.com comes outfitted with top and bottom page navigation bars to get anywhere site-wide. They make it real easy to just strap in and go without a checkflight or walkaround. The menu's simple: Find an Airplane (free), Add an Airplane (also free for a limited time), Welcome to New Users (nice, brief intro), Add/Edit Accounts, and the ever-present shameless promotions.

Just know up front the database of worldwide planes is huge. Take advantage of the search criteria form to limit your choices. Some limiting criteria include: make, model, year, power type, cruise speed, max rental rate, avionics, total time, ratings required, airport identifier, special characteristics, and more.

No, you probably won't uncover a Cessna 150 outfitted with a stormscope and TCAS, but you will find everything in an airworthy rental based upon your reasonable perimeters.

Fee or Free: Free at review time.

Crashpads.com

http://www.crashpads.com
e-mail: iads@gte.net

BRIEFING:

You're getting sleepy, very sleepy, and the FAA says you're out of duty time. Get to Crashpads.

Fee or Free: Free. Membership is required to access Crashpad's database, and you must work for an airline. All the other resources don't require a membership.

Frames or no frames. That's your first of many convenience options at Crashpads.com. Me? I usually go frameless, but it's your choice. With that out of the way, you'll be pleasantly bombarded with a host of site solutions and niceties for flight crews searching for some in-between downtime.

Just listed crashpads, special offers, and a huge resource center for flight crews are just what the FAA ordered. To view the enormous and secure crashpad database, however, you must become a member (verify your employment with an airline). For those listing crashpad accommodations no membership is required, just submit the required info.

Even if your accommodations are covered, crash here anyway during your ground time. An aviator's array of delightful resources are surprising helpful with just a few clicks. Check airline flight availability, follow an interactive flight tracker (courtesy of TheTrip.com), or get hotel phone numbers. Look up the airport codes of the world. Read about airline world news. Even check into a live, real-time chat room.

If you're in the commercial carrier business, Crashpads.com tucks you in and keeps you refreshed.

The Pilot's Resource Page

http://www.pilotresource.com

e-mail: webmaster@pilotresource.com

RATING

BRIEFING:

A hastily designed, but thoughtfully compiled page of aviation enthusiast resources.

The Pilot's Resource Page. How descriptively accurate. Oh yes, you'll be delighted with link resources o'plenty. Especially if you're not aesthetically inclined, you'll breeze through without a care and a smile on your face.

The best way to dig in? Just begin scrolling. This frameless page employs mere descriptive topic text to guide you into its interior pages. Leave your quest for visual perfection behind and ride right seat through a collection of categorized aviation goodies. Stay alert, the pattern's filled with hordes of ad banners and nonrelevant obstacles. The fog clears when approaching your destination. Flight Planning reveals weather, regulations, insurance, and other preflight needs. Aircraft and Flight Gear lists aircraft and aviation supply dealers (only the best seem to have made the cut). The Makers identifies your favorite aircraft, avionics, and aviation accessories companies. Flight Training steers you toward some of the better training and testing centers around. Flying Opportunities puts you in touch with those looking for pilots (military and civilian). Areas of aviation appreciation, adventure gear, and AOPA membership round out your options.

Fee or Free: Free.

Air Routing International

http://www.airrouting.com

e-mail: techsupport@airrouting.com

BRIEFING:

Get on track and stay there with a newly emerging site from a long-time air routing pro.

One of the pilot's greatest resources? Yes, that's right, it's information. Take an online trip with Air Routing International, and you'll discover why it's now an award winner.

The site wasn't even complete at review time and still coasted to a mention here. Why? A couple key features are sure to become the international pilot's best friend: airport locator, pilot feedback, and the AIRMAIL newsletter. Although excellent page presentation and link organization should command some attention and review, I'd rather concentrate on these functional flight facets. Use the airport locator (by city or identifier) to retrieve location data on a huge list of airports worldwide. Even get time and distance info using a handy calculator. Just enter departure location, arrival location and airspeed in knots (calculator will automatically include a 15-minute bias on takeoff). The pilot feedback form, offering real experiences from international pilots, launches you into a long, city-alphabetized list of hints, suggestions, and warnings. It's a huge compiling of interesting, yet informative remarks.

And, if ground time permits get plenty of air routing news from around the globe from AIRMAIL by the AR Group.

Fee or Free: Free. Hints to fee-related air routing services.

Worldwide Airport Path Finder

http://www.calle.com/aviation/airports.cgi

e-mail: carl@fallingrain.com

RATING

++

BRIEFING:

Fun functionality is the rule, flashiness isn't. Data-heads and the research-oriented will enjoy this ride.

First have a little fun with the Worldwide Airport Path Finder (WAPF), then be suspicious. As any careful aviator would agree, planning with current and correct info is the only way to go. That said, the WAPF is fast and full of features. Though it's not fancy by any stretch, this bare bones database interface fruitfully finds multi-step great circle paths from one airport to another.

Input fields take your data to return great circle flight paths, maps, and weather. Your data for ICAO airport codes, mapping options, nautical mile range, average speed, departure day/time, and altitude range begin the adventure. Multiple push buttons serve up weather info, airport info, navaid info, waypoint codes and more.

The coolest feature for those just toying with this tool is the mapping and quick click weather options. Great real-time topographical maps identify airports and selected areas. Weather-wise, an entire menu of forecasts, TAFs, and METs come in all directions and distances from the supplied airport ICAO.

Fee or Free: Free.

Air-News

http://www.air-news.com

e-mail: none available

BRIEFING:

Real opinions from world travelers shine light on the globe's best and worst.

Worldwide flyers take heart and take note, Air-News is for you. Avoid any advertised hype about eating out, hotels, and entertainment and jump straight to real opinions from real people who speak their minds online. Air-News collects experiences and presents them using a fashionably designed database. The categories are many and the comments are candid.

Initially a handsome interface welcomes you aboard with an at-a-glance world region choice to begin your journey. Select from: Europe, North America, Asia, South America, Africa, Australia/NZ, Worldwide, or In Flight. You may even opt to go straight to the newest articles or search via a host of left-margin methods.

Whatever your searching methods, suffice it to say that finding your category and region is easy. Once you begin reading the real-life opinions, you'll be hooked. Categories within which folks offer suggestions include: hotel, fun, nightlife, shopping, warnings, eating out, entertainment, travel, health/medicine, hints & warnings, and passenger matters. The entries themselves are fresh and non-edited. Each record offers info for location, category, subject, remark (the opinion or suggestions), author/e-mail, and age of entry (nice!).

Fee or Free: Free.

Aviation Aspirations

http://www.aviation-aspirations.com

e-mail: online form

RATING

BRIEFING:

Worldwide depository of flight training recommendations.

Aspiring to be an impartial purveyor of flight school recommendations, Aviation Aspirations blows past the pay-to-play level of Web promotion. We're assured that what lies before us in pixilated glory is an unbiased compilation of enlightening information for finding a flight school. What's more, the free info contained reaches beyond our continental confines and goes global.

Sure it's easy enough to navigate through Aspirations' offerings, but don't expect to be dazzled aesthetically. The pages were obviously meant for speed. Although you'll notice a few ad banners poking around, loading time is good, and the information is better.

A colorful assortment of language/country codes points you to country-specific info and appropriate translations. The all-encompassing "world emblems" signifies relevant info to all visitors. The simplest way to the goodies is via the World Site Chapter Index. Here you'll find the jumping off points to: Choosing a Flight School (good!); Our Short List of Reputable Flight Schools; Training Courses & Rental Requirements; Location & Training Environment; Medical; and much more of the like.

Fee or Free: Free.

QuickAID

http://www.quickaid.com

e-mail: online form

BRIEFING:

Invaluable airport info resource is free and fast. What more could you ask for?

Perhaps you've already tapped into the airport-related travel info dispensed by a QuickAID information kiosk found at many major airports. If not, you need only grab a mouse, dial in, and search QuickAID online. By simply following their easy-to-use system of menus, you'll quickly uncover a wealth of info airport ground transportation, shops, services, area hotels, and even terminal maps.

Personally, I had no interest in company-related details (personnel profiles, company background, and contact info). If you're like me, you'll simply skip the corporate stuff and make a beeline to QuickAID's cyber heart: airport information.

The compilation of data's huge, but the site's surprisingly fast nonetheless. Begin by clicking your airport of choice (a list of airport names with identifiers is provided). Though not every airport is represented, lots of the majors are here. Get info on: ground transportation (taxis, busses, shuttles, etc.), area lodging, airlines, airport services and facilities (restaurants, banks, business services, children's services, parking, and more), terminal map, and Airport Yellow Pages.

Fee or Free: Free.

Travelocity

http://www.travelocity.com

e-mail: online form

BRIEFING:

Mega travel haven does everything but fly the plane.

While it's not impossible, getting the full grasp of Travelocity's rich information wonderland isn't a carefree endeavor. The interface, though perfectly designed for ease-of-use, is intimidating at first. But, fellow aviators need only gather their courage and begin clicking.

Frankly if you're just in it for the destination guide and not the reservations stuff, your choices will be that much simpler. Certainly, with Travelocity you can do a lot of things online: book a flight, rent a car, reserve a hotel, book vacations and cruises, and more. If you were so inclined you could spend weeks pouring over this site's saturation of travel lore.

At least at review time, I was more intrigued by the destination guide, maps, and weather. Just narrow the search to a selected city and get the scoop online. City facts, Activities, Orientation, Overview, and When to Go are written well and packed with current information (courtesy of Lonely Planet Publications). Weather reports, including current conditions and five-day forecasts, are available for over 740 cities. And, street maps make directions a breeze.

Fee or Free: Free.

The Professional Pilot's Wait Time Web Site

http://www.pilotwait.com

e-mail: Webmaster@pilotwait.com

RATING

BRIEFING:

Real recommendations of dining, lodging, and things to do from fellow flyers.

Waiting for weather to change? Waiting for a passenger? Waiting for an engine overhaul? Whatever your wait state, The Professional Pilot's Wait Time Web Site invites you to make good use of your ground time. Maybe it's time to become a little more enlightened concerning great places to eat and stay and fun things to do worldwide. Gathered by people who travel for a living, the accumulated local knowledge provides real-life recommendations and honest observations.

The page presentation's simple. Keeping a "down to earth" theme, the offerings are friendly and understated—just right to host a free fellow pilot forum for real-life recommendations. A left-margin column gives the stats at a glance: revision date, new listings for which states, and a listing count of restaurants, places to stay, and things to do. Listings are encouraged to be of a local nature (big chain establishments are discouraged). Most recommended listings offer establishment address and phone with non-edited description. A corresponding rating (in stars) and cost scale (in dollar bills) give you an even clearer picture into each recommendation.

As of review time there were well over 500 listings, representing 48 states and 19 countries. Now that's substance!

Fee or Free: Free.

AirCharterNet

http://www.aircharternet.com

e-mail: hq@aircharternet.com

RATING

┿ ┿ ┿ ┿

BRIEFING:

**Air charter
made easy and
almost
automatic with
a virtual charter
agent.**

Without compromising your Web time with cheesy graphics, The AirCharterNet travel site reigns supreme in many cyber-areas: content, design, page navigation, and organization. Just take the interactive demo tour and see for yourself.

Air charter passengers, air charter operators, and frequent travelers in general need to make room on the bookmark list for this resourceful Web wonder. Once you've become a member (it's painless and free), you'll meet the efficient virtual charter agent who automatically takes care of everything. Without charging a nickel more for your flight, the virtual charter agent will identify qualified air charter operators for specific trips; swiftly and easily solicit price quotes from any one of them; e-mail price quotes to you; and help you reserve flights.

Beyond the vast resources of the virtual charter agent, you'll also find the site helpful for the travel-related topics of: vacation planning, ground services, worldwide weather, and filling empty charter legs.

Fee or Free:
Membership is
free.

Fillup Flyer Fuel Finder

http://www.wdia.com/ff/ff

e-mail: comments-ffff@voyager.wdia.com

RATING

┼ ┼ ┼

BRIEFING:

Finding your way through this fuel finder is worthwhile.

Maybe someday Fillup Flyer Fuel Finder will find the time away from the pump to clean this confusing, yet bookmarkable online presence. Don't misunderstand, Fillup Flyer is in this book for a reason. Under the thin veil of design lurks a very useable fuel resource that is worth the initial effort.

Fee-based, Fillup Flyer provides members and nonmembers fuel price reports based on routes, nonstop, multi-destination, area, or statewide. What are your options for report info delivery and requests? Most choose computer, but fax, voice, or mail are also available. Once you gather your visual orientation you'll have the major topics in sight. Click into: About Fillup Flyer, Admin, General Info, Membership and Costs, Member Reports, Nonmember Reports, Premier FBOs, Sample Reports, Nationwide Fuel Station Price Statistics, and more.

Hey, if a little extra scrolling and clicking is worth saving up to a dollar per gallon on your next trip, then tough it out and assign this one to your favorites list.

Fee or Free:
Fee—sign up annually (recommended) or pay by report.

UK Airfields Online

http://www.uk-airfields.co.uk

e-mail: sam@sand.co.uk

BRIEFING:

UK-only airfield directory dazzles with simple brilliance.

Okay, my aero Web search narrowed here just a bit. But, such a simple, yet functional gem deserves its moment in the limelight.

Handsomely designed, UK Airfields is aptly named with a singular purpose—giving you instant access to popular UK Airfield info. Site navigation is basic. Simply use the pull-down menu, find your desired destination, and click "visit." Yes, that's it. There aren't any ads, banners, or membership requests. UK Airfields is around for your benefit—really.

As of review time, the list of possible airfields to visit includes: Aberdeen, Belfast, Birmingham, Cardiff, Compton Abbas, Denham, Duxford, Edinburgh, Exeter, Gatwick, Glasgow, Headcorn, Heathrow, Ipswich, Isle of Man, Lasham, Lundon Luton, Manchester, Manchester (Barton), Southampton, Stansted, White Waltham, and Wycombe Airpark. Once you make your choice, each airpark maintains its own pages. A sample selection? Belfast International Airport's site includes valuable info, like: getting there, Northern Ireland, business profile, airport facilities, flight schedules, flight arrivals, flight departures, and airport news.

Fee or Free: Free.

Aviation Information Resource Database

http://www.airbase1.com

e-mail: sales@airbase1.com

RATING

BRIEFING:

Let your mouse do the clicking through this big yellow book of online aviation resources.

Cleared for an informative flyby, you are invited to mouse your way around this resourceful labyrinth aptly tagged the Aviation Information Resource Database. Brought to all cyber-flyers free of charge by AIRbase ONE, this dominating database equates to a computerized Yellow Pages.

Flip through its topics and you'll see what I mean. Delve into over 12,000 aviation businesses listed in over 1,100 categories. In addition to thousands of service-related listings, there's a complete facility directory of all public/private airports and heliports. Also at your curiosity's convenience are: aircraft and engine parts, FBOs, avgas or jet fuel suppliers, and an exhaustive general aviation events calendar.

When you're really ready to pinpoint a preference, searchable subjects get you there with powerful queries. Just pick a topic: aviation businesses, airports, fuel suppliers, fuel prices, DUATS planning, lodging, restaurants, ground transportation, general aviation events calendar, and other aviation Web sites.

Although hard to do, getting lost at this airbase is corrected easily with a handy "Need Help?" button. It's a progressive taxi through an industrious airpark.

Fee or Free: Free.

Flight Watch

http://www.flightwatch.com

e-mail: FlightWatch@compuserve.com

BRIEFING:

Flight Watch
directs you to
aviation's finest
legal resources
with your own
online attorney.

The legalities of aviation? Although most of us are way off course, fluttering around helplessly in the complex airspace of law, may I propose a source of refreshment? Keep your eye on Flight Watch—Resources for Pilots and Aviation Lawyers.

Normally I prefer my legal resources less flashy. But, this sophisticated design wreaks of credibility. Some of the bulleted topics offer descriptions before you link up, but most do not. Regardless, you'll encounter a nice variety of FAA documents, databases, and handy look-ups.

Even if you're not in any legal trouble, being familiar with Flight Watch's facts, figures, and federal resources might just help you to avoid any forced hangar time. Clean up your bookmark list and make some room for this one. You never know when legal questions will arise, so look through the site's links to find: aviation legal resources, federal legal resources, government publications, law libraries, legal search engines, private sector publications, and much more.

My closing argument? It's a free, resourceful hub for aviation's legal questions. Case closed.

Fee or Free: Free.

Equipped to Survive

http://www.equipped.com
e-mail: dritter@equipped.org

RATING

BRIEFING:

The survival
instinct is alive
and well with
this must-
bookmark site.

Long flights over water. A perilous single-engine journey over mountainous terrain. What if disaster strikes? Will you be prepared? The fact of the matter is survival—you may have only one chance. Make it count with the online excellence of the Equipped to Survive site.

First a note on aesthetics—don't expect any. Honestly proclaimed up front, the site's author emphasizes information, not imagery. Second, site navigation simply consists of links to topics and "previous page/next page" buttons. So, nothing fancy here either. However, dip into the third criteria of content and you strike gold. The focus, you'll find, is on equipment—what is useful, what works, and what doesn't. Most of the site info is based upon the author's research on wilderness and marine survival from an aviation perspective.

Fantastically insightful articles worth printing and saving include: The Survival Forum, Basic Aviation Survival Kit, Ditching (for pilots), Aviation Life Raft Reviews, Survival for Kids, Survival Skills and Techniques, Aviation Life Vest Reviews, and more.

Fee or Free: Free.

TheTrip.com

http://www.thetrip.com

e-mail: feedback@thetrip.com

RATING

BRIEFING:

A travel agent, a taxi driver, a map interpreter, a hotel concierge, a maitre d', and an airport TelePrompter all rolled up into an online info-fest.

Straying a tad from my aviation-only focus, I must include this favorite of mine for the frequent traveler. Whether you're the pilot in command, or some other MD-80 crew is getting you there, TheTrip.com becomes the ultimate in travel insurance.

Wonderfully educated design pros weave their obvious skills and combine perfect page scripting. Thoughtful navigational bars and subtle icons guide you effortlessly through fantastic travel data. Under The Flight, you'll become your own travel agent—checking flight availability and actually making reservations. There's even a real-time flight tracking query to check any flight's status. Trip Planner helps you to book a flight, car, or hotel. The Complete Traveler magazine offers an unlimited number of tips and news articles. And, saving the best for last, Guides & Tours category ably spews out specific weather, lodging, dining, or city map data based upon your chosen city.

Tired of business travel stress? Settle into TheTrip.com for a pre-departure briefing.

Fee or Free: Free.

Air Safety Home Page

http://airsafe.com

e-mail: tcurtis@airsafe.com

RATING

Airline safety analysis gives you the hard truth and worthwhile advice for airline travel.

Odds are you were bombarded with media overload from the last airline disaster. Newspapers, radio, cable, and even Internet news join the bandwagon when heart-wrenching air carrier tragedies occur. In the interests of safety, this site's veteran airline safety analyst brings to light important industry info not easily found in one source.

Some events you may painfully remember, other airliner mishaps may have escaped your attention. In any case, the facts and observations found in the Air Safety Home Page may open your eyes to valuable passenger advice.

Complex navigational gizmos and graphics are virtually nonexistent. But, Air Safety's claim to acclaim is hard, reliable data and important advice. Read about the last ten fatal jet airliner mishaps, fatal jet airliner events by model, the top ten air traveler safety tips, child safety, top ten questions about airline safety, and more.

I know it may not be the most cheerful topic, but I urge you to point your browser here for safety's sake.

Fee or Free: Free.

The Air Safety Investigation Resource (ASI)

http://startext.net/homes/mikem/

e-mail: mikem@mail.startext.net

RATING

++++

BRIEFING:

Strategic
selection of
quality aviation
links with
safety in mind.

Similar to my publication's goal of rounding up worthy sites, The Air Safety Investigation Resource seeks to narrow the infinite sea of aviation's online cache. Simply organized into a "catch-all" table of contents, the site topics dribble down the page.

Although you'll be keeping your scroll bar arrows and "back" button busy, this site's worth the extra hunting time. Navigation and aesthetics rank among the ho-hum variety, but the thoughtful collection of hyperlinks catapults it onto the bookmark list. Obviously the time spent sifting through and collecting quality reference sources took priority—and rightfully so.

Check into these summarized link areas: databases of accidents, ADs, NTSB investigations, service difficulty reports, weather maps & text based forecasts, aviation organizations, and airport info.

Until an official online aviation library takes center stage in cyberspace, this is it.

Fee or Free: Free.

Aircraft Technical Publishers (ATP)

http://www.atp.com

e-mail: info@atp.com

RATING

+ +

BRIEFING:

Constantly searching for Airworthiness Directives? Free up the modem and cruise through ATP's instant list!

While other reasons exist for visiting ATP's site, my bookmark list increased by one because they offer a thorough list of Airworthiness Directives (ADs). Even better, the list is continuously updated with all ADs issued within the last 30 days. The value for repair stations is obvious. It means fast, thorough research. Even air charter operators, brokers, and owners will benefit from its timely information.

At the heart of ATP's AD offerings is a quick interface. The somewhat confusing nature of ADs disappears with a summarized list of ADs less than 30 days old. The AD number, effective date, manufacturer, short description, and recurrence status are conveniently simplified into a clickable table. To actually view a chosen AD, you'll need the Adobe Acrobat Reader. Download it from the ATP site if you don't have it. Go on, it's free!

More marginal site attributes involve some maintenance products and services, *FLIGHTLine Newsletter* info archive (Adobe Acrobat Reader needed), employment opportunities, and more.

Fee or Free: Free.

Aviation & Aerospace Medicine

http://www.ozemail.com.au/~dxw/avmed.html

e-mail: dxw@ozemail.com.au

RATING

╈ ╈

BRIEFING:

A no-frills one-stop shop of aerospace medicine knowledge.

It's not pretty. But topics like hypoxia, G-LOC, and the leans never are. The site's visual style seems to mirror the somewhat serious nature inherent in aviation medicine discussions. Don't expect any frivolous pictures or illustrations. The focus remains solidly on aerospace medicine. Period.

Once you click in, you'll be astounded at the worldwide collection of articles and publications. The phenomenal scope and breadth spills into just about anything currently troubling you. Selections like: Alcohol & Aviation, The Senses During Flight, and Laser Corrective Eye Surgery for Pilots are just the beginning. Read on for a whole series of articles relating to hyperbatic medicine combined with foot ulcers, oxygen therapy, wound healing, and strokes.

Looking for a specific aerospace medicine contact? A convenient alpha search quickly locates any one of 556 practitioners in 48 countries. Or, you may be more interested in tracking down a specific aviation medicine organization. This site puts you in touch with groups like: The Aerospace Medicine Association, Safety and Flying Equipment Association, and The International Academy of Aviation & Space Medicine.

The medicinal resources are endless. The value here is obvious.

Fee or Free: Free.

Great Circle Distance Calculator

http://www.atinet.org/~steve/cs150

e-mail: steve@atinet.org

RATING

┿ ┿

BRIEFING:

Dialing for distance? Call up this nifty 'Net calculator.

Born out of a software engineering project in 1994, the Great Circle Distance Calculator pinpoints distance faster than you can say "GPS." Obviously not meant to impress with grandiose design or layout, this global distance tool quietly does its job, perfectly. You'll crack an appreciate grin the moment you need a flight distance in a hurry.

The site simply computes the flight distance between any two points on Earth, called the Great Circle Distance. As you may have guessed, the two points are generally derived from latitudes and longitudes (degrees, minutes, and seconds—or decimal format). However, if you're a little thin on "longs" and "lats," you're still covered. Just enter the desired three-letter airport codes. You'll get the same result. When shopping for more generic distances, try the clickable map. Though it's not as accurate, you'll probably get your global distance questions answered.

Whatever the input method, your resulting data may be viewed in statute miles, nautical miles, or kilometers. It's your choice, and it's free. How many online aviation tools can say that?

Fee or Free: Free.

EarthCam

http://www.earthcam.com

e-mail: cammaster@earthcam.com

RATING

╪ ╪ ╪ ╪

BRIEFING:

Be everywhere at once with a 24-hour peek into the world's live video cams.

Room with a view. Window on the world. An eye in the sky. Whatever your description, EarthCam is the source. Blossoming into a global cyber-cam hub, EarthCam compiles and categorizes the limitless, living directory of live video cameras on the Web.

Generally used by aviation enthusiasts as a quick destination peek, these handy cams offer glimpses of live weather conditions—instantly. Though obviously not worthwhile for navigation or flight planning, the cams do give some quick insight into current conditions. Better still, the wide variety of cams isn't limited to airports or large cities. You'll get a look at the Bay Bridge traffic, or Chicago's lakefront, or Disney World.

Colorful page presentation, clever icons, and convenient searching tools cheerfully guide you into an unbelievable array of cams. Peer through traffic cams, weather cams, business cams, educational cams, scenic cams, and more. Or, get a bit more serious about weather with a clickable world map broken down into regional satellite views.

My favorite part? Previewing text descriptions before downloading the pictures saves hours of frustration. Be sure to read them prior to clicking—there are some time-wasters in the mix.

Fee or Free: Free.

The Air Charter Guide (ACG)

http://www.guides.com/acg

e-mail: webmaster@guides.com

RATING

BRIEFING:

A must-be-viewed site for charter operators and passengers.

Whether you're on the passenger side or the cockpit side of air charter, you simply must have a printed and online version of ACG at your fingertips. The printed 700-page reference edition teams up with this online guide to give you hundreds of charter operators and brokers worldwide. The index conveniently sorts: charter operators by location, name, or specialty and U.S. & international brokerage services by name and specialty. There's even a complete list of aviation services providers—from insurance to sales.

Although the printed edition tells the complete story about each operator, the online "zine" makes retrieval of basic info easy. Also on tap: charter industry info, discussions, and news. Industry reference topics give you a peek into: travel weather, city guides and maps, airline reservation systems, limousine and car rentals, and travel publications and associations.

The site is expertly organized, fast, and helpful. Chartering? Dial this one up!

Fee or Free: Free.

Introduction to GPS Applications

http://www.redsword.com/gps

e-mail: jbeadles@pobox.com

RATING

BRIEFING:

Position your browser here to find worlds of info on global positioning systems.

Aimed at new users of global positioning systems (GPS), this site voluntarily offers up great insight served in a plain brown wrapper. But, faster than you can say "spaced-based radio positioning systems," you'll be overwhelmed by GPS topics, issues, definitions, Q&As, products, and more. Congratulations to the author for such a monumental informational effort. If you're expecting graphics or English perfection, your cyber-hopes will be dashed. You will, however, find lots of pages relating to global positioning systems.

Just sifting through the loosely organized list, you'll discover there's more to GPS than push-button navigation. Highlighted subjects include: How GPSs Work, GPS Acronyms, Definitions of GPS Terms, Types of GPS Receivers, Policy Issues, Industry Applications (agriculture, surveying, photogrammetry, etc.), The NAVSTAR Signal Specification, GPS Satellites, and more. All online documents are color-coded with symbols representing the status of the document—from substantially complete to a proposed, but non-existent page.

You'll learn about the author and his qualifications, find links to frequently asked GPS questions, unearth an archive site for GPSs, and be presented with sponsorship opportunities. Get ready to take notes, this online GPS class is in session.

Fee or Free: Free.

Aero-Tourism

http://www.yi.com/home/RogerEtienne/aerotourism

e-mail: etienne@vcn.bc.ca

RATING
✝ ✝ ✝ ✝

BRIEFING:

An organized treasure chest of practical info for globally minded flyers.

Thinking about taking the Cessna 150 to Switzerland? Okay, bad example. But, for those who like to break out of the familiar and spread their wings globally, Aero-Tourism is just the ticket. This site, simply designed for aerodynamic functionality, boldly avoids Uncle Jim's cross-country pictorials and limits the content to useful info.

The subjects are focused solely on global private pilotage. Topics include: foreign licensing procedures, places where one can rent, things to do, places to visit, and stories of flight abroad (caution: may need some multilingual skills here). The country-related info (as of review time) includes: Alaska, Australia, Canada, Colombia, France, Kenya, New Zealand, Portugal, South Africa, Switzerland, and Zimbabwe. Generally, the country resources are independent links to country-maintained sites. In almost every case, the content is useful and thorough. Specifically, you'll run into tidbits on overflight authorizations, ATC costs, civilian permits, prior notifications, The Aeronautical Information Publication (a global version of the AIM), airports of entry, and foreign exchange rates.

For fascinating facts and international flying insight, this is your first fix.

Fee or Free: Free.

F.E. Potts' Guide to Bush Flying

http://www.fepco.com/Bush_Flying.html

e-mail: none provided

BRIEFING:

Online book represents its printed predecessor with an unequaled reference for the bush pilot.

For those pilots who slip the surly bonds of crowded airspace, this unique online book should be a required flight manual. Wonderfully organized into a slick index and clickable chapters, the guide's content is crucial for bush pilots and fascinating for everyone else. This text-based resource is well written (no fluff—just the useful stuff), with easy-to-follow tips and techniques. Generally, the topics and scope assume the reader carries at least a commercial ticket. But, everyone will enjoy a look at things like: partial stall landings, STOL landings, pre-heating, ground handling, and many images. The table of contents breaks down into the following categories: General Information, Equipment and Environment, Flying Techniques, Images, Glossary, Illustration, and Author Photo.

The only thing that unsettled me during my visit was the author's disclaimer: "I am primarily a pilot, not a writer…" To the latter I must disagree.

Fee or Free: Free.

High Mountain Flying in Ski Country U.S.A.

http://www.tc.faa.gov/ZDV/high_mountain/

e-mail: donald_smith@admin.tc.faa.gov

RATING

BRIEFING:

A text-based summary of essential mountain flying info with specific emphasis on Colorado's ski country.

Tooling around the Rockies and other high altitude airports means extra sharp mountain flying skills. While expertly briefing pilots on the intricacies of Colorado flying, this educational site gives all mountain-bound pilots a great heads-up!

Brought to you by the concerned folks at the Denver Air Route Traffic Control Center and the FAA, this site's a great resource for explaining high mountain distinctions. Do's and Don'ts of Mountain Flying, in particular, is a well-written laundry list of hints, guidelines and safety essentials. Print it and keep it in your flight bag—it's excellent. Winter Flying is an equally informative masterpiece reminding pilots of the hazards of winter weather and aircraft operation. And, appropriately, there's a valuable refresher on density altitude.

If you're planning a flight into Colorado's Ski Country, check out these clickable topics: Commonly Flown Colorado Mountain Passes, Ski Country Airways Structure, Ski Country Airports, Flight Watch, Colorado Pilots Association Mountain Flying Course, and more.

Bookmark this site for safety's sake—it's a keeper.

Fee or Free: Free.

The Hundred Dollar Hamburger

http://www.tpwi.com/burger.html

e-mail: jpurner@tpwi.com

RATING

BRIEFING:

Looking for fly-in eats? This burger's well done!

Yes. I've mentioned the Hundred Dollar Hamburger before, linked to other sites. But, something this good deserves its own check ride.

Love to fly? Love to eat? Point the GPS toward the Hundred Dollar Hamburger—a Pilot's Guide to Fly-In Restaurants. Conscientiously updated, you'll get first-hand reviews and information on just about every general aviation fly-in worldwide.

First, click on your desired state or country (sixteen as of review). Second, choose the selected city to get an honest, straight-from-the-pilot's-mouth review. And, third, view your selection, complete with reviews. Write-ups are awarded one to five burgers, with five being best.

Be responsible. Use the burger rating form and serve up a PIREP of your favorite or not-so-favorite fly-ins.

Fee or Free: Free.

Pilot Portal

http://www.pilotportal.com

e-mail: none available

RATING
✝✝✝✝

Trying to quickly compare a Citation II's range with a Lear 35's? Curious about the crew requirements for a Cessna T-37 trainer? Simply defined, the Pilot Portal's Datacenter is a data intensive, interactive handbook. Review full descriptions, brief history, and technical data for each of the over 800 included aircraft.

Currently, clickable categories include: Top News, Web Links, Community, Product Reviews, Pilot Shop, and Classifieds.

Fee or Free: Free.

Webflyer

http://www.webflyer.com

e-mail: webmaster@webflyer.com

RATING

BRIEFING:

A knowledgeable resource for those collecting, cashing in upon, and seeking insight into the fine print world of frequent flyer programs.

Quite simply, Webflyer soars triumphantly into the murky abyss of frequent flyer (FF) programs. Skeptical? First, a few stats. At review time, Webflyer offered up over 1,000 online pages of pertinent info. There's 3,600 hyperlinks and 70 chat rooms. Second, the guy controlling the content has some experience with this sort of thing. How much? He's accumulated over five million frequent flyer miles/points, and conducted over 3,000 interviews on the subject with folks ranging from Congress to *Good Morning America*. Third, and most importantly, seeing is believing. Webflyer's organization and lofty style take flight with quick return menus, expertly tailored graphics, and nice subject area descriptions.

With so much to cover, I'll only tap into some highlights: The Top Ten Mileage Bonuses; InsideFlyer magazine—monthly "zine" that takes you into the heart of frequent flyer news; the Boarding Area lists and links every FF program known to man; and the Programs Area clues you in on program reviews, enrollment, accounts online, and more.

More FF fun begins by clicking into FlyerTalk, LiveFlyer, AirPoll, and ScreenFlyer.

Fee or Free: Free.

SkyCentral (DUATS)

http://www.skycentral.com

e-mail: duat@duat.com

RATING

+ + + + +

BRIEFING:

With free online flight plan filing and weather briefing info, this site should be every pilot's first stop.

Still one of the best resources in civil aviation today is GTE DUATS—Direct User Access Terminal Service. This valuable site provides current FAA weather and flight plan filing services to all certified civil pilots. The service is available 24 hours a day, seven days a week at no charge to the user—fees to operate the basic GTE DUAT service (weather briefing, flight plan filing, encode/decode) are paid by the FAA. With DUATS you'll access completely current weather and NOTAM data. Instantly select specific types of weather briefings: local briefings; low, intermediate, or high altitude briefings; and briefings with selected weather types. The DUATS computer also maintains direct access lines for flight planning filing. You can file, amend, or cancel flight plans.

A tad computer shy? Never used DUATS before? No problem. Help areas take you by the hand with: Connecting, How to Log On, Weather Briefings, Flight Plan Filing, Entering Data, and more. If you fly... If you're a pilot... If you file flight plans... If you require weather info... Look no further and make room for a bookmark.

Fee or Free: Free.

Flight Data

http://www.flightdata.com

e-mail: webmaster@flightdata.com

```
 RATING
 +++
```

BRIEFING:

This aviation
data player
weaves a
quality web of
data-driven
information.

Among the aviation data sites that spin Webs of wonder, Flight Data ranks right up there, where oxygen is needed for extended periods of time. If you're a data site admirer, odds are you'll virtually hyperventilate at this site's volume, speediness, and succinct design.

A surprisingly quick-to-load list of clickables represents your introductory menu—complete with clickable main directories and subcategories. As you would expect, data oozes out of area. Scan FAA Databases for: FAA examiners, mechanics, FARs, N-numbers, and pilot data. Get pointers to instruction with Ground School's FAA exams, AC recognition, and flight schools. Or, tap into the Classifieds for aircraft and employment listings. True aviation junkies might even want to delve deeper into its link lists for: supplies, owners, builders, simulation, and more.

If you're not into the intensive data searching, skip over to other site niceties. Visit a few Air Traffic Control centers with the live link provided, click through a Graphs area for graphs based on 300,000 registered US aircraft, or get a quick peek of your area weather.

Fee or Free: Free.

Bookmarkable Listings

GoldenWare Travel Technologies
http://www.traveldesk.com
e-mail: webmaster@GoldenWare.com
Free travel information including hotels and car rentals.

Shareware Aviation Products
http://www.look-up.com
e-mail: webmaster@look-up.com
Aviation software tools for flight planning and management.

Aerodynamics and Flight Simulator
http://www.web-span.com/afs/
e-mail: afs@club-internet.fr
Information and demonstration for aerodynamics and flight simulator software.

Exotic Aircraft Company
http://www.barnstormers.com
e-mail: baron@skyguy.com
Tips, procedures, and information on restoring vintage aircraft.

Airwise Hubpage
http://www.airwise.com/
e-mail: feedback@airwise.com
An independent guide to worldwide airports and aviation/airline news.

Best AeroNet
http://www.bestaero.com
e-mail: chuck@bestaero.com
Business aviation fuel network with jet fuel uplifts at over 700 sites worldwide.

GPS WWW Resource List
http://www.inmet.com/~pwt/gps_gen.htm#intro
e-mail: none provided
Huge list of global positioning system (GPS) links and related references.

The Homebuilt Homepage
http://www.homebuilt.org
e-mail: webmaster@homebuilt.org
Central reference to homebuilt/experimental-class aircraft.

Flight Training & Flight Schools

Student Pilot Network

http://www.ufly.com

e-mail: spn@studentpilot.net

RATING

++++

BRIEFING:

Reach into this network for tips, discussions, and experiences about student pilots.

C'mon, we were all students once. Maybe you still are. Regardless, every seasoned and not-so-seasoned pilot can relate to the Student Pilot Network's enthusiasm, insightful forums, and first-time stories.

I think you'll agree the presentation is flawless, adding to your visiting experience. Menus are carefully placed in nonintrusive frames. Links, icons, and site specifics are clear and easy to find. The content of articles and page summaries are written well and nonintimidating. What a great secondary resource for those in pursuit of flight.

Obviously Student Pilot Network endeavors to make flight school searching relatively painless. Identify schools meeting your particular needs and make quick comparisons with the many schools in their database based on your criteria. Other site offerings include: sharing experiences among pilots in the Discussion Forum, providing excellent Learn-to-Fly-Articles, offering tips and Q&A from aviation experts, and pointing to aviation scholarships.

My favorite feature, however, was the pilot interviews. Loads of informative Q&As will fill your screen based upon type of pilot. Read about the successes of the seasoned pilots. And, live the day-to-day realities of a student pilot. Whatever your skills and aspirations, Student Pilot Network is invigorating and entertaining.

Fee or Free: Free.

StudentPilot.com

http://studentpilot.com

e-mail: neil@studentpilot.com

RATING

BRIEFING:

An honestly thorough student pilot resource. Free instruction, tips, and more. How can you go wrong?

Fee or Free: Free.

When just starting to break out sectionals for the first time, beginning aviators appreciate any and all educational tools. Yes, there are always plenty of books, maps, charts, and fellow aviator tips at the pre-pilot's disposal. But, technology shines again with StudentPilot.com's worthy learning resource online.

Obviously not meant as a substitute for personal flight instruction or comprehensive reference material, StudentPilot.com's brilliance is in its ability to summarize neatly and present clearly. Just take a preflight walkaround of StudentPilot.com. Page design and organization are model examples of Web perfection. Simple menus and lack of time consuming graphics make page piloting a breeze. Taxi easily into listed, yet well organized articles, instruction, and forums.

Sure page mechanics pass with high marks, but the true test of aptitude surfaces with a content checkride. The virtual flight school truly delivers a self described "one-stop teaching tool for student pilots" with thorough description of the basics. Preflighting an aircraft, navigation techniques, ground reference maneuvers, and weather report analysis are just a few. True students will enjoy a huge compilation of fellow pilot experiences—uninhibited and easy to relate to. Read about: First Night Flight, July Checkride Story, Caught by an Engine Problem, CFI Checkride Report, Small Airports, and more. I counted more than 100 articles categorized by topic. They're inspiring, enthusiastic, and real.

The Aviation Ground School

http://209.150.150.129/school/

e-mail: sushil@usa.net

BRIEFING:

An excellent educational array of ground school basics. It's more thorough than you might expect.

Serving as sort of a Cliff's Notes for volumes of aviation reference and training materials, The Aviation Ground School thoroughly summarizes many important areas of flight and training. Topic selection seems well thought out, with everything from aircraft controls to human factors. Page layout isn't necessarily flashy, just purposeful. However, sounds, animations, and pictures are scattered throughout, adding a touch of fun.

The aviation wisdom site-wide reads pretty much like a textbook; it's just summarized. The excellent assortment of left-margin topics steer you into: news (site updates), aircraft controls, aerodynamics, aero-engines, instruments, fuel systems, electrical system, air navigation, meteorology, flight environment, and human factors. Once clicked into, each subject gives a brief overview and serves up its own set of subcategorized topics. For example, the airplane controls area gives specific analysis and description of the ailerons, elevator, rudder, trim, and flaps. You get the idea. Each educational area involves text almost exclusively, but photos and other media wiggle in occasionally.

For an excellent primer or simply a refresher, The Aviation Ground School rings the bell for flying enthusiasts. Click in with questions in mind. Class is already in session.

Fee or Free: Free.

Interactive Learning Systems (ILS)

http://www.flyils.com

e-mail: info@flyils.com

BRIEFING:

A fun little free tease to an innovative fee-oriented study site.

Billed as an interactive study guide, the ILS site hides nothing in its solicitation for those interested in a fee-related test prep course online. But, before you toss this book in disgust because I'm seemingly promoting this product-oriented site, hear me out. While it's true most of ILS's benefits will be derived after you buy in, some subtle freebies shouldn't be missed. For example, the free demonstration offers a nice introductory Learning Center. After dabbling in the Learning Center, move on to the Testing Area to sharpen your skills. There are quite a few questions to toy around with as you get a taste for the full blown interactive study guide. Try your hand at multiple choice questions that ask: what conditions are necessary for the formation of thunderstorms?; the pitot system provides impact pressure for which instrument?; and to get a complete weather briefing for the planned flight, the pilot should request what? Anyway, you get the idea. There are many questions and corresponding answers. Have fun with this quick trial refresher.

If in fact you do become intrigued with ILS, the complete program involves a live chat room, cool graphical interfaces, cyber instructors, interactive learning centers, graded quizzes, and practical final exams.

Fee or Free:
Reasonable fees apply for interactive study. Many free test prep questions in the Demo area.

Spartan School of Aeronautics

http://www.spartan.edu

e-mail: spartan@mail.webster.com

RATING
+ + +

BRIEFING:

Spartan's online
brochure peeks
into the school's
training haven
for aeronautics
hopefuls.

Faster than you can say "aviation maintenance and professional pilot training," the Spartan site captivates the eager aeronautically inclined to pursue their dreams. The intro page gives you an inquiry form on startup (they waste no time) and prompts you through a doorway to the full blown Spartan Web site.

It's easy to get jazzed with so much information at every turn. Wind your mouse through a myriad of main menu highlights, like: the Spartan Executive, the latest school news, and financial aid info. The long list of left-margin site links takes you further into your Spartan search. One of the better site aspects, especially for those contemplating an aeronautics career, is the Excerpt Area detailing the nature of work, working conditions, employment outlook, and qualifications and advancements for each Spartan career specialty. Learn about aviation maintenance, avionics/instruments, nondestructive testing, communication electronics, and professional pilot. Obviously though, more than just industry information can be had at Spartan online. Tap into the course catalog, college newspaper, student housing, international enrollment, school calendar, and more.

Fee or Free: Free.

Sierra Academy of Aeronautics

http://www.sierraacademy.com

e-mail: info@sierraacademy.com

BRIEFING:

Future airplane pilots, helicopter pilots, dispatchers, and mechanics need only point their mouse here to begin.

On initial page load, quick changing aircraft photos whet your appetite to get serious about an aviation career. Snapshots of pilots in training, singles, twins, and torn down engines give you a visual taste of what could be.

With perfect presentation, Sierra Academy's site takes on an air of professionalism, which is just the kind of start you'll want when choosing a career-level flight school. The introductory options are simple and nonthreatening. Avoiding the complex maze of online tours peppered with boring school news, Sierra Academy of Aeronautics' online vision is a bit clearer than most. Great information is at the heart of the hype for Sierra. For instance, each career path program is thoroughly detailed and thoughtfully arranged. Just call up the Airline Pilot & Corporate Pilot section. You're pleasantly greeted with industry info, program particulars, and related info (financial aid, job placement assistance, and low-cost college degree options).

To begin, though, you're invited to read through a nicely succinct introduction of Sierra Academy information concerning women in aviation. Move on into your field of choice with the details of airplane pilot, helicopter pilot, aircraft dispatcher, and aircraft mechanic.

Fee or Free: Free.

College of Aeronautics

http://www.aero.edu

e-mail: mariez@aero.edu

BRIEFING:

Prep for the College in your pj's. Get the scoop on College's aeronautics programs.

With 80 percent of College of Aeronautics grads employed with aviation industry giants, College's promotional Web site almost demands respect. But, even if you don't know the school's stats, its online presentation is inviting nevertheless. With a host of possible clicking directions, the site introduces you to its information and resources via button menu or site map. It's your choice.

There's no question the navigation's good. Pull-down menus, buttons, and text links get you anywhere site-wide. Dial in the GPS on the mouse pad and depart. You simply can't get lost. Opening into an aeronautical arena of options, College's menu prompts you to: President's Message, News & Information, Academic Programs, Admissions Information, Student Gallery, Alumni, Employment, Air Challenge, and Hot Links.

Obviously, as you'd expect, degree programs are introduced and thoroughly explained. From maintenance degrees to avionics, each area is summarized with no-nonsense prose. After researching College's program options, test your aeronautics trivia skills with the monthly Air Challenge quiz. My quiz was ten questions, and I'm happy to say I passed easily—after skipping to the answers.

Fee or Free: Free.

Mountain Flying

http://www.mountainflying.com

e-mail: sparky@mountainflying.com

RATING

✝ ✝ ✝ ✝

BRIEFING:

Generous
assortment of
mountain flying
tips, complete
with handy
illustrations.

There's just no getting around them. Our world contains mountainous regions. And, even plains-prone aviators should understand the important distinctions that peaks provide. Based on info from Sparky Imeson's book, *Mountain Flying Bible*, Mountain Flying's online resources dip into specific tips and teachings.

Almost an online textbook for mountain flying, Imeson's site speaks to basics as well as the advanced techniques of mountain flying. The chapters conveniently available from the left margin include: Must Know Info 1,2 & 3; Mountology; Mother Nature's Tricks; Book Reviews; Scud Running; Adverse Yaw; About Stalls; Emergency Landing; Night Flying; Spot Method; and Oxygen. As you can plainly see, there are numerous topics here and lots of online reading. The writing is superb, typo-free, and augmented with an occasional illustration or table.

In my opinion the best way to get the most from Mountain Flying is to go straight to the site map. Here you'll have a list of chapters and nice description of each section's contents. Learn about stuff like: mountain meteorology, density altitudes, leaning the mixture, updrafts/downdrafts, terrain modification, and more. What an excellent important resource.

Fee or Free: Free.

University of North Dakota (UND)— Aerospace Sciences Aviation Department

http://www.aero.und.edu/Academics/Aviation

e-mail: www@aero.und.edu

```
RATING
+ + +
```

BRIEFING:

UND's Aerospace Sciences Aviation Department showcases its educational wares online.

The Aviation Department counts about 1,200 majors in seven different programs. Students come from all 50 states and nearly 20 foreign countries. Good, now that I have your attention, click into UND's Aviation Department online composite for a well-described peek into why the school is so revered in aviation instruction.

One of the leaders in aviation-related training, the John D. Odegard School of Aerospace Sciences Aviation Department is a mouthful to say but is respected when said. Widely known as one of the major players, UND's Aviation Department promotes itself with expected grace online as well. Layout, presentation, text, and navigational components all mesh together perfectly with a harmonious hum. Just skim the five-button menu to begin. Info relating to degree programs, aviation courses, flight operations, flight training centers, and faculty make up your initial investigative options.

Then, get a bit more enlightened as to the degree programs of air transport, commercial aviation, flight education, air traffic control, aviation systems management, and more. Still more details can be had in the way of classes and curriculum for each program.

Fee or Free: Free.

American Flyers

http://www.americanflyers.net

e-mail: help@amercianflyers.net

RATING

BRIEFING:

Handsome training and supplies presentation courtesy of American Flyers.

Emblazoned with their flying eagle logo, American Flyers soars onto the cyber-scene with expected grace, style, and worthy resources. Self proclaimed, "the world's finest pilot training since 1939," the American Flyers site expands beyond school info and instruction into an arena of pilot necessities as well as niceties. The flawless interface gives you a hint as to what lies beyond the startup screen.

High flying page design lifts American Flyers into the elite group of Web pros who "know what they're doing." Use the fancy menu or a no-nonsense index to begin your journey. The Pilot Shop (new at review time) features headsets, flightbags, supplies, and more. Pilot Resources steers you into weather, forms, FAA documents, and "cool" aviation links. A Chart Room makes it too easy to avoid flying around with expired charts. Actual school information (domestic and international) is also available for those so inclined.

Then, have some real fun with a free online ground school test prep. If you're rusty, sign up for the full blown online ground school course (fee-related). It's handy 24-hour instruction for a variety of levels: private, instrument, commercial, ATP, and more.

Fee or Free: Free. Online instruction series is fee-related with a few free samples.

The Academy

http://www.theacademy.net

e-mail: programs@theacademy.net

BRIEFING:

Class is in session on the Academy's professionally polished program presentation online.

With vistas of tropical Lakeland, Florida, in mind The Academy is one of the world's most unique vocational colleges offering three distinctively different programs. Your virtual Web tour takes you into The Academy's programs for the professional pilot, aviation maintenance technician, and culinary arts gourmet chef. While the latter may not be to your taste, the former programs do offer a tempting array of flying fare.

A helpful guide to those searching to fulfill career dreams, The Academy's site uses subtle, easy-to-read page layouts and steers clear of time-wasting graphics wizardry. Programs are carefully summarized, complete with snapshot photos of training in progress. Specifically, the Flight Program discusses occupations for graduates, certificates, ratings, and training conducted. Similarly, The Aviation Maintenance Technology Program area highlights general curriculum, airframe curriculum, powerplant curriculum, and course details.

Join The Academy online for thorough insight into their programs, credentials, and capabilities. Even an admissions area answers your questions about acceptance, transfers, foreign students, and payment policy.

Fee or Free: Free.

FlightSafety International

http://www.flightsafety.com

e-mail: webmaster@flightsafety.com

RATING

BRIEFING:

Company info
perfection from
world respected,
high-tech
aviation
trainers—it's
what you would
expect from
these folks.

What better way to emphasize a professional approach to training than with a top-notch site. FlightSafety's expertise seems now to stretch into the cyber-arena. The company's objectives and content descriptions are written well, avoiding long-winded sales pitches. Content links to FlightSafety particulars give you up-front and current information. There's a left-margin site index for quick page navigation. And, best for beginners, a colorful link menu points the way. Everywhere you go, though, you're always an e-mail icon away for more information on any topic.

Content links include: Course Schedule, Crew Resource Management, Maintenance & Crew Resource Management, Simulations Systems Division, Learning Center Network, People@flightsafety, News@flightsafety, and Airline/Corporate New Hire Program. Also, flip through Courses and Schedules to be introduced to the corresponding course material by aircraft manufacturer.

There's a reason why corporations, airlines, the military, and government agencies rely on FlightSafety. Tap into this site and you'll get a feeling why.

Fee or Free: Free.

Aviation Communication

http://www.flightinfo.com

e-mail: instruct@flightinfo.com

```
RATING
┿ ┿ ┿ ┿
```

BRIEFING:

Summed up succinctly as "serving the aviation community, as well as potential flyers who just want more information on aviation."

Aviation Communication refreshes the experienced and preps the beginners with an information-rich heads up. You'll fall smack into insightful tips and solid info from seasoned pros. I even copied a few noteworthy tricks in Rules of Thumb, reminisced at the good advice in Checkrides, and refreshed myself with distances and separation in Airspace.

Don't expect online flying manuals or serious studying. This great source simply highlights and summarizes important topics. For example, Rules of Thumb combines helpful suggestions regarding: descent, ground speed, wind computation, bank angle, true airspeed, horsepower, pressure altitude, temperature, climb, instruments, and airworthiness.

Although there's not enough room here for details, you'll need to trust me and spend time clicking into: Learn to Fly, Logging Time, Message Board, Medicals, Post Resumes, Airline Addresses, Classified Ads, Flight Schools, Instructing Hints, and more.

It's aviator info euphoria. Enough said?

Fee or Free: Free.

Be a Pilot

http://www.beapilot.com

e-mail: online form

RATING

BRIEFING:

Dreamt of learning to fly? Fantasized about a well-organized intro-to-flight site? Touch down here for some encouraging reality.

Hey, stop dreaming and start browsing Be a Pilot's online taxiway to flight. Along with words of encouragement, you'll find visual page wizardry made up of handsome graphics that are quick to load. Omni-present top and left-margin menus give you the guidance of a slick GPS. And plenty of efficient page layouts give you the "white space" to stay focused.

At the site's heart is an easy-to-use flight school search tool sortable by state. The surprisingly complete flight school list gives you many schooling options in your area, including brief descriptions and contact information. When you've narrowed your options and chosen a school, be sure to take advantage of the $35 introductory coupon. Just fill out the registration form (fairly lengthy) and print out the introductory flight coupon.

Other topics to call upon include: Welcome to Flying (nice, encouraging intro), What's New, Aviation Links (companies involved with and endorsing Be a Pilot), and the helpful Flying Library. The Library gives you a quick but accurate peek into safety, steps to getting your license, costs, and more.

Fee or Free: Free, but make sure to fill out the survey and receive a $35 intro to flight coupon.

Applied Aerodynamics: A Digital Textbook

http://www.desktopaero.com/appliedaero/appliedaero.html

e-mail: info@desktopaero.com

RATING
☩ ☩ ☩

BRIEFING:

A scholarly online lecture that gives aerodynamic buffs a lift.

Kudos to Professor Kroo and the rest at Stanford University. This digital textbook arouses the awe of aerodynamics for aviators worldwide. Intended to supplement a more conventional aerodynamics textbook (the printed variety), the online version of Applied Aerodynamics peeks into some winged wonders via the Web.

Similar to a textbook, this digital resource provides thoughtful site organization with right-margin topics, detailed table of contents, instructions, and index. Although graphic design gurus weren't called upon to send viewers into a GIF frenzy, the pages are simple and clean. Taking the place of visual perfection, interactive attributes within the text takes the form of analysis routines that were directly built into the notes. (See, for example, the streamline calculations, airfoils, wing analysis, and canards.) You'll also stumble across cool charts and various depictions throughout.

Intrigued as to topics covered? Here's a taste: fluid fundamentals, airfoils, 3D potential flow, compressibility in 3D, wing design, and configuration aerodynamics. Sound like pocket protector stuff? Trust me and jump into the slipstream—it's drag-free.

Fee or Free: Free.

Aviation Ground School

http://www.geocities.com/CapeCanaveral/3819

e-mail: thend1@ibm.net

If you're like me, the actual wheels-up instruction was always more fun than memorizing FARs in ground school. It probably stands to reason that we could all use a tiny refresher now and then. Though not volumes of rocket science, Aviation Ground School gives your clicking fingertips a pointer to solid info vital to private pilots and wanna-bes.

With a simple, easy-to-understand manner, our educated author provides online instruction for a variety of topics. Particularly well written with charts and diagrams are: Components of the Fuel System; Aerodynamic Principles; Effects of Air Density on Performance; Airspace Definition, Airport and AIM Data, and Federal Aviation Regulations; Aeronautical Chart Symbols and Their Meanings; Navigational Methods; Principles of Weather; Terminology and Procedures of Radio Communications; and more.

After you shuffle a few site typos under the rug, the overall site organization is pleasantly simple and quick to load. Mostly text-based, the information employs appropriate diagrams and avoids gratuitous pictures. After clicking into a subject you may either move on to the next topic, or return to the index.

You will find a few other links here, but the online instruction is your real reason to stay.

Fee or Free: Free.

SimuFlite Training International

http://www.simuflite.com

e-mail: wmcewen@simuflite.com

RATING

╈ ╈ ╈ ╈

BRIEFING:

Advanced center
for professional
simulator
training checks
in with their
own advanced
promo site.

I'll readily admit the reason I initially visited SimuFlite's site didn't include simulator training. I clicked in for the link to live conversations between air traffic controllers and pilots in the Dallas/Fort Worth (DFW) area. Of course, now there are many ways to get to the DFW live link, but I must say taxiing through SimuFlite's site opened my eyes to their quality offerings.

For those interested in simulator-based training, SimuFlite straps you into their cyber-stopover for a well-designed intro. Clicking into any of the following exemplifies the site's layout and organizational skills: About SimuFlite, What's New, Press Releases, Aircraft/ Simulators, Training Schedule, Aviation Links, SimuFlite People, Cockpit Movie, Employment, and Ground Chatter.

Even if you're not SimuFlite-bound, do visit the weekly Ground Chatter collection of thoughts, sayings, and trivia. Depending upon your capacity for nonessential entertainment, it might just be worth a bookmark.

Fee or Free: Free.

See How It Flies

http://www.monmouth.com/~jsd/fly/how

e-mail: jsd@monmouth.com

Set aside your AIM, the FARs, and your operations manual for the moment. Buckle into the right seat for a little online instruction from FAA safety counselor, John Denker. Then, get ready to learn something—even if you think you know it all. See How It Flies might surprise you with thought-provoking commentary on the perceptions, procedures, and principles of flight.

Easily arranged in table of contents format, See How It Flies packs unlimited tips and worthwhile piloting techniques into a refreshingly candid resource. Clicking into the chapter file folders unearths no-nonsense tricks and useful procedures to help you fly better. Learn how to use your eyes, ears, fingertips, and seat of your pants to gather info. Find out about using your hands and feet to make the airplane do what you want. And, read about how to organize your thinking.

Well-written, practical prose skims the surfaces of: vertical damping, roll damping, and stalls; angle of attack, trim, and spiral dives; slips, skids, and snap rolls; take off; landing; cross-country flying; and more. You'll find chapter contents are easy to understand with well-defined concepts and corresponding diagrams. Thankfully absent, however, are meaningless plane pictures and inappropriate graphics. So, enjoy and learn in frustration-free peace.

Fee or Free: Free.

AviationWeb

http://www.AviationWeb.com

e-mail: webmaster@AviationWeb.com

RATING

++++

BRIEFING:

When your flights of fancy have turned to something more than dreaming, check into this inexhaustible U.S. flight school directory.

Hey, these guys concentrate on one thing: flight schools. Not a lot of extra stuff that throws you off course. When you're ready to move into a twin, wrestle around a Boeing 777 commercially, or just flutter around in a trusty 152, climb into the left seat with AviationWeb. This searchable database easily finds your area's best schools via three criteria: city, state, and/or zip.

Certified flight instructors and pilot schools are invited to create an online company or personal profile FREE through an update form. This is a great resource designed for an international base of pilots (and pilot wanna-bes).

Fee or Free: Free.

Neil Krey's Flight Deck

http://www.crm-devel.org/neilkrey/

e-mail: neilkrey@aol.com

RATING

+++

BRIEFING:

Welcome aboard the Flight Deck for an educated view on training and learning.

Whether you're relying upon the instructor in the right seat for guidance, or an airline pilot to get you home, experience factors into the background of most longtime pros. Captain Neil Krey of Neil Krey's Flight Deck site has quite a background. This man, who is in the business of training and education programs, is an accomplished commercial pilot with an eye toward many aviation research areas: crew resource management, training & learning, the future, and more. In the Flight Deck you'll find links and info to important topics, such as: Web-based Training, Aviation Safety Reporting System, and Scenario-based Planning.

There's an educated look into aviation's future, as well as many fascinating studies and papers published by Captain Krey. Make yourself comfy in the jumpseat— you're going to learn something here!

Fee or Free: Free.

FirstFlight

http://www.firstflight.com

e-mail: tjs@firstflight.com

BRIEFING:

No plane. No stalls. No talking to the tower. No expense. It's the cyber-way to pilot a Cessna 152 for the first time.

Although a crafty approach to enticing new recruits, FirstFlight wildly succeeds in captivating potential flyers with some fun cyber-152 instruction. Excellent content and organization make FirstFlight easy to use for Net novices as well as aviation novices. Unlike a flight simulator, this site steps you through the private pilot certification process via a series of "flights." Although not intended as a substitute for actual instruction, the evolving list of "flights" (new ones are added monthly) are a great preview to the real thing.

Scan through the current private pilot requirements. Read the private pilot syllabus. Examine checklists. Take an online preflight. And strap into the left seat. Following the script in each "flight," you'll become familiar with your cyber-Cessna: taxi, communicate via radio, take off, and land! You'll encounter embedded checklists throughout each "flight"—they're excellent references. Much of the information is basic and well suited to a flying introduction.

Congratulations to this innovative, educational, and interesting site. (How many sites can claim all those wonderful adjectives?) This guy's good...where do I sign?

Fee or Free: Free.

Embry-Riddle Aeronautical University

http://www.embryriddle.edu

e-mail: online form

BRIEFING:

A perfect demonstration of how smart folks (well, they are aviation educators) can grab the technological reigns and capitalize upon appropriate Web applications.

From the minute you type its address, the Embry-Riddle page exceeds your expectations—even from the world's largest aeronautical university. This online equivalent of a university brochure reeks of outstanding aesthetics while satisfying content-hungry surfers. Page navigation is simple with well-designed, omni-present menus and clickable buttons.

Main topics are clearly labeled as: Visitors, Students, Admissions, Catalogs, Directories, and Faculty/Staff. Its content, quite simply, overflows the cup of perfection. From university info to research links to aviation links, you could easily spend days here. Education seekers will find admissions stuff, financial aid info, and a cool clickable campus map tour. Students (and anyone else) can tap into Career Info, the Avion Online (University-sponsored "zine"), and Associations. There's general campus news, library info, and more research areas. You'll even have at your fingertips: faculty/administration info (including phone numbers), colleague information, and more.

In person or online, this university offers quite an education.

Fee or Free: Free.

Learning to Soar

http://acro.harvard.edu/SSA/articles/learn_soar.html
e-mail: gei@cfi.harvard.edu

BRIEFING:

A nondescript gem of useful, GIF-less information about learning to pilot a glider.

Hidden deep in the darkest reaches of the Web, way past the glitzy bandwidth-hogging pages, you'll find Learning to Soar. Shunning the hindrance of noisy engines, this soaring sites sets you free to discover everything you've always wanted to know about becoming a private glider pilot.

The text-only information is accurate and thorough. The author spends a tremendous amount of time stepping you through the entire private glider pilot process. Topics include: glider ports, gliders and instructors, minimum training requirements, medical requirements, student pilot certificates, the written exam, training schedules, the flight test, total costs, glider vs. airplane training, private pilot privileges, and a few important soaring contacts.

Sidestep the search engines (and those graphic-intensive sites) to find glider knowledge o'plenty here. It's an uplifting experience.

Fee or Free: Free.

Bookmarkable Listings

SimCom Training Centers
http://www.simulator.com
e-mail: readback@simulator.com
Simulator training programs and information.

GG-Pilot
http://www.gg-pilot.com
e-mail: online form
Directory of America's top flight schools.

Aero Data Files
http://www.tcsn.net/adf
e-mail: aero@tcsn.net
Free, online reference material for aviation historians, researchers, writers, and scholars.

Aeroflight
http://www.netlink.co.uk/users/aeroflt
e-mail: john@jhayles.demon.co.uk
Find detailed profiles of lesser-known aircraft types, info on NATO and non-aligned European air forces, and more.

Aviation Online Magazines & News

PlaneBusiness

http://www.planebusiness.com

e-mail: pbadmin@planebusiness.com

RATING

✝ ✝ ✝

BRIEFING:

PlaneBusiness plays the role of airline industry publishers.

Anything but plain, PlaneBusiness is always on time with airline industry stats, daily business news and financial tidbits. Better yet, it's pretty entertaining.

Written well, designed well, and updated daily, PlaneBusiness is your carrier correspondent full of news, insider talk, and dry wit. Presented in summary menu format, the features and articles load instantly with no need to get on the standby list. Just pick your linked topic and begin boarding: PlaneBusiness DailyBanter (the only daily financial wrap-up of the airline industry); PlaneBusiness Banter (headlines and more from their subscriber-based weekly e-mail newsletter); PlanePerspectives; PlaneBusiness Message Boards (enjoy some airline industry buzz); and more.

Even if you're searching specifically for a favorite or not-so-favorite airline article, just type it in to reveal a list of all PlaneBusiness mentions. Or, simply dig through the recycle bin for a mound of old airline-related stuff. It's all in there, just don't forget the rubber gloves.

Fee or Free:
Everything's free site-wide, except for PlaneBusiness Banter (a weekly e-mail newsletter).

FAQs About Amateur-Built Aircraft

http://www.provide.net/~pratt/ambuilt/faqhmblt.htm

e-mail: pratt@provide.net

BRIEFING:

Questions,
answers, and
insight for
homebuilders.

Homebuilts and certification? Jim's got the answer. Not really sure of Jim's credentials, but it's obvious he knows his stuff and/or where to find correct information. We are clued in on his authority to inspect amateur-builts and issue Experimental Airworthiness Certificates. Enough said?

If you're new to homebuilts—building, certification, or the FARs, I encourage you to begin your journey here. The questions are many and the answers are thorough. Just don't expect any attempt at visual style. Simply remind yourself you are visiting for solid information not imagery. Keep your hand steady on the scroll bars and "back" button. And, away we go.

Sample question topics include: FAA publications for homebuilts, how to get an "N" number, test flight programs, yearly condition inspections, the skills necessary for homebuilding, rules for experimental aircraft, medical certificates, researching the best homebuilt kit companies, safety, and more.

Jim also serves up forms used in applying for an airworthiness certificate, FAA documents, advisory circulars, and the checklist he uses when inspecting an aircraft.

WARNING: As stated explicitly on this site, always contact your local FAA office before relying on any Web-based information. Information contained here is meant only as a reference.

Fee or Free: Free.

AeroSpaceNews' Leading Edge

http://www.aerospacenews.com

e-mail: editor@aerospacenews.com

RATING
+ + +

BRIEFING:

Mega multimedia medley of entertaining news, views, and movies.

Fee or Free: Free.

I suppose when all is said and done I would probably be considered a sucker for bells, whistles, and gizmos. But, aren't most pilots? Anyway, if you're like me and enjoy a good multimedia online experience, I've uncovered a bookmarkable addition for you. AeroSpaceNews' Leading Edge "e-zine" incorporates just about every sense but smell.

Although not gracefully visual as Web pages go, the site's variety of aviation topics combine with cool sights and sounds to get you quickly involved. Begin with a quick look through your list of weekly news pages—General Aviation, Airline, Space, Military, Feature of the Week, This Week in History, Editorials and Commentary, Humor and Other Fun Stuff, and more.

A word of caution to those technically challenged: you'll need many plug-in applications to see and hear this site's good stuff. RealAudio, QuickTime VR software, RealVideo, and Java capabilities are simply a must. With the latest versions of either Netscape or Explorer you should have no problem. But, if you're lacking a specific plug-in, AeroSpaceNews provides handy links to free download areas.

Streaming NASA TV broadcast, the Virtual F/A-18 E/F Cockpit Tour, Audio of the TWA-800 Tapes, Airforce Radio News, and a Virtual Boeing B-777 Cockpit Tour are among my favorites.

Aviation International News

http://www.ainonline.com

e-mail: ain@compuserve.com

RATING

++++

BRIEFING:

An astounding array of features, current news, and pilot reports for the business aviation world.

Real reporting. In-depth insight. A bonanza of breaking news. Aviation International News (AIN) means business. With the precision and professionalism you'd find in today's corporate aviation world, AIN shines with "suit-and-tie" appearance with something between the ears too.

Matching its printed sibling in style and wit, AIN online displays its mastery in Web design and organization. The pick lists are clear. Articles are easily intelligible. And, the Top Story list spans a couple of pages with summary links. Photos are few, articles are written well, and nonobtrusive menus are everywhere.

Content-wise AIN is just as enriching. Only one click away, the top stories touch on topics like: flight testing of new business jet aircraft, fractional ownership news, FAA & NASA studies, big-name FBOs, buying pre-owned aircraft, FAR commentaries, technology breakthroughs and more.

As an added bonus, pilot reports pick apart the latest in business aircraft. Real pilots. Real analysis. It's just the sort of reports that should be of interest if your company's shopping for some wings.

Fee or Free: Free.

Aviation Week Online

http://www.aviationweek.com

e-mail: mangann@mcgraw-hill.com

RATING

╪ ╪ ╪ ╪

BRIEFING:

An expectedly satisfying variety of aviation news, resources, and stuff to buy.

Fee or Free: Some free articles. Printed magazine is subscription-based.

Okay, let's pause and take a quick inventory of the Web's aviation "zines." Lots of monthlies. A fair amount of quarterlies. An unlimited number of those "randomly updated." But, weekly? Yes, Aviation Week Online is a weekly. Religiously updated each week (actually daily if you count the handful of "Today's Top News Stories"), Aviation Week Online is everything a well-crafted Web "zine" otta be.

Beauty and brains. Quick link menu of resources. New featured stories teased on start-up. All in-depth articles, well-written from the name you know: Aviation Week. But, here's the twist. You'll be invited to delve into a smattering of newsworthy tidbits from two major sister publications: *Aviation Week & Space Technology* and *Business & Commercial Aviation*. Look for topics like: Testing Live Tomahawks, Wings Over Antarctica, Industry Trends, Commercial Carrier Market Turbulence, The Era of Mergers and Acquisitions, and more.

Many linkable choices can take you in many directions. There are lots of resources and pointers to sibling publications (McGraw-Hill being the proud parent): *World Aviation Directory, A/C Flyer, Overhaul & Maintenance,* and a host of aviation newsletters just to name a few. Other aviation pursuits line the menu too, like: jobs, gallery, Safety Resource Center, an interactive forum, and lots of stuff to buy.

Ultralight News

http://www.ultralightnews.com

e-mail: buzzman@ultralightnews.com

BRIEFING:

Ultralight news madness runs amok.

Just when you thought you knew all there was to know in aviation, don't forget about those who gravitate toward the open air thrill of ultralights. They're pilots too. And judging by the content and commentary dribbling all over Ultralight News, the industry is cruising along nicely thank you.

Frankly, even I was a bit surprised to find such a huge melting pot of ultralight events, announcements, tips, technical tips, kit ratings, trouble shooting, aircraft alert bulletins, for-sale stuff, and show coverage. Yes, it's everywhere site-wide hiding under a paper-thin veil of organization.

Get your wings wet with a careful scan of the intro page. There's lots of reading, a few hidden gems, and site links everywhere. The best hope I can offer you in navigation is a one-through-eight section index, which carefully outlines each section's contents. Just a taste of your ultralight news stay might include: flight training, propeller resources, engine maintenance schedules, accident data, product reviews, cross-country adventures (interesting!), industry watches, and so much more. Oh, and my favorite—read about "what to do when your !@#$% engine won't start."

Fee or Free: Free, although small donations are readily accepted. Even ultralight classifieds are free.

The Southern Aviator

http://www.southern-aviator.com

e-mail: webmaster@southern-aviator.com

RATING

+ + +

BRIEFING:

Punch in
Southern
Aviator on your
bookmark GPS
if you're a
southern states
flyer.

Bursting at its southern-style seams, the Southern Aviator's online complement to its print cousin serves up southern hospitality. The official voice for southern states aviators (and those transitioning through) speaks volumes with such a handy info-rich resource.

Take for instance the daily postings of area news and events. You'll get a nice summary first with an invitation for more. Example articles deal with topics like: Southern Carolina Increasing the State Share for Some Important Airport Projects; Kissimmee Plays Host to What Could be the Largest Gathering of P-51 Mustangs in Recent History; and An Historical Perspective of the Civil Air Patrol Wing Commander of Louisiana. Well, you get the idea. Topics vary, but southern-related news is always at hand.

Once you've read the latest, browse the left-margin menu of essentials. Serious resources, product presentations, and light-hearted entertainment find their way onto your screen. Get some last-minute points of interest in Specials. The Virtual Hangar highlights products, services, and FBOs. And, Southern Aviator's Sections steer you into the best of TSA, Calendar, Flying Places, Hangar Talk, Classifieds, and more.

Fee or Free: Free to browse, but there are many things to buy.

Are you a southern aviator? Hey, "smart birds fly south" by pointing their browser here.

Interplane

http://www.inter-plane.com

e-mail: topgun@inter-plane

BRIEFING:

U.K.-based aviation info buffet serves up variety to worldwide aviators.

No stranger to awards, Interplane deserves one more for such an outstanding multidimensional offering to aviators. Although U.K.-based, Interplane knows no borders when offering its worldwide collection of news, aviation links, and commercial aviation information.

Who ever said "trying to be all things to all people doesn't work" weren't anticipating the hard-working folks at Interplane. Featuring news, links, humor, employment, air show events, and aircraft/helicopters for sale at even a minimal level of completeness is a truly daunting task. But, a quick look through Interplane's news, long link directory (with handy summaries), growing humor page, and others demonstrate effective site organization and dedication to an all-around aviation resource.

Humor submissions were particularly entertaining with these selections (be sure to check them out): Ten Dollars, Hard Landings, Fifteen Things You Don't Want to Hear on an Aeroplane, Flight Attendant & Pilot Announcements, I Have to be on This Flight!, and others.

Fee or Free: Free. Subscribe to a free monthly e-mail list to be updated on Interplane additions.

AirDisaster.com

http://airdisaster.com

e-mail: Kilroy@db.erau.edu

RATING

+ + +

BRIEFING:

AirDisaster is sometimes gruesome, sometimes enlightening, but always disturbing.

Yes it's an ominous URL. But skip to the site's sub-head: "solutions for safer skies." With a stated purpose of "providing an Internet resource for the latest in aviation safety," AirDisaster does offer a well-organized forum for air safety and observations into preventable situations. The bulk of the content, however, delves into the disturbing pool of airliner accidents. And it is disturbing.

Certainly photos are everywhere. Small and large. Graphic and innocuous. The continuously updated Safety Scale counts the fatalities and accidents. And, the latest fatal accident is summarized on start up with a link to more details.

Relatively well organized and tasteful in presentation, AirDisaster's purpose isn't to glorify the gruesome. Rather, its offerings combine a series of articles, reports, and statistics identifying the nature of airliner accidents. Clickable topics quickly move you into: Top 100 Crashes, Air Safety Forum, Crash Database, Voice Recorders, Crash Photos, Special Reports, Eyewitness Accounts, Accident Reports, and more.

NOTE: As stated by the site Webmaster, viewer discretion is advised. The subject matter lends itself to disturbing depictions of airliner accidents in the form of photos and video.

Fee or Free: Free.

GPS World Online

http://www.gpsworld.com

e-mail: editorial-gps@gpsworld.com

RATING

++

BRIEFING:

GPS stuff and
then some gets
pinpointed from
Web to your
screen.

A capable complement to the printed version of *GPS World* magazine, GPS World Online pinpoints topics of interest with uncanny precision. While not undermining its flair for design and organization, the site's star performers are the limitless features, resources, and articles.

The nicely presented intro page offers up a selection of menu buttons together with a few feature story teasers. While not solely devoted to aviation uses of GPS, a wide spectrum of insight and resources is plentiful. Site topics include: The Annual GPS Buyers Guide, GPS Solutions Database, Features (articles and columns), Resources (calendar, links, and article index), Products and Company News, Services, Employment Opportunities, and more.

The Buyers Guide, relatively new at time of review, is especially handy for narrowing down specific companies for specific GPS-related stuff. For digital compasses, antennas, electronic charts/maps, radiometers, seminars/training, integrated instrumentation with GPS, and about a gazillion others just click for associated companies.

Fee or Free: Free.

Plane & Pilot Magazine

http://www.planeandpilotmag.com

e-mail: editor@planeandpilotmag.com

RATING

BRIEFING:

Popular *Plane & Pilot* roars onto the Web's cyber-scene with pilot resources and a few articles.

The popular magazine for active piston-engine pilots, Plane & Pilot teases a bit with its online offerings. The presentation and left-margin menu are certainly capable enough for the interested surfer, but content serves largely to whet the appetite for the printed pub. Get a handy list of summarized feature stories in this month's and past issues. Generally, one feature story is offered in its entirety.

Plane & Pilot magazine has been one of my favorites for years. So, it stands to reason that your reviewer would include its site as an award winner if it brought its standards of excellence to the Web. I think you'll agree its online sister is a winner, not for savvy self-promotional offerings, but for its schools directory and monthly feature article. Obviously trying to be thorough, Plane & Pilot's school's directory links up to all the majors and many minors in the category of aviation training. Relatively comprehensive in scope, you'll be pleasantly surprised with such a quality collection.

Even if you're not in search of training, Plane & Pilot keeps your attention online too with full-blown topical features monthly. Scan the back issues if you crave a bit more.

Fee or Free: Free.

Crashpages.com

http://www.crashpages.com

e-mail: editorial@crashpages.com

RATING

++

BRIEFING:

Dedicated to family members of those that died in all aviation accidents is the memorial archive of Crashpages.com.

Publishing "not just the facts" on airline safety and fatal disasters, Crashpages.com serves up a bit of editorial comment too. Yes, you'll find horror and heroes, tragedy and transcripts. But, Crashpages.com still seeks to encourage safety in the skies. Here's some site perspective: "you would have to take a random flight every day on a commercial aircraft for almost 30,000,000 years to be insured of being in a fatal plane crash."

The fact is, airline disasters do happen. Maybe not to you or someone you know. Nevertheless, we are all still affected by the news. In Crashpages.com the light shines bright on past tragedies—ones you may have forgotten. Swissair 111, Delta Flight 1141, TWA Flight 800, and others come to life in words, pictures, and voice recorders. Site options include: a message board, news articles, image gallery, annual crash reports, voice recorders, links, and more.

Sprinkled into the mix of history, pictorials, facts, and statistics is the author's editorial thoughts. Almost surely provoking your ire or agreement, the opinions are candid and earnest.

Fee or Free: Free.

AirConnex

http://www.airconnex.com

e-mail: webmaster@airconnex.com

RATING

BRIEFING:

Award-winning site for airline news and air travel links.

At first AirConnex appears a bit simplistic: nice design, fast loading, and just a few summarized site categories. Certainly scud-running the cyber skies of gaudiness, AirConnex has chosen a new route. A less complex and flashy route in its quest to "answer as many of your air travel needs as possible." Where's the huge out-of-scale plane pictures and endless dead link directories found at most information sites? Not here. Climb aboard yourself and see what I mean.

Mostly text description greets you on start up, which foils most time wasters. Each category is revealed before clicking with a more than adequate peek into content. Probably harboring the most value is the wonderfully independent Air Bulletin. This weekly global airline newsletter keeps you current on commercial carrier news and events, complete with photos and side links. The Aviation Bookstore serves up a nice interface for book ordering (via Barnes and Noble) with categories like: accidents, aircraft, history, pictorials, travel, airlines, and more. Or, if you're just searching for your favorite airport, tap into an easy-to-use compilation of airport Web site links.

Fee or Free: Free. Leave your e-mail address for future updates.

Be sure to add AirConnex to your favorites list, because surfacing sometime in the near future is a formidable list of site additions. Look to the horizon for sections on laughter in air travel, tips & hints to travel for less, specs for hundreds of commercial aircraft, and more.

CyberAir Airpark

http://www.cyberair.com

e-mail: webmaster@cyberair.com

RATING

+ + + +

BRIEFING:

Touch down at The Park for tantalizing tidbits, prizes, entertainment, and handy safety stuff.

Once you land at CyberAir Airpark, you've got a myriad of stops right off the taxiway. Click on an Airpark map or select from the site index for: Control Tower and FAA Info, The Museum, the RealAudio Area (have your audio player geared up), The Press and Media Center, The Office Center, The Fixed Base Operations Building, Links, and more.

Although the above locations certainly warrant a visit, you may want to skip directly to Hot Stuff selections, including: Last Week's Aviation History, Free BFR at CyberAir Airpark, CyberAir Beacons—updated weekly, Aviation Safety Pages, and Aviation Trivia (monthly winners receive better-than-expected prizes).

Page navigation skims the surface of simple, with clickable map or index options. Nifty additions include a scrolling info banner and a link to Chicago Approach Control—live!

Fee or Free: Free.

AeroWorldNet

http://www.aeroworldnet.com

e-mail: online form

RATING

BRIEFING:

International aerospace news that's updated weekly and written well—the perfect ingredients for a bookmark.

The global aerospace perspective—you'll find it online at AeroWorldNet. Current and updated weekly, this international aviation news source gives you efficiency and excellent insight. Topics covered: feature stories, weekly headlines, industry news, briefs in aerospace, event archives, and more. Great, short summaries capture the essence of most articles before you click into the full story.

Mostly text-based with some banner ads and logos floating around, the pages are quick to load and easy to navigate. Left-margin links take you to additional subjects like: Aerospace Jobs, People and Places, Industry Literature, Industry Products, Aerospace Events, Industry Message Board, Aerospace Companies, Industry Associations, and Membership (sponsorship) in AeroWorldNet.

With not many places to turn for solid, aerospace news online, you will be rescued when you land on AeroWorldNet's informational oasis. Lacking are a plethora of typos, giant pictures, and old news. It's a world of positive difference compared to your other Web options.

Fee or Free: Free memberships—sponsorships are available.

Planet Aviation

http://www.planetaviation.com

e-mail: none available

RATING

++++

BRIEFING:

Web radio show just for us aviation types.

A radio show on aviation? Yes. But, better still, you don't need a radio and you can tune in live—worldwide! Self-dubbed as "where the best of aviation hang out every single week," Planet Aviation rides the radio waves of Web innovation and brings aviation enthusiasts this unique approach to industry news.

Traveling at 186,000 miles per second, Planet Aviation's aeronautical "audiology" comes together into entertaining shows. Left button topics move you into your audio preferences of: About, Audio Present & Archived, Video Interviews to Download, Aviation Links, Contact, Feedback, and Who Won? (prizes given away to listeners).

Crank up your 14.4 kbs (or hopefully faster) modem and point your browser here to hear.

Fee or Free: Free.

General Aviation News & Flyer

http://www.ganflyer.com

e-mail: comments@ganflyer.com

RATING

BRIEFING:

Online "zine" mirroring the printed one—no teasing here, though, there's plenty of articles and features.

This online complement to its printed twin glides with effortless site navigation and hearty aviation news. Unlike other publications, which try to sucker-punch you into subscribing, this online sibling actually gives you the printed features, current articles, and commentary without teasing. Sure, they invite you to subscribe. But they're low-key about it.

Get to the heart of the site by clicking into Read the News. You'll tap into the current issue, as well as hordes of archived articles. Regular categories include: News, Features & Opinions, Alaska Flyer, Oshkosh Preview, Homebuilts, Products & Services, Books & Videos, and Cessna Mods & Maintenance. Want more general aviation? Click About The Flyer, Flyer Archives, Read the News, Search the Classifieds, Calendar of Events, RoBen Aviation Books, and a few links.

Fee or Free: Free.

Rotorcraft Page

http://www.rotorcraft.com

e-mail: norman@rotorcraft.com

BRIEFING:

Here's enough info to keep your head and your gyrocopter spinning.

Grab the stick and go for a gyro spin with Rotorcraft.com. Probably not for everyone—especially dedicated fixed-wing folks—Rotorcraft.com does a great job of gearing you up with endless screens of gyrocopter info. The at-a-glance Reports section delves into current events and fly-in reports, as many more categories stand by in the margins. Scroll down to reveal your clickable options: Upcoming Events, Chapter News, Aviation & FAA Sites (only a few as of review time), International Organizations, PRA Connection, Manufacturers List, Instructors List, Classified, Gyro Store, New Products, In Development (homebuilders development page), and E-mail Lists & Expert Contacts. Among the gyro insight offered, you'll find answers to: How much do gyros cost?; Is a license required?; How much does training cost?; and How can I get a test ride?

Looking for more rotor fun? Rotorcraft.com happens to be the home server site for the Popular Rotorcraft Association, Air Command International, and Rotor Flight Dynamics, Inc.

Fee or Free: Free.

Business & Commercial Aviation (B/CA)

http://www.awgnet.com/bca

e-mail: mangann@mcgraw-hill.com

BRIEFING:

Business and commercial aviation "zine" that gives you more than just a hard sell into subscribing to its printed twin.

Unlike some online versions of printed magazines, Business & Commercial Aviation reaches beyond the GIF-driven solicitation for subscription. Sure, an online subscription desk is still ready for your order. But, you'll find substance here too—more than you might think.

Through an excellent labyrinth of well-positioned frames, news and opinions are everywhere. Well-written gems include monthly columns from legendary pros, current events, and in-depth feature articles. Your always-present topic menu moves you quickly into the mainly magazine topics of: B/CA Intelligence, B/CA Observer, B/CA Viewpoint, Safety, Top Stories, Columns, About B/CA, Subscription Desk, and Gallery.

Sure the articles below will change monthly, but to give you a taste read on. Lively discussions and professional analysis are at your clicking fingertips with articles like: "Reinstatement of Aviation Excise Taxes is Temporary;" "FAA Says Mid-Air Close Calls are Declining;" and "All-Inclusive Warning System is Under Development."

Also, a fun little sidebar features a gallery of images, videos, and sounds. The convenient mini search engine helps to browse for the latest gallery additions. I think you'll find the unending list of newsworthy GIFs to be pleasantly overwhelming.

Fee or Free: Free, unless you subscribe to the printed version.

FlightWeb

http://www.flightweb.com

e-mail: rparrish@best.com

RATING

++

BRIEFING:

An air medical must-see. Check in for current, thorough industry information.

Faster than you can say "E.R.," FlightWeb bursts onto your screen and serves up no-nonsense air medical resources. Homebuilders have their own sites. Aerobatic buffs have theirs. And, now the air medical pros have an online forum to gear up for air medical transport readiness.

This dedicated breed of specialists comes together with their own well-organized cyber-support staff. Not limited to just pilots, FlightWeb dips into content designed for worldwide air medical folks who are flight medics, nurses, medical doctors, communication specialists, dispatchers, and more.

Your blue button menu links you up with a wide range of worthwhile reasons to add a bookmark. Industry professionals will want to scan through: Air Medical Web Pages—links to flight programs, associations EMS, Medevac, vendors, and others; Chat Room; Flightmed Mailing List Archives—a searchable grouping of posted messages; Resources—air medical clip art, mentors, medical protocols, legal issues, and various FAQs; White Pages—e-mail directory of air medical pros; Associations; Vendors; and more.

Scrub up and join FlightWeb in this well-educated online operatory. The air medical doctor will see you now—24 hours a day.

Fee or Free: Free.

AircraftBuyer.com

http://www.aircraftbuyer.com

e-mail: dmperry@access.digix.net

RATING

BRIEFING:

A great aircraft "e-zine" that steers clear of "smoke-and-mirrors" information.

More than mere "e-zine" camouflage, *A/C Flyer's* AircraftBuyer.com dutifully avoids the cheap subscription-only tease and serves up meaty aviation delights. This flashy electronic version of its popular sibling in print may surprise you with helpful formats and regularly updated news.

Well-organized search engines guide you to endless listings of aircraft, products/services, and dealers/brokers. Current resale news and industry info is always at the ready, along with lots of flight training, financing, and insurance. And, the informative Ownership Articles touch on many important topics. Aviation links, About AircraftBuyer.com, performance charts, and info on the Premium Club round out your thorough options.

Moving through the useful content is a snap. The subtle use of appropriate design elements balances nicely with useful navigation. Left-margin menu buttons help categorize your selections. And, well-thought-out input forms guide you like a finely tuned GPS.

Fee or Free: Fee-based to list your aircraft, free to search for one.

Aviation Safety Network

http://aviation-safety.net

e-mail: webmaster@aviation-safety.net

An award-
winning, yet
dark view into
the world of
airliner disasters.

Morbid and sometimes somber, Aviation Safety Web Pages may seem at first to cater only to the accident curious. Those who are drawn to the disaster scene with fascination will certainly get their fill of fatality statistics and gory details. If you reach a little further, though, you'll notice this airliner accidents site employs descriptive accident data—the kind that may lend a hand with your own accident prevention preparation.

Religiously updated, the site contains a wealth of airliner accident info found in features like: The Aircraft Accident Database, Statistics, Accident Reports, CVR/FDR ("Black Box Transcripts"), safety issues, and accident specials. Lists of accidents by year reveal endless summary tables of data. Event details like aircraft type, operator, and flight route combine with phase of accident, fatality counts, and remarks to paint a graphic accident picture. Links to additional articles, photos, and other reference sources round out your research options.

Have an unfulfilled curiosity about airline disasters? New fatal airliner accidents are added within one or two days. Sign up to receive free, e-mail "digests" to keep you apprised. Site update notification is also available for the asking.

Fee or Free: Free.

Jane's Information Group

http://www.janes.com

e-mail: janes.webmaster@janes.co.uk

For those who may not know, "Jane's" refers to the legendary English pioneer, John Frederick Thomas Jane, who began the widely regarded source for defense, aerospace, and transportation information. How appropriate that the world renowned resources of Jane's have found their way onto the cyber-info highway. Jane's boldly celebrates its 100 years of information solutions with its stunning example of Web design excellence.

Whether you choose to view the wondrous graphical imagery and organizational delight or opt for the speedy text version, you might catch yourself muttering praise as you click. Fascinating information and thorough descriptions are everywhere. Find out more about Jane's with The Product Catalog, Who's Jane?, or Editor's Notes. Take a ride into What's Hot with Photo of the Week, Interview of the Week, News Briefs, New Products, and more. Then, with your curiosity piqued, move into the information gallery. Here you'll uncover regional assessments, defense glossary (over 20,000 defense-related acronyms and abbreviations), and resource links (categorized by government/intelligence, defense/aerospace, space, and transportation).

Don't misunderstand. There's a lot of publication selling going on here. But, from the people that brought you the bible of the aviation industry, *Jane's All the World's Aircraft*, you can expect to be more than satisfied with brilliant content.

Ultralight Flyer Online

http://ul-flyer.com

e-mail: flyer@ul-flyer.com

RATING

✝ ✝ ✝ ✝

BRIEFING:

Get airborne
with this
ultra-organized,
ultra-balanced,
ultra-designed,
and ultra-
bookmarkable
ultralight site.

Boldly buzzing within aviation's online airspace, Ultralight Flyer Online gets in the cyber-pattern too with its own "ultra-site." Its award-winning offerings flutter around freely with simple euphoria. While layout, organization, and aesthetics are thankfully in line with some of the better aviation sites, my favorite facet is informative link summaries. Mostly, I've noticed Web sites enjoy launching you into unexpected territory, under the hood with no instruments. I'm sure you've been on the frustration end of "follow-me" site topics that never rise above ground effect. Ultralight Flyer Online begins to erase the link maze stereotype with handy menu descriptions before you click—even sub-menus give you a nice preflight before departure.

The thoughtful site framework doesn't fly solo however. The site's notable organization teams up with a nice collection of content. Menu items include: UltraAuction—buy & sell in real time; Prop Wash—introducing you to an online digest for ultralight and sport aviation enthusiasts; Ultralight News—in newsgroup or newsletter format; Ultralight Reference Library—source for flying clubs, aircraft showcase, flight instruction, regulations, books, and videos; and UltraLinks Web Directory—pointing you toward other cool ultra-offerings with a handy search tool.

Fee or Free: Free.

FlightLine OnLine

http://aafo.com

e-mail: submit@aafo.com

RATING

BRIEFING:

This "quasi-zine" (they've steered away from the traditional magazine boundaries) serves up flying features and news.

When an aviation information site offers such an obvious dedication to current updates, I'm immediately interested. Combine continuous updates with fascinating feature stories, and I'm hooked. FlightLine has the "zine" ingredients most have come to expect, but their flair for variety is unique.

Sort through great air race info, gallery photos, feature articles, news, links, and flight simulator info. Read the latest news, topical features worldwide, or delve into some fun audio and video clips. Whatever your fancy, a constant text menu flies right seat with you—always ready with new topic coordinates. Expect to uncover the latest in global air show news, be bombarded with a great collection of photos in the gallery, and pointers to some highly regarded links. Finally, this award-winning info gem rounds out your cyber options with flight simulator news and tips, and ongoing messages from the Editor's Desk.

Other innovations you may appreciate include the latest news from the American Forces Press Service and a "Your Shots" collection of viewer submitted photos.

Fee or Free: Free.

Airfax

http://www.airfax.com

e-mail: ifenews@airfax.com

BRIEFING:

Unlatch your tray table and prepare for a virtual smorgasbord of inflight entertainment tidbits and juicy rumors.

Just the facts on inflight entertainment are now only a click away. Airfax Online skims the commercial carrier scene for the latest inflight industry insights and conveniently serves up the behind-the-scenes info. Onboard amenities, seat back video screens, air phones, meal services, and current carrier stats seem to be among the hottest topics. Aircraft purchasing contracts and passenger marketing complete the update.

This proficiently pleasant site eases you into recline mode with a well-designed layout of five menu categories and interspersed current events. Browse the summarized feature story or click into the full text. Press the topic icons for: a summarized list of industry news & special reports; company services; references for surveys and statistics; various links; and a prompt for site feedback.

Do keep in mind the actual *Airfax Newsletter* is a subscriber service. Although you'll be introduced to an online sample, a fax or e-mail version will arrive twice monthly with your subscription. If you're in the business and rely on what the insiders have to say, this is your ticket. Have a nice flight.

Fee or Free: Free for some news and info—fee for newsletter subscription.

US Aviator

http://www.av8r.net

e-mail: usav8r@gate.net

```
RATING
+ + +
```

BRIEFING:

Current aviation
news that won't
waste your time.

Expanding upon their print version magazine, USA's
Netflight Central is your Dan Rather for aviation news.
Current event "news flashes" as well as weekly e-mail
updates keep you flying-wise. Special features key in on
events and guide you through a wide assortment of
aviation updates and links. Use the left margin to jump
into a sea of goodies: news/flash, resources, Sportplane
Resource Guide (publication for sale), USA Magazine
Online ("Best of" articles—January 1996 to present),
FAA, FAA accident summaries, USA Consumer Adviso-
ries (mini product reviews), and a host of hotlinks.

Browse the resources or peruse back issues. Design is a
little large and clunky, but it's relatively uncluttered and
written well.

Fee or Free: Free,
but leave your e-
mail for weekly
updates.

AVWeb

http://www.avweb.com

e-mail: editor@avweb.com

RATING

BRIEFING:

Free membership after completing a survey entitles you to competent aviation related journalism.

A daily info resource. Yes, daily. One of the best, most competent online aviation publications around. Get your news each day, or browse in summary form with the weekly e-mail edition—AV Flash. The managing group are seasoned pros—writers, editors, and publishers with years of experience. You'll recognize names of well known regular contributors—the best in aviation journalism.

Selections include: NewsWire, ATIS, Safety, Airmanship, System, Avionics, Places, Products, Shopping, Classified, Brainteasers, Weather, Sites, and more. Also, dip into an organized database of: FAA Aircraft, Airman and Mechanic Registries, the Medical Examiner and Repair Station Lists, U.S. Airman Directory, the FARs and others.

You'll find a host of site navigation features, including menus everywhere you go, clickable topic icons, and convenient descriptions. The "New" section is a great personalized version of the table of contents. It shows you exactly which sections, articles, and features have been added or changed since your last visit.

I've been an avid subscriber for well over two years now, and let's just say it's tops on my bookmark list.

Fee or Free: Free, but sign up for all the good stuff.

Air Chronicles

http://www.airpower.maxwell.af.mil

e-mail: editor@cadre.maxwell.af.mil

RATING

BRIEFING:

Brought to you by the folks at the Airpower Journal, Air Chronicles gives you online insight into today's modern Air Force.

Air University Press, publishers of Airpower Journal, has opened the door to this interactive Air Force info resource. It's about Air Force doctrines, strategy and policy, roles and missions, military reform, personnel training, and more. Jump into a discussion group, or read what others have to say.

A host of categories include: Airpower Journal, Contributor's Corner, Airpower Journal International, Current Issues, and Book Reviews. My favorite, Contrails, gives you a mixed bag of aviation stuff, like: news, weather, tools, references, government sites, symposia, professional development, fiction, and professional journals.

Military authors, civilian scholars, and people like you and me create this heads-up, intelligent review of our modern Air Force.

Fee or Free: Free.

Aviation Digest

http://www.avdigest.com

e-mail: webmaster@avdigest.com

BRIEFING:

Mainly a look into flying clubs and flight museums with a couple of fun additions. One hundred dollar hamburger anyone?

Do you enjoy bed and breakfasts, flying into Canada, or just soaring in Houston? You'll find a club that meets your needs. Search throughout the U.S. or Canada for a new group of buddies who share your interests aloft. Specifically, clubs you may find interesting include: The B&B Fly-Inn Club, The International F104 Society, South Central Section (SCS) 99s, Southwest Flying Club, TSS Flying Club, and Wings Over Canada. Still mesmerized by the abundance of info? Just type keywords into a handy site search—you'll find your way.

Scan through museums, helicopter services, the Advanced Maneuvering Program, links, and classified ads. You'll even discover sumptuous fly-in-and-dine hot spots nationwide—brought to you by the One Hundred Dollar Hamburger people.

Fee or Free: Free.

Aviation From Pilot— the UK GA Magazine

http://www.hiway.co.uk/pilot

e-mail: tonyf@pop3.hiway.co.uk

```
RATING
+++
```

BRIEFING:

An OK UK online "zine" (representing its printed sister) with a fantastic A-to-Z list that sheds light on acronyms, abbreviations, and jargon.

Revolving upon the general aviation scene in the UK for over 30 years, *Pilot* magazine's printed version has made its mark in over 27 countries. Now with the online edition stretching out worldwide, those interested in UK aviation stuff need only check in here.

Not a UK flyer? Well, don't go just yet. There's a few things here for everyone: book reviews, CD ROMs, videos, past *Pilot* articles on instruction, flight tests, touring articles, and yes, a great reference resource for aviation acronyms, abbreviations, and jargon. Just click on a searchable alpha letter and get a succinct aircraft definition. From Accelerate-Stop Distance to Zulu, it's excellent for beginners and others puzzled by aviation jargon.

Fee or Free: Free.

Aviation & Aerospace

http://www.mcgraw-hill.com/aviation/aviation.htm

e-mail: webmaster@mcgraw-hill.com

BRIEFING:

Aviation & Aerospace gives you a peek into your favorite McGraw-Hill aviation publications— featuring advertising and subscription info.

For leading edge insight into aviation, turn to the pages of McGraw-Hill's popular printed resources. If you're like me, you just can't get enough aviation info— whether online or in print. This aviation index page gives you at-a-glance briefings on the industry's leading magazines and newsletters. Perfect for planning your upcoming advertising schedules or just getting more details before subscribing, this site provides you with contacts, phone numbers, related products, leading advertisers, and demographic data.

Take a sneak peek into *Aviation Week & Space Technology*; Aviation Week Group Newsletters (seven publications ranging from business aviation to airports); Aviation/Aerospace Online (news and data available by subscription); *A/C Flyer* (corporate aircraft sales); *Business and Commercial Aviation*; and the *World Aviation Directory*.

Fee or Free: Free to peruse, but various fees apply when subscribing to magazines.

In Flight USA Online

http://www.inflightusa.com

e-mail: editor@inflightusa.com

BRIEFING:

Here's an in-flight magazine you'd actually want to take with you. Lucky for you this handy little "e-zine" is on the Web—no need to waste an airline ticket to get it!

Stow and lock your tray table. Return your seatback to its upright position. Give your flight attendant all that garbage you're holding. And, most importantly, don't forget to snag that in-flight magazine! Okay, truth is, they're only good for a captive audience. But, this online magazine (also existing in print) piques your in-flight interest a little better.

Soaring with juicy, current aviation info (stemming from each monthly printed version), you'll tap into a variety of hot topics. Dive into: news, editorial, features, and executive reports. Or, get info on a variety of special topics like: flight instruction, homebuilts, air shows, new products, and more. During your online stopover, you'll also be invited to get sidetracked with a nice selection of stable links (lots of NASA stuff).

Oh, and if you just can't fly without the printed version, you can simply e-mail a subscription request. They make it so easy.

Fee or Free: Free for online viewing, fee for printed magazine subscription.

Internet Business Air News

http://www.bizjet.com/iban

e-mail: john@bizjet.com

RATING

+ + + + +

BRIEFING:

A down-to-business air news site—efficiently designed to foil time wasters.

Enough flying fun, let's get down to business. With Internet Business Air News you immediately get the impression that dedicated, responsible adults are pulling the strings on this site. It's mostly text, organized well, with a few photos (I'm a fan of bandwidth efficiency).

Specifically focusing on daily business aviation news, the opening page has all the current events you can handle—no clicking necessary. All newsworthy articles load initially by default (from most current to least current). Then, should you need to scan back issues with past articles, just search to access.

After you've caught up on today's headlines, you'll find: a great directory of maintenance/FBOs/handlers (mainly Europe-based), directories, other sites, Virtual Air Show, and *European Business Air News* (printed magazine subscription info). Or, if you're a plane shopper, the Aircraft Market makes use of a pull-down list of aircraft manufacturers. All are easy and convenient.

Fee or Free: Free.

Journal of Air Transportation World Wide (JATWW)

http://cid.unomaha.edu/~jatww

e-mail: journal@fa-cpacs.unomaha.edu

```
RATING
+ + +
```

BRIEFING:

A scholarly online endeavor which will pique interest among enthusiasts.

Before sifting through this site, it may be appropriate to fix your bow tie, position the specs on your nose just right, and have aviation theory volumes at the ready. Before intimidation sets in, browse through the offerings—you *will* learn something. The Journal's goal is to eventually become "the preeminent scholarly journal in the aeronautical aspects of transportation." Lofty? Yes, but the JATWW will offer an online sounding board for peer-reviewed articles in all areas of aviation and space transportation, research, policy, theory, practice, and issues. After article review, approved manuscripts will circulate via list server free to all subscribers.

At year end, bound volumes, including all accepted manuscripts, will be available for sale and library reference. If you're not interested in being a part of the free global distribution, you can still visit the site and review any articles of interest. Topics include: aviation administration, management, economics education, technology and science, aviation/aerospace psychology, human factors, safety, human resources, avionics, computing and simulation, airports and air traffic control, and many other broad categories.

Fee or Free: Free, but you'll need to add your e-mail address to their list—follow the specific instructions carefully.

The Avion Online Newspaper

http://avion.db.erau.edu

e-mail: avion@avion.db.erau.edu

RATING

BRIEFING:

An online university "zine" that spreads its wings and intrigues more than just its fellow students.

No stranger to aviation news, the talented folks at Embry-Riddle Aeronautical University continue journalism excellence with this award-winning online newspaper. Mostly written for students, The Avion Online harbors a wealth of fascinating info for every flying enthusiast. You'll uncover the most current events in aeronautics. Find headline newsmakers on the front page and enjoy a host of University stuff. Categories include: Campus News, Metro News, Student Organizations, Space Technology, Data Technology, Diversions, Opinions, Sports, and Comics.

Technically organized with perfection in mind, clickable action buttons and eleven illustrated icon boxes make navigation simple. An online search engine requires only a concept or keyword for subject look-ups.

Billed as "for students by students," The Avion gives us all an educated peek into aviation.

Fee or Free: Free.

Air & Space Smithsonian Magazine

http://www.airspacemag.com

e-mail: online form

RATING

┼┼┼┼

BRIEFING:

An online "zine" sibling to the printed version with its own distinct personality.

As your collection of unread aviation magazines continues to pile up (due to too much flying time), stroll on over to the keyboard and tap into this award-winning online magazine. Sure, you'll be encouraged to subscribe to the well-respected print version, but if you're interested, the online way is easy.

Just here to browse? Well, stay awhile—it's worth it. The Air & Space Web site gives you a peek into the current hard copy issue and provides many additional online articles and features. For quick text-based navigation, the table of contents lists everything, including pages not referenced in the home page. Capitalizing on a history of journalistic excellence, Air & Space continues the tradition here with fantastic current events, interviews, review and previews, marketplace, associations, and more. You'll even find quite an endless array of QuickTime movies, including a C-130 takeoff, a C-130 landing, the Reno Air Racers, an F-104 launch, the Flying Wing, and an X-14 take-off.

After you've sampled and read through Air & Space's offerings try the visitor contact InfoBase. It's a handy all-purpose bulletin board and contact center. Get in touch with other aerospace enthusiasts with this searchable resource—it's excellent!

Fee or Free: Free (fee for magazine subscription).

Bookmarkable Listings

The Controller
http://www.thecontroller.com
e-mail: feedback@thecontroller.com
Sneak peek into *Controller* magazine with for-sale classified
and broker listings.

UK Airshows
http://www.uk-airshows.demon.co.uk
e-mail: paul@airshows.co.uk
Personal UK air show reviews, complete with future show
information and past pictorials.

AeroCrafter
http://www.baicorp.com/aerocrafter
e-mail: aerocftr@baicorp.com
Online complement to the printed magazine offers homebuilt
aircraft info and sources.

Skydive!
http://www.afn.org/skydive
e-mail: online form
Award-winning skydiving archive, complete with equipment,
training, and organizational information.

Flight Forum
http://webusers.anet-dfw.com/~toddc/flight.htm
e-mail: toddc@anet-dfw.com
Newsletter subscription site for aviation-related safety issues
and information.

United Space Alliance
http://www.unitedspacealliance.com
e-mail: communications@usahq.unitedspacealliance.com
Online space info center features Space Shuttle news, virtual
facilities tours, and space-related resources.

National Championship Air Races
http://www.airrace.org
e-mail: online form
Official news and information site of the Reno Air Racing
Association and the National Championship Air Races.

Aviation Parts, Supplies, & Aircraft

JETplane

http://www.jetplane.com

e-mail: info@jetplane.com

BRIEFING:

Expert design, organization, and professionalism, take the active with JETplane. Don't forget your checkbook.

For-sale sites need only check here for a model of site aesthetics and function. JETplane site engineers earn accolades and a 300-knot flyby for this award-winning showing.

Prop planes, business jets, transport jets, helicopters, miscellaneous aircraft, and parts combine to form the mix of online classified ads. Yes, they're fee-oriented to list, but value seems obvious. If you're shopping, search by category. Scan the lists, use a keyword search, or just view the recent listings. Oh, and if you're the type who wants info to come to you (instead of the other way around), join the e-mail list to get notification of your specific product interest.

Scanning the listing and finding your million-dollar turbine baby is painless. Narrow the search any way you desire (manufacturer name, year of manufacture, location, airframe hours, etc.), and move to a summarized list. Click an active listing to get the details: up to a 1,000-word description, photo, and all the particulars. Then, use the response form to contact the seller directly.

Hmmm, I wonder how much G-IVs are going for today?

Fee or Free: Free to search; fee to list ad.

South Valley Aviation

http://www.svconnect.com

e-mail: inquire@svconnect.com

RATING

++

BRIEFING:

Pilot supplies fast, affordable, and secure with online ordering.

C'mon, aren't we all looking for the best deal for pilot supplies? Headsets, books, flight computers, and other needed gadgetry can wreak havoc upon the family budget. Enter South Valley Aviation.

Similar to the generic brand isle of your local supermarket, the plain brown wrapper site isn't flashy, but value is abundant, nonetheless. Big-name pilot products litter these online isles. Start by selecting your category: books, charts, FAR/AIMs, headsets/intercoms, transceivers, GPSs, flight bags, flight computers, flight logs, flight planning, software, training, or videos. For search-savvy shoppers, it might be faster to just type your specific product with the search text box. Next, tap into pages and pages of "Internet coupons" worthy of a look to further discount your purchase. How many coupons? You won't be disappointed with the obligatory one or two. There are many, offering substantial savings on special products. There's no rhyme, reason, or expiration dates associated with the coupons, so check in often as they're changeable.

Finally, standard shopping cart technology applies here. You know: select quantities, view the basket, check-out, and so on. Transactions are said to be secure, so pull out the plastic man and shop 'til your mouse hand drops.

Fee or Free: Free unless you buy something.

Helicopters Only

http://www.helicoptersonly.com

e-mail: Helo@helicoptersonly.com

RATING

+ + +

BRIEFING:

A nifty little one-stop chopper shop.

If the truth be known, Helicopters Only isn't only about helicopters. They've sprinkled a few fixed wing goodies into this online supply stew too. But, the focus is helo stuff, and rotor pilots should think "bookmark."

Relatively new, but obviously growing into their goal of "your one-stop chopper shop," Helicopters Only begins your online shopping experience with solid—not superlative—interface. A left-frame menu gives you the heads up site display, while the main frame gets into detail. Initial site loading brings featured products to your attention, as well as a free contest to win a Pathfinder Flight Computer (at review time, it'll change no doubt). Read and click the product photos leading to headsets, book library (great selection of hard to find helicopter books), cockpit supplies, test prep guides & materials, gifts, and even some children's stuff. For more specific gotta-haves, click into the online catalog, or view the new product additions (efficient!).

Once you've spent your limit, check out with "shopping cart" technology. It's simple, painless, and secure. By the way, it's encouraging to know that satisfaction is guaranteed at Helicopters Only. All products offered have been tested and approved by site administrators themselves.

Fee or Free: Free.

Cessna

http://www.cessna.com

e-mail: corpcomm@cessna.textron.com

RATING

BRIEFING:

Model corporate
site showcases
its aircraft,
company
philosophy, and
skill at public
communication.

Stuffy? Dry? Humorless? Visually boring? No, not
Cessna. This giant aircraft industry leader leans towards
fun and fanciful when it comes to its online showcase.
Pushing my "five-plane" scale of excellence, Cessna
creates the perfect corporate template of Web style.
Employing every site mechanism known, the Cessna
site gives you frame-driven menus, drop-down navigation, text links, running text scripts, changing photography, and more. It's almost enough just to sort through
all the gizmos. But, when you're done gawking at all the
plane pictures and gadgetry, steer into a menu topic or
two. Customer building cheerleading comes in the form
of A Culture of Commitment and A World of Support.
The good stuff, though, is found scanning the pictures
and info on leading edge aircraft. Read, see, and hear
snippets on Citation aircraft, Caravan aircraft, and
single engine aircraft—all broken down further by
model.

And, when you're tired of scanning aircraft (no such
thing for me!), there's much more taking the form of:
becoming a pilot, a Cessna career (employment opportunities), and Cessna financing.

The Cessna site. It's a showy showpiece of Web mastery.

Fee or Free: Free.

pilotslounge.com (ShopNet)

http://www.pilotslounge.com

e-mail: customerservice@pilotslounge.com

RATING

BRIEFING:

No lounge
lizards here.
Just the sound
of credit cards
singing with
pilots shopping
online.

You won't find blue smoke here or sultry jazz vocals. But, this lounge does spotlight aviation. Lurking in the online sales stage of pilotslounge.com, an ensemble of aviation-only entertainment keeps you glued to your seat.

Even though junior-level design and typo-ridden warm up acts begin your adventure, don't despair. The main acts of supplies, discussion groups, and chat room make up for any downside. Pilot supplies, ordering info, and name-brand product banners are everywhere. The online store is customer satisfaction certified by WebWatchdog, and convenient product/price update status loads onto the main page. Even track your purchase shipment 24-hours with online tracking. That's right, you almost can't help but buy something with such a healthy helping of categorized products. Click through airport guides, apparel, gift items, avionics, books, checklists, flight simulators, headsets, training materials, videos, and more.

Aviation news, employment listings, message board, classifieds, airline interview info, aviation links, and others serve as competent back-up singers at this lounge. Drop in when you're feeling saucy. There's no cover.

Fee or Free: Free.

The Mooney Mart

http://www.mooneymart.com

e-mail: coy@mooneymart.com

RATING

+ + +

BRIEFING:

Interactive
Mooney
emporium
delights, dazzles,
and disseminates
Mooney-only
matters.

If there was an inaudible way to be loud and boister-ous, Mooney Mart's online presence has discovered it. Longwinded run-on commentary fills the pages, together with haphazard typos, clip art, sales pitches, and more. But, for the true Mooney enthusiast, you simply must make room for a bookmark.

Just take a deep breath and click in knowing you'll be bombarded with the Web's equivalent to used car sales propaganda. To provide appropriate content, the site prompts you to enter through one of three Web portals: existing Mooney owners; enthusiast/perspec-tive buyers; or general aviation industry vendors, dealers/brokers, etc.

Once in, everything Mooney may be found here in the form of: sales, maintenance, modifications, forums, supplies, classifieds, links, and current events. Step into the introduction to get your feet wet with the five basic differences that Mooney Mart's site offers: interactivity (Autopilot Al asks for info to personalize your online experience); Mooney-specific supplies; Mooney discussion groups, Q&As, etc.; free Mooney-oriented classifieds; and current events with "Mooney Memories."

Mooney owners will be pleasantly surprised with automatic features like: Mooney Service Center SDRs (service difficulty reports), NOTAMS (notices to all "Mooniacs"), Mooney factory service bulletins, and FAA ADs.

Fee or Free: Free.

List a Plane

http://www.listaplane.com

e-mail: online form

RATING

++++

BRIEFING:

Classy for-sale
site speaks
volumes with
organization and
good design.

Departing the hordes of unseemly and unsightly aircraft listing sites, List a Plane rises out of the sales cesspool depths and rewards us with style and substance.

It's a perfect place to park your plane for sale. Menus, illustrations, and fancy site organization leave you feeling comfortable to sign up with those guys. Certainly they claim prompt, efficient service. But, you'll have to evaluate this on your own. The easy listing format and examples guide you effortlessly into the arms of online sales. Even if you're on the buying end of the sale, you'll be equally impressed with helpful info request forms and a courtesy instruction section describing every search field. Search by manufacturer, model, N-number, aircraft age, price range, engine type, and more.

Based upon your search criteria, a multitude of flying for-sale listings pop up with: TTAF, SMOH, instrumentation, price, contact (e-mail and phone), and other detailed info. Some listings even serve up a photo or two.

Fee or Free: Free listings for a limited time (as of review time). Hurry, it will become fee-based.

AircraftDealers.net

http://www.aircraftdealers.net

e-mail: info@aircraftdealers.net

RATING

BRIEFING:

What's the big deal at AircraftDealers.net? Over 2,500 listings, that's what.

Wheeling, dealing, and displaying, AircraftDealers.net may at first seem like that used car salesman that's immediately in your face when you pull into the lot. There's banners, multiple menus, and lots of announcements that seek your attention via various colors, styles, and sizes. But, hold firm and press on. AircraftDealers.net is loud (note the site's use of exclamation point punctuation), but thoroughly resourceful.

Your first clue to the resourcefulness of AircraftDealers.net is the series of four pull-down menus sitting atop the site's chaos. With only a click you'll go directly to message boards, weather info, site mission, a quick tour, and lots of site advertising opportunities (including banners, business ads, and aircraft listings). Once you stumble across the aircraft search engines, you'll become entranced with the sheer volume of listings. How does over 2,500 listings sound? Now, to be fair, the listings come from many sources (Aircraft Shopper Online, Wings Online, Controller, Aircraft Buyer.com, and others). But, give credit to Aircraft Dealers.net for tying them together and offering a centralized picture of aircraft offerings.

With such volume, the proper search engines aren't just nice they are necessary. In this respect, AircraftDealers.net rises to the challenge. Search by aircraft, state, year of aircraft, dealer(s), date added, and more. Sort by year, aircraft type, dealer, state, or date submitted.

Fee or Free: Free to browse, fee to list your aircraft.

Pilot Toys.com

http://www.pilottoys.com

e-mail: controller@pilottoys.com

BRIEFING:

Well-named site stores the essentials for flight.

Ah, the name—how apropos it is. Except these toys at Pilot Toys.com aren't of the stuffed animal or Tonka truck variety. Most, however, are just as fun to us pilot types. Fun has its price though, and you'll find prices, products, and promotions o'plenty at Pilot Toys.com.

A modest, yet workable interface brings you the whole online store, sans the bells and whistles. In fact, you can expect minimal photos, Java scripts, and ad banners that can often slow the searching progress. Take flight quickly with an immediate clearance for site navigation. A nondescript text menu presents the choices, while a main frame displays the contents. Although the name is Pilot Toys.com they stock mostly basics: test preparatory materials (books & software), flight computers, plotters, CD-rom reference, textbook & student kits, aviator's library, and the new FAR/AIM series. Shoppers will receive good description, adequate photos, and simple-to-use shopping cart technology.

A secure server (approved by SiteInspector) assures ordering protection, and plenty of instructions make purchase painless.

Fee or Free: Free.

Aircraft.Customads.com

http://aircraft.customads.com

e-mail: admin@customads.com

BRIEFING:

Custom doesn't have to be complex. Find, sell, or trade aircraft easily online.

Fee or Free:
Aircraft searching is free and members receive one free, pictureless ad. Fee-related advertising is available.

Emerging as a worthy resource is Aircraft.Customads.com—not necessarily for volume of listings, but for overall site organization. Its automated systems make placing and updating ads simple. Expecting a complicated cockpit of controls? Grab the yoke and find only the essentials for easy flight. The topmost menu, which is eerily similar to browser menus, keeps you on a steady course with some site basics: Help, Search, Site Map (good!), FAQ, E-mail, and Home. Then, roll into the free data havens of: FAA database searches, aircraft sale listings, aircraft trade listings, aircraft wanted listings, classified parts/services listings, and dealers and brokers listing. Yes there's a lot to search through here too. Become a member (free), place an aircraft sale listing, place an aircraft wanted listing, or place a dealers and brokers listing. Even review or update your ads.

Aircraft searching (if that's your game) is well organized with lots of narrowing fields: aircraft make & type, price range, ads listed within a user specified number of days, and year range. Or, find your flying dream machine based upon N-number or airport ID search.

Pilots' Web

http://www.americaworks.net/aviator

e-mail: none available

BRIEFING:

Joining the aviation shopping fray, Pilots' Web's strength is found in variety.

Spinning a modest web of visual delights, Pilots' Web steers clear of presenting its shopping center with any hint of flashiness. If you're in the mood for quality supplies, gifts, books, manuals, and specialty kid stuff, then prepare for mundane presentation. Your scroll bar, back button, credit card, and patience are about all you'll need. Don't misunderstand. While style (any hint of it) is not this site's strong suit, the store is well stocked.

Break out the plastic for secure ordering of any number of supplies. The telling icons organize the variety. An Altimeter Quadrant has the pilot and student pilot products. Snoopy identifies aviation stuff for little flyers. And, the Flying Aircraft leads you to online help with a free locator service. Specifically you'll encounter: aviation videos; home schooling aids; kneeboards, tripboards, and clipboards; books, study guides, and manuals; headsets; flight planning software; aircraft toys; flight computers; and more.

While Pilots' Web certainly avoids any hint of visually friendly design, it makes up for it with fast loading times and simple searching. Just be ready to use the scroll bar and back button—mine are still smoking.

Fee or Free: Free.

AeroMall

http://www.aeromall.com

e-mail: feedback@aeromall.com

RATING

+++

BRIEFING:

Aeromall's stringent selection process makes these chosen aviation merchants the cream of the crop.

The old saying, "there's strength in numbers" certainly becomes evident as you stroll through the compilation at AeroMall. The difference? AeroMall maintains an affiliation of independent merchants who are hand-picked and "approved as legitimate, time-tested operations." Yes, that's a big deal to the growing community of savvy aviation shoppers.

Although the pages are relatively attractive and organization is good, the real story is in the content. This one-stop-shop resource slips only the best and brightest aviation merchants in front of you. Curious about some of the requirements to be included on AeroMall? The merchant must have a professional, easy-to-use design, use industry standard encryption (for credit cards), and display a telephone number staffed during normal business hours. Hey, now that's a beneficial selection!

So although the rule here is quality over quantity, it's pleasantly surprising to see that the quantity is here too. Just browse the departments: aviation software, books & videos, pilot supplies, aircraft for sale, aircraft insurance, hardware & software, luggage, specialty, and gifts and collectibles. Clickable merchants line the pages in an organized table offering at-a-glance info on each.

Fee or Free: Free, unless you're prompted to buy at a featured site.

Aviation PartsBase

http://www.partsbase.com

e-mail: webmaster@partsbase.com

```
RATING
++++
```

BRIEFING:

Click into this parts mega mall for 24-hour shopping and no waiting.

The stats are impressive even at review time: 30 million parts online and 7,000 PartsBase members. Add in daily updating and good site organization for a truly useful aviation parts locator service. Worthy of award-winning recognition, Aviation PartsBase plays the perfect middle-man for both buyers and sellers of aircraft parts.

The participation among industry players certainly gives you reason to take notice—the list is long and well rounded. This worthy resource does require fee-related membership, but the site's organized nature and huge parts base has me feeling at ease. Membership ties you into all the goodies, like: unlimited parts searching, unlimited inventory listing, automatic "Request for Quote" via e-mail or fax, complete access to TradeCenter (an aviation bulletin board for buying, selling, or trading), aviation related links, PartsBase discussion group, weekly e-mail newsletter, and free tech support.

Although not complex to use, PartsBase does require some pre-use tutoring. Their "how-to's" and helpful pointers make searching and listing a snap. Just click through the tutorial, FAQs, and new member info for thorough instruction.

Fee or Free: Fee-related services. New members receive a free 14-day trial run.

Aviationsite.com

http://aviationsite.com

e-mail: webmaster@aviationsite.com

RATING
┼ ┼

BRIEFING:

Having the right idea, Aviationsite.com offers innovation for aircraft buyers and sellers.

The concept is right on the mark. The execution could stand some improvement in the areas of page design and organization. Overall, with everything considered, free Web sites to those individuals trying to sell their aircraft just can't miss. A quick audio/video intro by your host introduces you to Aviationsite.com—an online used-plane lot without the pushy sales guys.

If you're an aesthetics sort of browser, page presentation may disappoint. Bury your initial skepticism and climb into the left seat anyway. For prospective owners, all you need to do is press one button: "Aircraft 4 Sale" and skip everything else. Next, click to locate a manufacturer: Beechcraft, Cessna, Citabria, Mooney, Piper, Commander, or experimental. When you reach an actual listing turn a blind eye from the lackluster page design, because all the essential info is there.

For sellers, there's certainly value here, especially with a giant, candid "tutorial" covering some of the pitfalls involved in selling an aircraft. While not intended as a comprehensive seller's guide it does identify many important considerations.

Fee or Free: Free to individuals. Fee-related ads for dealers.

Skywagon

http://www.skywagon.org

e-mail: webmaster@skywagon.org

RATING
‡‡

BRIEFING:

Skywagon-specific smorgasbord of thoughts, pictures, fly-ins, and tips.

Those not familiar with the Cessna 180/185 series may incorrectly envision a flying 1970 Ford stationwagon hybrid with swept back wings. Shake this silly scene from your mind and click into Skywagon's online tribute to this worthy workhorse. A word of caution though: if you're not fondly fanatical over the 180/185, you may want to move on because info contained here is dedicated to the Skywagon.

Jump aboard and clear prop. Skywagon is launched and serving up tribute-oriented praise and insight to Skywagon drivers. Even if you haven't wrestled around a Skywagon in your lifetime, you probably know someone who has. If so, pass along the address (www.skywagon.org) to them instead. They'll appreciate it.

Enthusiasts will marvel at the site's clean, simple style and dedication to its namesake. Initially you'll have the opportunity to click into the fly-in catalog, post a question to the 180/185 list server group, read what's new in the world of Skywagons, browse the photo gallery, buy & sell, and more. Perhaps the most favored resource, though, is Knowledge Base. Here, you'll review a helpful FAQs area, tips & tricks section, product reviews, and columns.

Fee or Free: Free.

Aviationgifts.com

http://www.aviationgifts.com

e-mail: depar@firstdial.com

RATING
++

BRIEFING:

Fluff-free supply site makes shopping simple and secure.

For flight gear sans the fluff, step into Aviationgifts.com's stellar supply site. Relatively easy to use and devoid of time-wasting extras, this site skips directly to a huge menu of aviation gifts and necessities for sale online. Using the industry standard shopping cart system, Aviationgifts.com gets you through the store and the checkout line unscathed. Click and buy worry-free with customer satisfaction guarantee and secure server technology.

Though not a vision of perfect online beauty, Aviationgifts.com does an adequate job of presenting its wares. Organization and navigation are well designed with omni-present menus and photographic icons. Item descriptions are succinct and pricing is clearly marked on everything.

Categories from which to choose include: apparel, novelties, outdoor products, mouse pads, books and videos, aviation software, headsets, handheld navigation, flight cases, aviation art, glasses, kneeboards, log books, plotters and flight computers, timers and watches, and more.

Fee or Free: Free.

Aviation Industry Resource (AIR)

http://www.air-air.com

e-mail: webmaster@air-air.com

RATING
++++

BRIEFING:

A versatile, searchable link library with handy aircraft-for-sale resource.

Just as most modern libraries provide computerized searching to quickly locate your needed advice, Aviation Industry Resource has online volumes at the ready. Free to everyone, this international aviation registry and listing service quickly finds links, aircraft, and navaid info based upon your specifications.

For me, quick and easy page navigation is "resourceful" enough never mind AIR's simple searching forms. Jump into the link registry, pick your category, click a location, and type a keyword or two. You'll be thrilled with response time and the sheer volume of thousands of links. Adding your own Web site address (if you have one) is completely free and easy. The aircraft-for-sale listings work similarly. Simply pick a desired make of aircraft and get a corresponding list. Additions to the for-sale list are also free. I didn't uncover much in the listings area as of review time, but the collection seems to be growing—especially with no fee.

Other clickable site topics include: Sponsorship, Web Sites, Flight Planning (a few helpful links), and the fairly popular Bulletin Board.

Fee or Free: Free, even to list a for-sale aircraft or add your Web site address.

Aerosearch

http://www.aerosearch.com

e-mail: webmaster@aerosearch.com

RATING
✝✝

BRIEFING:

Dip into Aerosearch's huge database when looking for tools and parts.

Yes, the buttons are bland and overall site aesthetics leave you wondering who was flying left seat on the layout mission. But, before you make a mad dash for your favorite bookmark, dig a little deeper into the heart of the content. Disappointment completely subsides when you engage in a search for aviation parts and tools.

Touted as the "#1 source for aircraft part inventory location information on the Internet," Aerosearch does require new user registration (free) before you're underway. After login and password credentials are checked, you'll enter part numbers, alternate part numbers, or the national stock number. Then, click "start search" for your comprehensive list of suppliers. And yes, it's comprehensive.

The AeroPort section has more in the way of searches and info. New Equipment Manufacturer, FBOs, Aircraft for Sale, Repair Stations, Engine Shops, Airports Around the World, Flight Schools, Avionics, and Rental/Charter topics are all a bit sparse (as of review time).

My advice? Just stick to parts and tools searching for now.

Fee or Free: Free.

VisionAire Corporation

http://www.visionaire.com

e-mail: info@visionaire.com

RATING
☩ ☩

BRIEFING:

Peek in for visionary vistas of succinct corporate information.

Sure you've got your Boeings of the cyber-world spewing out online magic with infinite resources standing by. But, while obviously not the manufacturing powerhouse of Boeing, the VisionAire Corporation demonstrates its Vantage aircraft and other company topics with skill and purpose.

Its compact, yet finely tuned Web offerings give you concise insight into six main topics. Click on What's New to stay abreast of site changes—you can even register to receive automatic page updates. About VisionAire moves you into: The VisionAire Story, Meeting the Team, Company Locations, and Our Mission & Values. The Vantage Link supplies info regarding why you should consider a Vantage, Airplane Specifications, Aircraft Comparisons (under construction at review time), Prices & Terms, Partners & Suppliers, and Photo Gallery. You'll also get more insight with VisionAire News & Events, as well as the latest employment opportunities.

Fee or Free: Free.

AvShop.Net

http://www.avshop.net
e-mail: pilots@avshop.net

RATING

Even though it's graphically oriented, AvShop.Net's online catalog loads fast. The layout people (who are obviously talented) must have meshed perfectly with the site mechanics people, because the final result exemplifies teamwork.

Once the initial welcome page instantly appears, you begin to sense that the interior will be just as fancy as the exterior. Click to enter the catalog and you won't be disappointed. Because lurking under the cowl of this aerodynamic machine beats the heart of a full-blown aviation supplies catalog. Mostly magnifying its software selections, AvShop.Net still provides a wider selection of necessities than you're led to believe. A nicely presented main menu moves you quickly into stuff like: books and study guides, aviation videos, cockpit and aircraft accessories, pilot supplies, and a healthy dose of software specialties.

The site's beauty and brains also rise to the occasion during the "checkout." Once you've filled your basket with goodies, a well-organized system of ordering ensues. Review your basket contents, change or remove items, and proceed to either an electronic or offline "checkout." It's easy and convenient.

Fee or Free: Free, unless you're tempted into ordering.

Spinners Pilot Shop

http://www.spinnerspilotshop.com

e-mail: comments@spinnerspilotshop.com

RATING

BRIEFING:

As online supply shops go, Spinners tops the list with revolutionary completeness.

Few pilot supply sites handle the complete online ordering system flawlessly. In fact, only a handful come to mind, with Spinners propelling its way onto my list. Layout and design work well together with little waiting time. Colorful menu topics are always a click away. Online transactions are given secure routing. But, the best part revolves around Spinners' huge inventory. It's not the online mirage that most aviation supply sites throw together— just read some of their customer testimonials.

Without even touching the subcategory list, I'll give you a taste with: headsets, Jeppesen, pilot supplies, books, logbooks, software, flight computer, flight bags, videos, training aides, kneeboards, flashlights, GPS, intercoms, handhelds, plane supplies, and more!

Shopping is relatively painless with the standard "shopping cart approach." Simply view product photos, read descriptions, review prices, and add items to your "cart." Then, checkout online or offline. Simple instructions guide you through either method.

Get online, grab a mouse, find your favorite plastic card, and spin your way into a buying frenzy. It's easy to do.

Fee or Free: Free.

WWW.Plane-World.com

http://www.plane-world.com

e-mail: WebPilot@ComMark.com

RATING

BRIEFING:

Kick the tires, rattle the flaps, and check for prop dings online with Plane-World.

Fee or Free: Free to browse and to add your own classifieds.

All review criteria aside for a moment, the real test for aircraft-for-sale sites comes down to volume of listings. Selection is key, and to be frank, most aircraft-for-sale sites fall dramatically short in the listings area. Worse still, fly-by-night cyber-brokers tend to throw up visually forgettable Web tangles, expecting you to find your way through their meager offerings.

Rising above the scattered masses with Vx climb, Plane-World blasts onto the for-sale scene like a trusty Cessna 172 gone turbine. Appropriately simple menus and well-designed layout clear your way into a huge variety of classified listings. Following a left-margin menu that changes into sub-menus with each topic, page reckoning is of the 100-mile visibility variety. Start with For-sale or Wanted. Then, try the handy search engine or place your own free classifieds.

Although picture-less, the listings couldn't be more efficient and informative. The lack of pictures may put off some, but that's why the site's so fast. It's a trade-off I'll take gladly.

Aeroprice

http://www.aeroprice.com

e-mail: info@aeroprice.com

RATING

┼┼

BRIEFING:

Holding your hand through buying or selling, this site's cool features make for a worthwhile stopover.

Buying and selling aircraft. In the lifetime of most serious aviators, the murky abyss of either endeavor may be riddled with uncertainty—especially the first purchase or sale. But, breaking through the low lying fog of confusion, Aeroprice offers a progressive taxi toward understanding.

Though limited on any visual wizardry, Aeroprice provides some handy fee-related services, free tips & trends, and a gentle push toward additional resources. No, I'm not navigating under the hood. I realize that this for-sale site is subtly maneuvering toward cyber-sales of its QuickQuote online pricing and appraisal software. But, it's certainly worthy of a flyby if you're shopping or selling.

After entering info into a thorough online questionnaire, you'll be introduced to an excellent aircraft pricing analysis. Look for great insight into pricing adjustments based upon the average retail cost for your selected aircraft. Items analyzed include: airframe, engine, avionics, additional equipment, interior, exterior, and damage history.

Fee or Free: Free.

Bombardier Aerospace Group

http://www.aerospace.bombardier.com

e-mail: none provided

RATING

BRIEFING:

Jet shoppers or just dreamers will find the ultimate in online perfection with Bombardier.

If you were searching for that flawless corporate aerospace site against which to compare others, Bombardier Aerospace Group's Web presence is the model. Organization and page designs are among the cutting edge variety. Photo gallery images are professionally striking. And, page navigation is effortless. Though a fully functional and informative gem, the site is simply a standard-setting masterpiece.

Okay, so maybe you're not in the market for a Canadair Regional Jet or a Challenger, but most enthusiasts will agree that the company's line of aircraft are worth an appreciative peek. Luxurious business jets like Global Express, Challenger, Canadair, and Learjet grace the company's online pages with specs and pictures. Similarly, regional aircraft info for the Canadair Regional Jet and the de Havilland Dash 8 series are at the ready.

Those more interested in employment rather than jet shopping will appreciate their extensive online personnel department (originating in Montreal). Detailed job offerings are categorized into Administration, Customer Support, Information Systems, Engineering and Manufacturing.

Fee or Free: Free.

Northrop Grumman Corporation

http://www.northgrum.com

e-mail: none provided

BRIEFING:

Zero in on combat and weapons technology info with Northrop Grumman.

When you're talking about combat aircraft, precision weapons, or defense electronics, technologies developed by Northrop Grumman will usually wind their way into the conversation. When the discussion expands into online resources, Northrop Grumman's Web site must be in the mix. The company-wide facts, news, and knowledge flow endlessly within its online offerings. I suppose you'd expect a masterful site from a company who plays a major role in many of the world's most advanced weapons systems and technologies. After all, they're no strangers to design and systems integration.

The main menu guides you through the exhaustive company tour with broad categories of: What We Do, What's New, Executive Officers, *Review* Magazine, Photo Gallery, Corporate Directory, Career Opportunities, and more. Background info, product fact sheets, and key personnel biographies are well written and interesting.

Although you might be stifling a yawn, ready to turn the page, hold tight. There's fun stuff here too. I particularly enjoyed the great images in the video gallery of: B2 Missions and Testing, Various Aircraft on Display, Manufacturing, The F/A-18 Hornet in Action, and more. Quite frankly, the videos alone are reason enough to pay a visit.

Fee or Free: Free.

Microsoft Flight Simulator

http://www.microsoft.com/games/fsim

e-mail: tell_FS@microsoft.com

RATING

BRIEFING:

Get the real briefing straight from the source—before you fire up those flight simulator engines.

The Flight Simulator site combines a couple of magical components inherent in all award-winning sites: valuable online information and easy communication to a huge audience (I bet you know a Microsoft Flight Simulator user).

Sure there's software promo stuff everywhere. Ad banners and purchasing pages abound. But, looking a little further into the mix, Flight Simulator users will strike virtual gold. The latest product information and downloads can be found in News. You'll find lively discussions, topical chats, and tips in the MSN Flight Simulator Forum. Performance specs, flight scenery enhancement products, and current Flight Simulator news are also handy for cyber-flyers. And, for those not yet into the Microsoft Flight Simulator scene, a convenient demo movie gives you a free sneak peek at this wondrously real simulator.

Whatever your simulator readiness, all Microsoft Flight Simulator users need a quick refresher here. And, soon-to-be users? It's simply a perfect preflight walk-around.

Fee or Free: The info and tips are free. The software isn't.

The Aviation Online Network

http://www.airparts.com

e-mail: webmaster@airparts.com

RATING

+ + +

BRIEFING:

An easy-to-use, partly subscriber based resource—great for finding parts.

The selections here aren't endless, effectively narrowing the confusion factor. Simply and conveniently at your fingertips are: Parts Search (for members), RFQ bulletin submission form (an equipment buy & sell forum with free classifieds), Parts Search (demonstration), Show News, and Links (broken out by icon-represented categories).

If you're in the market for parts, you'll have good luck here. Some stuff is available without subscribing, but for parts you'll need to subscribe.

With a little extra ground time on your hands, you're invited to test your skills with the FAA Exam Man Question of the Day—you might even win a free video!

Fee or Free: Free, but you'll need to subscribe (name, address, e-mail, etc.)

Global Aviation Navigator

http://www.globalair.com

e-mail: webmaster@globalair.com

RATING

+ + +

BRIEFING:

Good internal database makes searching for aviation stuff pleasantly efficient.

Don't be fooled. It's not *2001—A Space Odyssey.* Punching any of the multicolored buttons will guide you to info and company listings. Useful topics and sub-topics narrow your focus in the aviation Internet directory for: FBOs, airports, dealers, weather, insurance, FAA stuff, financial services, and more.

Specifically, plane and parts enthusiasts will find a satisfying collection of classified ads—easily searchable with a text box prompt, "quick look" categories, or a laundry list of infinite sections. Good thing they make searching easy, because loads of listings are the rule here. From beacons to floats, and consultants to warbirds, the variety is pleasantly satisfying.

Fee or Free: Free. Fee for listing an ad.

PC Aviator

http://www.pcaviator.com.au/

e-mail: none provided

BRIEFING:

Lots of selling going on here, but good products abound. Become introduced to some quality flight simulator stuff—great for power off stalls in your pj's.

Find flight simulation hardware and software on this site Down Under (Melbourne, Australia). Approved for serious training purposes or just frivolous fun, PC Aviator's flight simulator products give you lofty experiences straight from your computer. To enter, click on the runway.

Although a hard sell for their simulator stuff, the site offers a limited selection of other flight simulator links, great list of worldwide aviation links, and downloadable software. Other clickable areas include The Latest Headlines (site news and miscellaneous flight simulator links) and *Computer Pilot Magazine*.

If you're interested in the PC Aviator full color catalog, just sign up here. This printed product catalog is full of screen shots and simulator product info. By adding your name to the mailing list, you'll regularly receive a copy of the catalog.

Be forewarned: graphics, sound, and Java wizardry are plentiful. Download speed may suffer.

Fee or Free:
Free—sign up for the catalog if you're a "sim" buff.

Aircraft Shopper Online (ASO)

http://www.aso.com

e-mail: webmaster@aso.com

RATING

BRIEFING:

It's an award-winning site for a reason. Unique searching capabilities smooth out online shopping turbulence.

Keeping the value of your time in mind (hey, you could be flying instead), ASO's pages are effortless and efficient. It's mostly text until you get to your selected destination. Once you plunge into over countless aircraft-for-sale listings and narrow your search, you'll get descriptions and photos. Serious aircraft shoppers should skip directly to "PowerSearch" for excellent sorting and criteria setting. Set price and date ranges, limit the search to one aircraft make, or scan the entire listing. If you are (or will become) a frequent ASO shopper, these crafty Web developers have even included a clickable area for new additions and changes—showing only changes added in the number of days you specify.

Also handy are: Dealers and Brokers, Aviation Links & Terms, Aircraft Partnerships, Success Stories, Aircraft Parts, Aircraft Avionics, and the online assistance of Help & Tips.

Fee or Free: Free.

Air Source One

http://www.airsource1.com

e-mail: service@airsource1.com

RATING

+ + + + +

BRIEFING:

Speed through this quick checkout line for student, corporate, military, and airline pilot supplies.

Grab an electronic shopping basket and stock up on your favorite aeronautical necessities with Air Source One. Simply put, you'll breeze through the quick check with no lines and everything you could possibly need.

This giant online pilot supply superstore expertly offers up isles of products from which to choose: headsets, GPSs, transceivers, charts, other electronics, FAA test preps, flight bags, aviation books, apparel, gifts, necessities, and software. Conveniently complete your order by credit card (they assure secure credit card processing), phone, fax, or mail. Online ordering can be next-day delivered and includes an e-mail confirmation.

If your basket gets heavy and you just want to find a particular item in a hurry, search by manufacturer or item description and simply type in your item. More minor site features include: weather, company info, and other aviation sites.

Fee or Free: Free, unless you buy something!

Jeppesen

http://www.jeppesen.com

e-mail: webmaster@jeppesen.com

RATING

✝ ✝ ✝

BRIEFING:

Artfully organized electronic catalog offers useful pilot supplies.

With over 60 years of industry leadership (from a man who invented aviation charts), Jeppesen Sanderson once again captures the aviation world's attention with a visually captivating, organizationally brilliant Web companion. From the world's leading publisher of flight info (computer flight planning services, aviation services, and training systems), Jeppesen's site provides a current, online look into its offerings. Conveniently located among the company's history and profile info, you'll find the promotional core: the Jeppesen catalog.

While most "e-catalogs" weave the shopper through time-consuming pictures and tangled disarray, you'll glide effortlessly through Jepp's: manual services, VRF flight information, airport & FAR reference info, Airway Manual accessories, GPS/NavData services, Jeppesen FS-200 Instrument Flight Simulator system, pilot supplies, maintenance training products, and CFI renewal program, and more.

When ordering you have three options: 1) e-mail order info, 2) call the listed 800-number, or 3) fax the order. No credit card online ordering systems were available at the time of review.

Fee or Free: Free.

Wings Online

http://www.wingsonline.com

e-mail: mailroom@wingsonline.com

RATING

++++

BRIEFING:

Aviation shopping is made easy with this site—crammed with specs and pictures of aircraft for sale, rent, or lease worldwide.

I'm always a fan of productive, visually appealing Web creations resulting from skill and a lot of elbow grease. The moment you grab the yoke here and finesse the controls, you'll also believe someone spent some late nights fine-tuning the many subtle nuances. This fantastic aircraft shopper resource gives tire kickers and eager buyers alike good info and many search choices. Sort by aircraft type, price, location, or the latest additions as of current date (marvelously efficient!). Search through related listings, such as: For Sale by specific "N" number and specific seller. Once you narrow your search and actually tap into the seller's wares you'll be instantly informed with important specs: TT, STOH, SBOH, SMOH, registration, avionics, interior/exterior, price, contact, and more. Most listings also include multiple pictures showing off such areas as: exterior, panel, interior, etc.

The best part for you Net-savvy shoppers is you'll actually find loads of quality listings—not a smattering of local rejects. When you're ready to really shop, try on this site, it fits perfectly.

Fee or Free: Free.

Optima Publications

http://www.pilotsguide.com

e-mail: webmaster@pilotsguide.com

RATING

+ + +

BRIEFING:

This Optima site deftly guides you through their popular printed airport guides.

Okay, so maybe I've slightly narrowed the geographic scope with Optima Publications. But, click through the Pilot's Guide Online and you'll see why they've become an award winner. With a focus on California, Southwestern, and Northwestern Airports, the Optima publications offer vital and current airport info.

You'll find convenient and thorough descriptions of product offerings, including: Pilot's Guide to California Airports, Pilot's Guide to Southwestern Airports, Pilot's Guide to Northwestern Airports, Fun Places to Fly, Aeronautical Chart Subscription Service, and more. Click on any product category for instant prices and ordering info.

Scan through info about the Pilot's Guide (history and what it is) and topics relating to current subscribers (revisions service, customer service, etc.).

It's a simple, well-organized sales pitch for some excellent pilot products.

Fee or Free: Free.

AirShow—Aviation Trading Network

http://www.airshow.net

e-mail: crewchief@airshow.net

RATING

BRIEFING:

This expertly arranged for-sale site combines thoughtful features and a wondrous assortment of quality aircraft.

You may, at first glance, give your own high rating to this site for its online design and user friendly layout. But, I urge you to discover the core of the AirShow's hidden talents. Just try looking up your favorite aircraft. While most aviation for-sale sites skimp by with only a few aircraft, the AirShow explodes with a huge variety of listings. It's a true resource for the buyer and seller. Clickable menu icons include: Find an Aircraft, Featured Dealers, Financing, Finding a Buyer, Showcase, The Sound File, Dealer/Broker info, and more.

The expertly developed searches within the huge database can be narrowed by: price range, aircraft type, special characteristics, year range, and aircraft make/ model. Serious plane hunters will rejoice at the brilliant What's New search—giving you only the latest additions since a user-specified date.

Not shopping, just selling? Well, you'll be equally impressed. All details for listing your unwanted flying machine are here—just click. Conveniently, you have a choice between an online ad form, or custom service (mail, fax, or e-mail your photos and info).

Fee or Free: Free. If you're interested in showing an aircraft, reasonable fees apply.

Raytheon Aircraft

http://www.raytheon.com/rac

e-mail: webmaster@raytheon.com

RATING

╋╋╋╋

BRIEFING:

Professionally prepared corporate look at Raytheon Aircraft.

Originating from the Raytheon company home pages, I invite you to skip directly to this nicely informative company page specifically devoted to Raytheon Aircraft. You'll quickly be enlightened about the company's broad product line. The nicely organized format gives you efficient descriptions of the Hawker 1000, Hawker 800XP, Beechjet, Raytheon Premier I, regional airliners (Beech 1900D), business turboprops (King Air series), piston-powered aircraft (Bonanzas and Barons), and military aircraft.

Current company press releases (timely and updated regularly) give you tidbits like: "Raytheon Aircraft Delivers 5,000[th] Beech King Air," and "E-Systems Montek Division Merging with Raytheon Aircraft." Company info sources guide you to stuff like: events calendar, newsletters & publications, shareholder info, aircraft in the news, aircraft services, Travel Air, Raytheon Aerospace, and a What's New section.

More clickable categories include: Key Business Areas, Shareholder Info, and Employment Opportunities. Still lost? A convenient site map makes finding a topic effortless.

Fee or Free: Free.

Boeing

http://www.boeing.com
e-mail: boeing@pss.boeing.com

RATING

BRIEFING:

The world's leading commercial airplane manufacturer blasts off with more Boeing brilliance.

Among the aircraft manufacturers vying for some of your cyber-time, nothing Web-wide comes within a nautical mile of Boeing's online extravaganza. You could easily spend hours (even days) and not unearth every informative tidbit. Graphics, page navigation, pictures, facts, and surveys masterfully combine to create this interesting look into the world's leading manufacturer of commercial airplanes.

In addition to its leading manufacturing position, Boeing commands respect with its capabilities in (and informational Web pages relating to) space systems, rotorcraft, military airplanes, missile/tactical weapons, electronics/info systems, business jets, and associated products. Get an insider's peek into this jumbo company with a quick look at Boeing (at-a-glance info); News (financial, shareholder information); and feature Boeing-related stories.

Also wonderfully prepared are the thousands of info pages relating to your chosen tours (complete with photos) and vast employment opportunities. The employment "area" is a grand affair with subjects relating to: college recruiting, internships, current opportunities, benefits, and submitting a resume.

Fee or Free: Free.

The New Piper Company

http://www.newpiper.com

e-mail: none provided

RATING

┼ ┼

BRIEFING:

Piper product pitch pages captivate with nice pictures and performance specs.

To get something out of the New Piper page you really don't have to own one or carry exclusive membership credentials from some elite Piper club. Even non-Piper junkies will enjoy browsing performance specs, pricing, and comparing equipment lists on the entire currently manufactured fleet.

Aircraft choices for further examination include: the Warrior III, Arrow, Seminole, Saratoga II, Archer III, Malibu Mirage, and the Seneca V. If the pages move you, a clickable map easily locates a dealer in your area. Or, if you're more an occasion flyer than a buyer, get the scoop on company tours with a factory tour info page, past Piper press releases, or browse pilot shop goodies.

Fee or Free: Free.

Lockheed Martin Corporation

http://www.lmco.com

e-mail: online form

RATING

+ + +

BRIEFING:

Lockheed Martin is light years ahead of its time in understanding how to appeal to aviation enthusiasts with the Web.

With ornate visual aesthetics riding shotgun, Lockheed Martin obviously sat the content people in the left seat for this highly informative site. Early on during this online flight you're inundated with visual introduction into company contents. Lists of topics literally fill the pages under category headings of: News & Announcements, Products & Services, Careers, Image Gallery, and Investor Relations.

You're looking for examples, aren't you? Remembering that these will change after review time, you'll be browsing articles like: "New U.S. Air Force F-16s Will Have Color Displays and Other Advanced Systems"; "Manned Space Systems to Produce Tanks for Reusable Launch Vehicle"; and "Lockheed Martin Competes Initial Design Review for Its Joint Strike Fighter Program."

Once you've muddled through lengthy topics and summarized tidbits, do check into the image gallery—the resources are endless. There's a Lockheed Martin photo archive, video library, and many television commercials in QuickTime format.

Fee or Free: Free.

Bookmarkable Listings

Aircraft Parts Locator Service
http://www.apls.com
e-mail: none provided
Free access to current inventory, overhaul capabilities, and other aviation supplier reference info.

Rockwell
http://www.cca.rockwell.com
e-mail: webadmin@cca.rockwell.com
Corporate information regarding Rockwell's avionics, communications, and navigation products.

Europa
http://www.europa-aircraft.co.uk
e-mail: sales@europa.co.uk
Detailed descriptions and information regarding the Europa kit plane.

Avsupport Online
http://www.avsupport.com
e-mail: info@avsupport.com
Fee-oriented aviation parts searching.

U.S. Wings Aviation Mall
http://www.uswings.com
e-mail: webmaster@uswings.com
Manufacturer and distributor of aviation products.

WSDN Parts Locator
http://www.wsdn.com
e-mail: webmaster@wsdn.com
Aircraft spare parts locator and repair/supplier database.

Internet Parts Locator System
http://www.ipls.com
e-mail: webmaster@ipls.com
Database of aircraft spare parts and repair capability for the commercial aviation industry.

007 Aircraft for Sale
http://www.web-span.com/acsales
e-mail: wright@web-span.com
Fee-oriented, aircraft-for-sale listings.

Airbus Industrie
http://www.airbus.com
e-mail: none provided
Corporate overview includes news, photos, videos, and history of Airbus aircraft.

Aircraft Suppliers Company
http://www.airsuppliers.com
e-mail: asc@airsuppliers.com
Online catalog features a wide assortment of aircraft parts and accessories.

Beech Aviation, Inc.
http://www.bonanza-aviation.com
e-mail: mail@beech-aviation.com
Beech aircraft-for-sale listings with photos, prices, and specs.

Nolly Productions, Inc.
http://www.nolly.com
e-mail: sales@nolly.com
Find videos, books, and software for training and career-related needs.

Aviation
Entertainment

Lost Birds

http://www.lostbirds.com

e-mail: doug@impulsestudios.com

RATING

BRIEFING:

Visually
spectacular site
introduces some
historic
perspective on
aviation
mishaps.

Generally a less than subtle sales pitch for its quarterly magazine, Lost Birds video, and for-sale accident reports, the Lost Birds site genuinely dazzles nonetheless. Visual perfection and historical aviation mini documentaries are top notch.

Skipping any purchasing choices, you'll be exposed to some visually intriguing and prose-stimulating accounts of aviation mishaps. Specifically, get a few fascinating articles in the Recent Mishaps monthly section. Uncover the background behind: F-100D—Training Maneuver Ends in Bail Out; HHG Pavehawks—Twelve Die as Two Helicopters Crash on Nevada Gunnery Range; Swissair Flight 111—229 Die as Plane Crashes in Ocean Near Nova Scotia; and F-15B meets F-5E— Two Jets Collide Over the Nevada Desert.

Morbid memories? Maybe. But, each topic stimulates intellectual reflection with first-class presentation and reporting. I read each article and certainly learned something. If you're more into the methodology, brief yourself with About Archaeology and Research Materials. They're equally insightful.

Fee or Free: Free
to browse summarized articles. Fee
for magazine
subscription and a
few products.

A multimedia site attraction not to be missed is the archaic news video stream of a Linea Aeropostal Venezolana Lockheed 1049 Super Constellation that tragically broke up and crashed into the ocean. The video report is short but impactful. Just remember to allow some downloading time—it takes awhile.

Plane Writing

http://www.xs4all.nl/~blago/planewriting/index.html

e-mail: blago@xs4all.nl

BRIEFING:

**Plane Writing—
your first, last,
and only
online stop to
reminisce about
the bygone era
of pre-fifties
flying.**

Wow! Top honors in the historical/entertainment categories go hands down to Plane Writing. Just moving through its stellar organization, I clicked along in wondrous delight. And the content? Yes, the featured selections of vintage writing is better than any I've seen. Specifically you'll become entranced with fascinating quotes from vintage writing about flying and early pilots' biographies.

It may almost be a disservice to describe the perfect style, artistry, and countless hours of organization obviously spent compiling Plane Writing. Suffice it to say, that frames, multiple menus, and text-link summaries play a role. But, you simply must experience it yourself.

Dive nose first into an array of quotes and story snippets from pre-fifties flying and living. Read about biographies and life from these heroes of an older era— one of exciting, new discoveries. This site takes you by the hand and subtly introduces you to history. Main subsections take you into separate long ago realms (each with its own menu of remembrances). Browse through selections entitled: On Leaving; Cities and Green Hills; Scraps and Pieces; WWI—WWII; Other Metaphors of Flying; Sounds and Smells; and Farewell to a Plane.

Fee or Free: Free.

A stopover at Plane Writing? They don't allow me enough room in this book to describe the reasons why. Just do it.

Patty Wagstaff Airshows

http://www.pattywagstaff.com

e-mail: PWAS@aol.com

RATING

BRIEFING:

**A dizzying
assortment of
Patty's pictures,
planes, and
people.**

If you're any part the true aviation enthusiast you claim to be, you must've strained your neck on more than one air show by now. How can you not get caught up in the flybys, aerial stunts, and big radial engine static displays? Well, something else tells me Patty Wagstaff enjoys air shows too. Her Web presence, Patty Wagstaff Airshows, is an obvious indicator that her organizational skills don't end at air shows. They've learned a bit about Web design too.

Sure the site sacrifices lengthy loading times in favor of glitz, but the compromise seems appropriate. We are talking air shows after all. The photographic picture gallery grabbed my attention first. There are many in Air Photos, as well as Patty and Her Fans. As you'd expect, her BFGoodrich Aeorspace Extra 300S fills the frames. But you may not expect a pretty fancy QuickTime movie of Patty in action—twisting, turning, and smoking. Have patience with loading times though; it's worth the fun.

Continue on through Patty's page and you'll read about her background, meet the staff, and have her next air show schedule at hand.

Fee or Free: Free.

Navy Flight Test

http://flighttest.navair.navy.mil

e-mail: online form

BRIEFING:

Navy Flight Test joins the military photo fray with a visually stunning selection.

Perfect visual mastery begins your Navy Flight Test journey into resources and photos. Just keep in mind the resources fall into the technical category of flight testing. You know, everyday stuff like: mechanical systems, propulsion, mission and sensor systems, ship suitability, weapon/stores, and more.

Yes, I'm more into the photos too, but the resources side deserves a bit more acknowledgment. Employment opportunities, flight test and safety lessons noted, weather, phone directories, and others also grace the pages of Navy Flight Test. Almost everything's way over my private pilot head, but it's still interesting.

When you've grown weary of too much of the vague and technical, skip over to an all-star cast of quality photos in the flight test gallery. All searchable photos are courtesy of the Patuxent River Naval Air Station Photo Lab. While most photo-related Web sites skew toward the amateur variety, this one is top-notch. Use the simple search for proof. Scan through pictures of an F/A-18 Hornet, C-12, C-130, AV-8B Harrier II, F-14 Tomcat, HARM Missile, aircraft carrier, and more. Even view by bomb drops, in-flight, missile shots, or ship operations.

Fee or Free: Free.

B-17 Flying Fortress—A Virtual Tour

http://www.b-17.com

e-mail: online form

RATING

BRIEFING:

This site's flawless execution rewards the QuickTime viewer with up-close B-17 nostalgia.

Virtually spectacular in concept and execution, B-17 Flying Fortress offers this online tribute to the nostalgic B-17 superhero. Obviously Web designers had fun in creating a visually succinct and inviting tour of this particular flying fortress physically located at the Lone Star Flight Museum in Galveston, Texas.

As you click in you quickly discover multimedia gadgetry was built into the source code. Don't worry though. You'll just need to be familiar with QuickTime VR panoramas and QuickTime VR Object Movies. Need a refresher? It's only a click away.

Once you've found your bearings, five panoramas take you inside WWII's most famous bomber. Sit in the cockpit. Peer out the top turret. Be a bombardier. Use the radio. Or, walk around the B-17, virtually, seeing every outside detail.

When you've become dizzy with too much multimedia video, check into the story behind the plane, the stats, and photography. It's virtually priceless.

Fee or Free: Free.

Airshow Action Photo Gallery

http://www.steehouwer.com

e-mail: peter@steehouwer.com

Oh Peter. So many air show photos, so little time. Thanks to an enormous collection of fantastic photos by Peter Steehouwer, our ground time is that much more palatable.

First, a warning about the objectionables: typos, layout, and organization fall into the seriously questionable category. But, once you've found the photos you become lost in smoke, sky, and high angels of attack. Peter has captured the thrill of speed and precision with an endless selection of high quality stills.

Just about every major worldwide air show somehow finds itself represented here with a collage of photographic reminders. From California to Arizona to Texas, and from Switzerland to the Netherlands to the U.K., Peter's Airshow Action Photo Gallery is a sight to behold. And, with Peter, quality is obviously key. Proudly, he reports all photos are aircraft in action, not ground shots. He shoots from ground to air, climbing atop of anything nearby (car, mountain, tower, step ladder, etc.) with some pretty powerful camera equipment. Just look at his quality. Peter's skill is obvious.

For frequent visitors I offer this hint: just skip directly to the scattered "new" tags and leave your e-mail address to be notified when the site is updated.

Fee or Free: Free.

Aviation Humor

http://www.snowhill.com/~harpo/Humor.html

e-mail: pplus@snowhill.com

BRIEFING:

Quantity, quality, and comedy. What more could you ask for?

Sadly, aviation humor tends to be a bit elusive in aviation's Web circles. Yes, there's some out there, but the offerings are often a joke themselves. For a great, no frills collection, Aviation Humor (a sub-site of the Unofficial U.S. Army Aviator Page) understands the need for lighthearted fare.

Without so much as a glimmer of page design or site organization, stories, jokes, and top ten lists trickle down the page separated only by a horizontal rule. The point is: don't expect the layout to hold your attention, because it won't. The scrolling pages of flying fun will, however, grab you by the funny bone and not let go.

While the quantity is good and growing, the selections are among the Web's best. Subjects poke fun at: a couple of United Airlines mechanics with nothing to do; short-tempered German air traffic controllers; Q&A featuring Iraqi fighter pilots; real stories from flight attendants; top ten things actually heard from ATC at Chicago O'Hare; and more.

Fee or Free: Free.

Airshowpics

http://www.airshowpics.com

e-mail: online form

RATING

BRIEFING:

Massive collection of aircraft pictures leaves you utterly dazzled.

Loaded with more pictures than even hard core collectors would own, Airshowpics completely dominates the very visual world of online air show pictures. As expected with such a massive collection, quality of photos varies widely, but most fall into the crisp and captivating category. With Airshowpics you need only sit back and click through the long menu of aircraft for a multi-hour visual show.

Featuring both flying and static aircraft on display, Airshowpics pumps adrenaline through your mouse and brings you up close and personal with the world's favorite flying machines. Begin by browsing the left-margin list. Display teams, fighters, bombers, airliners, airlifters, helicopters, vintage and special duty carry a collection of photos within. Actual selections within these categories include: Blue Angels, Snowbirds, Turkish Stars, F-16, Tornado, Dassault Breguet, B-52, Concorde, C-130, WWII bombers, and reconnaissance aircraft to name a handful.

Even when you've exhausted everything listed, go to the aircraft image archives for over 450 pictures. It's almost online overload.

Fee or Free: Free.

Paris Air Show

http://www.paris-air-show.com/
e-mail: Isiae@salon-du-bourget.fr

RATING

BRIEFING:

Get caught up in the "show of shows" with this online prep to the Paris Air Show.

Ah Paris. The lights. The history. The romance. Add in one of the world's most anticipated aircraft shows, and you have *the* definitive reason to visit. But, just make sure you plan your trip around June. You wouldn't want to miss nearly 2,000 exhibitors from 50 countries, 250 aircraft on display, and international aviation appreciation.

Okay, even if you don't plan to visit this electrifying spectacle, get a second-best thrill with past show facts, figures, and photos. Dip into last year's exhibitor's list and aircraft. Read about show history. And of course, peruse the pictures. Scan the exhibitors for the Concorde and Challenger 604. Get up close to the Boeing 777 and a little Skyhawk. There's Harriers and Hawkeyes, Appaches and Airbus A300s. Pick your favorite alphabet letter and be instantly transported to display aircraft.

What's that? You *are* planning to attend one of the greatest air shows in history? Great! Begin your planning here. Get the costs, the site layout, and general information for visitors. Handy public transportation maps, motorways, telephone numbers, and more are thoughtfully available for the clicking.

If it's supposed to get you excited, actually stirring you into a flying show frenzy, Paris Air Show online succeeds and then some.

Fee or Free: Free.

Europa #272 ZK-TSK, a Builder's Log

http://www.kaon.co.nz/europa/

e-mail: none available

RATING

BRIEFING:

Thorough builder's log puts you smack in the middle of foam, metal, resin, and glass.

The problem I've often tripped over among builder's log Web sites is lack of page updating. Not that I don't understand the concept, mind you. I put building an airplane way ahead of Web site documenting in my time inventory book. Finding someone accomplishing both—building and documenting with meticulous attention to detail and timing—is obviously rare.

So begins our online building adventure with Tony Krzyzewski's Europa #272 ZK-TSK, a Builder's Log. This extensive, almost daily account, summarizes the triumphs, tragedies, and tribulations in building an airplane. It's written well. Photos, when included, are appropriate, not gratuitous. And, the honesty of this first-time builder makes for fascinating reading. Each annual log (a bit over three years worth at review time) is broken down by month. Succinct titles give you a clue as to the log's content: The Adventure Begins; The Tail of a Plane; Winging It (At Last); Flapping On; Control System Rigging; Cockpit Module; Lower Fuselage; Getting Stuck In; and many more monthly entries.

Site navigation is simply scrolling, reading, and moving to the "next" entry. Or, use the monthly list of clickable bookmarks. Either way, you're guaranteed great aviation entertainment for your browsing dollar.

Fee or Free: Free.

Dean Garner—Impressions

http://www.deangarner.com/Impressions.htm

e-mail: online form

BRIEFING:

Visually captivating flight photo site reminds you why you began flying in the first place.

With thousands of badly designed aviation photography and illustration sites crowding cyberspace with bandwidth-hogging files, you may find this site's award mention surprising. But, Dean Garner's "Impressions" museum deserves a look.

The pages are clean, clutter-free, and visually spectacular. Even with gallery after gallery of photos, the site never stalled as my modem hummed along easily. So, the mechanics of my experience were good. But, the photos really earned the award-winning mention. Quite simply, they're breathtaking. Mostly military, these online gems stop you in your tracks and cause you to pause. At cruise, after take-off, in vertical climb, in formation, and against scenic backdrops, these aircraft photos remind you of the visual romance of flight.

At review time ten photo galleries (called "halls") introduce you to beautiful aircraft-in-flight photos. Just click to enlarge. From Tigre Maree Hall to Moore Hall you click into a limitless array of F-18s, A-7s, F-16s, F-4s, F-15s, and even an A-4 or two.

Fee or Free: Free.

Aviation Animation

http://www.avanimation.avsupport.com/

e-mail: jself@accn.org

RATING

✝ ✝ ✝

BRIEFING:

Fun and frivolous flying fancies o'plenty.

Purely of entertainment value, this toybox of aviation-related goodies guarantees a smile. It worked for me. With flying aircraft graphics, moving props, and more how can you go wrong?

An approved archive site from the Animated GIF Artists Guild (lofty credentials, no?), Aviation Animation serves up way more than just animated stuff. Although it doesn't offer up much in page design, its array of clickable fun is endless. Countless animations, aircraft sounds, and movies are scattered everywhere like hidden Easter eggs. Mostly, though, you'll be playing with over 249 aviation animations of antique, military, and present-day aircraft. Rotors spin, props turn, and background scenery goes by. Plan to have snacks and beverages at the ready; you might be here awhile giggling like a kid.

When you break from animation, try the sounds. The endless WAV files give you file size before loading (thoughtful!) and brief description. Hear running engines, flybys, communications, jet wind, and more.

If you're so inclined, there's even info here on how to make animations. I think I'll just click and enjoy thank you.

Fee or Free: Free.

Artie the Airplane

http://www.artiebooks.com

e-mail: none provided

BRIEFING:

A for-kids aviation site that's actually fun for everyone—moms, dads, and future aviators.

Whimsical, fun, friendly, and inviting, Artie the Airplane expands upon its popular children's books with a first-rate, just-for-kids Web site. Sure it's kind of a subtle promo for the books, but you won't mind a bit with this free aviation-rich playground for kids.

Your main stop, with kid in tow, should be the Fun Zone. Here you'll meet Artie the Airplane (a cute, happy looking rescue plane) and a menu of kid stuff to do. Click into the coloring book for black and white drawings to print and color (Jack the Jumbo, Waldo W. Wing, and Wally the Widebody to name a few). Next, have fun with mazes, connect-the-dots, and maps in the games section. Or, meet Artie's friends, complete with great illustrations and descriptions. There's Alice the Air Ambulance, Gramma & Grampa Cubbie, Superslim, and others—all worthy of a look. Finally, as night falls and your mouse hand is tired, read your little flying fan Artie's good-night poem, almost guaranteed to produce happy drowsiness.

All site illustrations are fun and inviting, teamed up with plenty of white space and easy reading for younger Web viewers.

Fee or Free: Free.

SkyFlash

http://www.sky-flash.com

e-mail: skyflash2@yahoo.com

BRIEFING:

Striking volume and quality launch this flying photo site onto your bookmark list.

I must admit, if it's not already obvious by now, I'm a sucker for flying pictures, no matter the subject. From military to airline to general aviation, quality aviation photos stir me up. Presentation has to be good, and picture quality needs to be above average to capture my viewing time. That's why SkyFlash moved into award-winning status in my opinion.

Mostly originating from air shows, military databases, and display team galleries, SkyFlash pictures fill up your non-flying ground time. Click into the grid/menu of gallery selections: yellow cells are new galleries and blue cells offer newly updated photos. Looking for a preview? Imagine the screaming action of: The Snowbirds, Blue Angels, Thunderbirds, high speed pictures, F-117 Stealth, SR-71 Blackbird, Harrier, Edwards AFB Show, close-ups, helicopters, Team 60, and strange/funny pictures (complete with editorial comments).

Links, special interest topics, and air show report news round out your site options, mainly serving as filler.

Fee or Free: Free.

South Atlantic Flight 1998

http://www.si-properties.com/sat98

e-mail: hgschmid@bluewin.ch

BRIEFING:

Marvelously
chronicled South
Atlantic journey
of a man, a
dream, and a
reality.

The vision is captivating and the flight a commemorative tribute. Dig into the history of events leading up to this spectacular journey and follow daily diary entries of flight progress. First, meet Hans Georg Schmid and his modern canard-type MD-11 as you click into this visually satisfying chronicle of past and present. Relive the daily events seen through the eyes of your pilot as he flew from Switzerland to South America back in November 1998.

Site design, mechanics, organization, and information-rich documentaries guide you through an inspiring journey. Click into the online presentation of: The History of Conquering the South Atlantic, The Pilot and Plane, The Route & Itinerary, His Reason for the Flight, and more.

Without divulging any flight details (I encourage you to click in and follow along yourself), get to the heart of his mission and read the daily news diary. It's packed with wit and wisdom, humor and horror. Become enraptured with entries titled: Interlaken—a Smallscale Oshkosh in Switzerland; The Flight is a Go!; Delhi, Osaka, and the Tragic Loss of 14 Dear Colleagues; Farewell; Simulator and Singapore; and more.

Forget the good book you're reading, and follow the adventures of plane and pilot over the South Atlantic. It's more entertaining and it's real.

Fee or Free: Free.

Wingspan—Air & Space Channel

http://www.wingspantv.com

e-mail: webmaster@wingspantv.com

RATING

+ + + +

BRIEFING:

A complete, current, and classy TV guide into Wingspan— Air & Space Channel.

Have you heard of Wingspan—Air & Space Channel? Me neither, but you will soon enough. The only all-aviation, 24-hour television channel is growing in number of markets nationwide (call your local cable company if interested). So stay tuned. For now, however, you can learn more about Wingspan, and get many of the Channel's newsworthy snippets online.

Just tune in, sit back, and click into this wonderfully designed aviation-only treat. The main topic menu spells out your choices with hyperlinks to: About Wingspan, How to Get Wingspan, Watch Wingspan, Aerospace News, Wingspan Store, Wingspan Interactive.

Sure most of the Channel's Web site is merely online promotion. However, a substantial amount of effort has been put into mirroring much of the newsworthy content here. For the new and current events, Aerospace News is where you want to be. A nice, summarized list of bulleted items quickly loads into view. Read about current airline news, financial reports, aerospace industry tidbits, and daily breaking headlines. Skip past the current stuff and head to the news archives if you're in the mood for more.

Fee or Free: Free.

On your Web viewing agenda should also be Wingspan Interactive. Here you'll stumble into interactive features, games, contests, and Wingspan Aviation Web Directory (links). The section's a bit sparse at review time, but additions are forthcoming.

Historic Wings

http://www.historicwings.com

e-mail: design@capstonesudio.com

RATING

BRIEFING:

This well-rounded presentation explores history in depth and sports a pretty fancy exterior.

Truly magnificent design draws you in, but the well-written history brings you back for more. Enter the visually spectacular world of Historic Wings.

Brought to you by Capstone Studio this gem of fun flying remembrances dazzles with such a wide array of Web savvy solutions. It's online design 101 and then some. Click into the main page just to see the visual theme change. I'm not sure how many "opening looks" there are, but each is well done. Once you delve in you'll find the simple frames-based navigation easily useful. The efficient menus offer only a few options, steering clear of clutter. "White space" makes online reading and viewing a pleasant experience. Even a Web site translation option offering six (yes six!) languages rounds out your thoughtful site features.

The wonderfully written historical features are changeable, but the selection and variety are endless. It's quality and quantity! My options (complete with summaries) at review time will give you a preflight inspection on what you can expect: Pretty Deadly (nose art); High Flight (poetry); Flight School 101 (interactive flying inspiration); Learn to Fly Forum; SR-71 Blackbird; B-52 Stratofortress; Aviation Posters (1910's–1940's); and more.

Fee or Free: Free. Subscribe by leaving your name and e-mail for updates.

Worthy of one of your top bookmark spots, Historic Wings delivers on style as well as content.

FlightDeck

http://exn.ca/Mini/Flightdeck

e-mail: flightdeck@exn.ca

RATING

+ + +

BRIEFING:

Mostly Canadian historical peek thoroughly delights.

Clean, charismatic, and clearly Canadian, FlightDeck provides a historical flyby courtesy of two respectable industry heavyweights: Discovery Channel Canada and the National Aviation Museum.

To thoroughly inspect FlightDeck's aviation museum online, you'll need full multimedia capability. Even if you have to get a free RealPlayer plug-in or download RealVideo, the time logged into FlightDeck is worth it. Step into The Hangar for a look yourself. Get the real-life historical perspective of an Auro CF-105 Arrow, a Bae AV-8A Harrier, de Havilland DHC-2 Beaver, Messerschmitt Me 163B-1a Komet, Submarine Spitfire, and many more. Every aircraft comes to life on your screen with RealVideo clips and brief commentary. See rare archival footage of the planes in flight or hear some engines revving.

Next, meet some aviators. Skip through a Milestone section of Canadian aviation. Glance into a searchable Image Gallery. Read about the many features, events, or just chat. Whatever your viewing perspective, you'll be visually delighted.

Fee or Free: Free.

The Flight

http://www.gruner.com/flight

e-mail: gruner@shareholder.com

RATING
+++

BRIEFING:

A fifty-year-old pilot and a fifty-year-old Cessna 195 trip the sky fantastic with this amazing personal account.

It's ironic that such an entertaining site devoted to hardy solo navigation offers slightly awkward Web site navigation. Just slip into the Table of Contents page; you'll be on course instantly.

Well-written chapters chronicle a 6,000 mile journey in a Cessna 195 radial engine beauty. Each online account uses powerful prose and striking photos to capture the essence of one man's fascinating skyward journey. His route includes: St. John's, Newfoundland (the most easterly tip of North America) and flying due southwest, over the Canadian maritime provinces, across the U.S., through northern Mexico, past the Tropic of Cancer to Cabo San Lucas, Mexico (the most southwesterly point of the continent). Scintillating chapters are titled: "Silent Giants of the Atlantic"; "Icing, Winds, and Silence"; "Flying the Gauges"; "Revolutionaries and Bandits"; "The Mythical Island of California"; "A Small, Dusty Airport"; and "The Pearl of Loreto."

This real account speaks of dark fjords, the brutal Sierra Madres, miles of oceans and deserts, and a mixed bag of weather. No, his wife didn't go.

Fee or Free: Free.

Dave English's Great Aviation Quotes

http://www.skygod.com

e-mail: english@skygod.com

Yes, there's some in jest, while others are rooted in seriousness. But, all the aviation quotes (more than you can imagine) do entertain. The hordes of quotes are conveniently broken down by category. Here's the list (take a breath first): Airports, Air Power, Balloons, Bums on Seats, Combat, Clichés, First Flights, High Flight, Humor, Last Words, Magic and Wonder of Flight, Maps and Charting, Miscellaneous Stuff, O'Hare ATC, Piloting, Poetry, Prediction (past and present), Press Corps, Safety, Space Flight, Women Fly, The B-17, The B-747, The Concorde, The DC-3, The F-117, The Harrier, and The P-38.

When you've finished absorbing these thoughts from meandering minds, click through Dave English's other site gems. Learn about the history of airport identifier codes. Plot a course through tremendous aeronautical chart resources. And, as always, stop by the links list—there's plenty.

Fee or Free: Free.

The Mile High Club

http://www.milehighclub.com

e-mail: info@milehighclub.com

RATING

✝ ✝ ✝ ✝

BRIEFING:

A scintillating site devoted to the erotic club that pilots, flight attendants, and daring airline passengers have been whispering about since early flight.

Tastefully exploiting the romantically inclined members of the Mile High Club, the Mile High Club Home Page boldly makes its online presence known. Mostly text-based, this mile high adventurer's site organizes a thoughtful mix of limited but appropriate graphics, page navigation perfection, and interesting stories.

Curious Mile High wanna-bes and members will find nonstop entertainment with this erotic fixation on skyward fantasies. Clickable sections include: All About the Mile High Club—membership requirements and rules/regulations; Mile High Adventures—info on one airline that specializes in this sort of thing; Mile High Club Store; and, of course, Tales of the Mile High Club—adult-oriented stories of those in pursuit of becoming a member; and more.

Okay, you're curious, right? Well, here's a taste of the tantalizing tales: "Full Aft Position," "Perks of the Job," "Commuter Fun," "Newlyweds," "Flight to Down Under," and more.

WARNING: Content of Mile High Club stories may contain language or situations not appropriate for minors.

Fee or Free: Free.

Plane Spotting

http://members.aol.com/planespot/main.htm

e-mail: PlaneSpot@aol.com

RATING

† † †

BRIEFING:

**Enthusiasts'
reviews are
categorized and
added to the
worldwide plane
spotting
database. It's the
right spot for
spotting.**

Whether you admit to it or not, all of us aviation types are apt to search the sky for a propeller's drone or a jet's roar as it goes by. For this reason it's always easy to spot the aviation enthusiast in a crowd.

Plane Spotting devotes itself to those who wouldn't pass up an opportunity to stop, watch, and revel in the wonder of flight. The site offers a plane spotting database of best aircraft viewing spots around the world. Entries that may be added by anyone are comprised of: directions to viewing spot, airport and identifier, city, type of aircraft frequenting the location, runway headings, frequencies, parking hints, and more.

Site navigation is simple with clickable links and short descriptions. A What's New section displays latest entries and info. Add an Entry provides an easy form to fill out. And, Aircraft Images does a great job of displaying some feature plane spottings without taxing your modem.

Fee or Free: Free.

The World of Aviation Poetry

http://www.gower.net/erst/airpoems.htm

e-mail: none provided

RATING

BRIEFING:

Don't let load time discourage your curiosity; these poems of aviation passion are timeless.

Hidden deep in this confusing cornucopia of online memorabilia, the heartwarming prose of Mr. E. Rowan S. Trimble summons you like an airport beacon. Hopefully, one reason you consult my collection of Web winners is to quickly arrive at such aviation gems as the World of Aviation Poetry.

The fantastic poetry is certainly worth waiting for—and you will be waiting for the disorganized jumble of a home page to load. Have a steaming mug of joe standing by, because efficient this site is not. The main reason you need to add this site to your favorites list? Heart-wrenching, thoughtful, inspiring, cleverly described words of wonder prevail. Some poems are short and powerful. Others linger through description and flowing recollection. My favorites are: "Vagabond Pilot," "The Final Cynosure of Fort Wolters," "Explaining Flight to My Son," "Broken Wings," "Echoes," and "Too Low." Yes, my favorites are many. I defy you to be more limiting.

Secondary reasons you'll enjoy your stay include: a series of great aircraft sounds in WAV format, Poetry in Aviation Pictures, Famous Flying Quotes, and much more.

Fee or Free: Free.

Dave, Carey and Ed's Super Lancair ES Kitplane

http://www.edlevine.com/lancair

e-mail: DaveCareyandEd@edlevine.com

RATING

++

BRIEFING:

Follow along as three first-time kitplane builders take us for a ride on their Lancair learning curve.

By including Dave, Carey and Ed's Lancair Super ES Kitplane Progress Page among the top 300 aviation Web sites, you probably think I've pulled a few too many Gs and rendered myself unconscious. While those around me may disagree, I assure you I'm fully aware and rational as ever. You'll just need to ride right seat with me on this one and follow my lead.

First, a few warnings. You'll be horrified by site design. Site navigation simply means using your scroll bar. And, the long-winded text tends to run on through carefree punctuation. Sweeping all of the negatives under the rug, however, reveals an entertaining over-the-shoulder look at the slow progression of building a kitplane. Complete with photos and brutally truthful chronicles of the construction, each entry summarizes the challenges and triumphs.

Although the site doesn't get updated regularly (hey, they've got building to do), you can request auto e-mail notification when updates occur. When it's completed in a couple of years, the kitplane will evolve into a 220 mpg sport plane. Read on about the Lancair and performance specs by clicking the hyperlink to Lancair.

Fee or Free: Free.

Virtual Horizons

http://virtualnorth.com/horizons

e-mail: Horizons@BushPilot.com

BRIEFING:

Expand your browsing horizons with an insider's account into the Canadian bush pilot.

Virtual Horizons—it's where the soaring spirits of Canadian bush pilots shower us surfers with cyber-collections of stories, articles, letters and photographs. Mostly navigating through the Great Canadian North, where even industry hardened pilots clamor for a window seat, some of Canada's best aviation writers and flyers give you a tour into their experiences.

There's talk and pictures of beautiful landscape, memorable journeys with Cessnas, Beavers, and Otters. Feature stories span a trip into the high Arctic to flying a Cessna Caravan in West Africa. Although giant, high resolution pictures run wild throughout the descriptive accounts, don't scroll past them unviewed. The download time might be a bit lengthy, but these romantic beauties deserve a peek.

The icing on the Virtual Horizons cake? Hints for best viewing and site navigation are plenty. Thoughtful tips on weathering the lengthy image loading waits will increase a beginning browser's enjoyment. And, descriptive links guide you with pinpoint accuracy before you click.

Fee or Free: Free.

Captain J's Aviation Page

http://www.geocities.com/CapeCanaveral/1274/contents.html

e-mail: justinr@geocities.com

RATING

✈ ✈ ✈

BRIEFING:

Briefing: Captain J has just turned off the "no-enjoying-yourself" sign. It's time for a romp in aviation distraction.

Fee or Free: Free, even if you have to download the plug-ins.

Getting down to serious diversion, Captain J's Aviation Page avoids the facts, the FARs, and the forecasts. Replacements take the form of more trivial, but worthwhile aviation endeavors like: movies, games, jokes, poetry, photos, and sounds. In fact, this fanciful virtual compilation offers nothing to make your flying safer, forecasting easier, or the regulations clearer. Captain J is here only for fun.

Certainly taking the low road to reach this shaky organization and design destination, Captain J shows concern solely for aviation entertainment—no matter the means. You'll forgive and forget, however, as you reach the series of online delights. Clicking into Sounds brings to life a 747 flyby, an F-16 on takeoff, San Francisco's ATIS (full 60 seconds), a jet taxiing, and more. Similarly presented, Airplane Movies, Aviation Games, and Photos are ripe for the clicking. Examples? Grab some popcorn for QuickTime movies like: The X-1 Released from a B-29. Avoid crashing your plane into the mountains with the Alaska Flight Game. And, scan through high resolution pictures like a 747 at an EAA Fly-In. Then, maneuver your mouse into the inspirational poetry and anecdotes. They're equally inviting.

Solo Stories

http://www.geocities.com/CapeCanaveral/3831
e-mail: fly@poboxes.com

RATING

BRIEFING:

**Sensational solo
remembrances—
sans instructor.**

The fact that the Solo Stories site is updated continuously, easily navigated, and packed with stories has nothing to do with my overwhelming recommendation. The brutal honesty and unbridled realism is why I've cleared room for a bookmark.

Granted, Solo Stories, brings back personal memories of my own solo and cross-country days, but I'm sure it will do the same for others. Whether you care to relive your solo adventures through the memoirs of others or learn from their mistakes before you fly, check in here for a taste of reality. For a cyber-ride of jittery, real-life flights, I suggest clicking into stories titled, "If You Run Into Traffic, Tell Them You're a Student on Your First Solo—They Will Get Out of Your Way"; "As I Latched the Door Behind Him, My First Words Were 'Oh Sh_ _'"; and "When I Landed Safely, I Felt Like Amelia Earhart!"

Then, when you're ready to recount your experience, a link guides you into adding your own solo story. It's simple to contribute, just look at the many entries already showcasing their maiden voyage.

Fee or Free: Free.

Fudpucker Airlines

http://www.infinet.com/~cuban8

e-mail: Cuban8@infinet.com

BRIEFING:

Frolicking in a hilarious haze, Fudpucker Airlines captures aviation's priceless perceptions.

Fee or Free: Free, unless you have an overwhelming urge to send them money as they request.

Way out in restricted airspace, cruising at oxygen altitudes, Fudpucker Airlines has obviously shunned the comfort of pressurization and opted for mind fog. Put another way, whenever your page introduction warns: "there's still time to back out and run for your life" you begin to realize your online airfare was cheap for a reason.

Just scanning the index of the Fudpucker Pages should give you a clue as to this site's comical content. All About Fudpucker; Ashley's Hot Tips for Cool Pilots; Where To Go; What to See; The Dudley P. Fudpucker Complete Guide to Aviation Terminology; Who Are Those Guys?!; and more feature pointless drivel you can't live without. Whatever your fancy, do remember to observe the online passenger rules. Among those of which you should be aware: "Don't get snooty with the crew"; and "Remember, your pilot is still learning to fly and he is more scared than you."

While you're online with Fudpucker, Night Flight must be among your site destinations. The countless stories (mostly true) are hilarious and ramble on for pages and pages. Simply put, these amazing tales are worth the bookmark space alone.

Paper Airplanes

http://www.net-www.com/planes.htm

e-mail: webmaster@pchelp.net

Remember when grandpa expertly added those taped ailerons to your simple paper airplane? Well, I'm sure a lot of aviation wisdom and engineering dreamers came up with this little jewel of a site.

Although under some updating at the time of review, the page and what it offers just screams, "STOP WHAT YOU'RE DOING AND HAVE A LITTLE FUN!" From an Origami Aerobatic Design to a Supersonic Fast Flyer to a Soaring Glider, anyone running the age spectrum will delight at these propeller-less paper creations. There's plenty of designs to try. Step-by-step diagram instruction glides you through assembly.

It really is simple, free fun. Click, print, fold, and enjoy!

Fee or Free: Free.

"Dad" Rarey's Sketchbook
Journals of the 379ᵗʰ Fighter

http://www.rarey.com/sites/rareybird

e-mail: dr@nbn.com

RATING

╋ ╋ ╋ ╋

BRIEFING:

An illustratively chronicled tribute to a WWII fighter pilot that deserves a look.

Painful at times and uproarious at others, this wonderful hidden gem of a site delves into a personal account of Mr. George "Dad" Rarey. Drafted into the Army Air Corps in 1942, this young cartoonist and commercial artist kept an animated cartoon journal of the daily life of the fighter pilots. Brought to the bookshelves and now cyberspace by his son and wife, this thoughtful reflection chronicles "Dad" Rarey's WWII life.

Skillfully prepared and graphically rewarding, this home page tribute has all the stuff that comes under the heading of great organization: excellent page links, clickable menu icons throughout, and tiny thumbnail pictures that don't waste time (and can grow at your command). But, by far, the best page features are the written descriptions and illustrations. Contributions you find here come from surviving members of the 379ᵗʰ Fighter Squadron, excerpts from Rarey's letters to his wife (Betty Lou), and Betty Lou's memoirs.

Clickable sections include: Cadet Life, Volumes 1–5, Nose Art, and Artifacts.

Fee or Free: Free.

Aviation Jokes

http://www.hojmark.org/aviation-jokes.html

e-mail: asbjorn@hojmark.org

RATING

╀ ╀

BRIEFING:

Non-graphically driven collection of flying flippancy and aeronautical amusement.

Quite frankly, I'm not sure how often or to what extent this humor driven home page is updated with fresh stuff. Whatever the update status, this page does deliver on fabulously funny flying fancies and the like. Albeit the page aesthetics take a winning position among the yawning variety, you'll forgive and forget as you read on.

Without revealing too much about these treasures, expect to stumble across stuff relating to: ATC communications, crew-to-cabin conversations, glossary, landings, lies, and other aviation anecdotes.

The Aviation Jokes page uncovers a hodgepodge of lists, one-liners, article excerpts, dialog stories, and questions/ punch lines. Even without any idea of page longevity, this site's recommended for frivolous flying fun. Take it in while it lasts!

Fee or Free: Free.

The Hangar

http://www.the-hangar.com

e-mail: webmaster@the-hangar.com

RATING

BRIEFING:

Hang out here for images, history, and hangar talk.

Step into this spacious hangar housing a delightful blend of history, images, and pilot career banter. Mostly steering towards worldwide military aircraft, your nicely framed selection features: Images of the Week—displays current week winners and links to favorite past selections; Aircraft in the Hangar—use a pull-down menu to select by alpha characters, type, or nation; Hangar Talk—join fellow enthusiasts in this lively bulletin board forum; What's New(s)—scan a list of additions and site modifications; Historical Calendar—just select a date with this cool, searchable history book of military aviation events; Comments/Suggestions; Odd Bird Quarterly—learn about unusual aircraft; Search!—quickly locate site contents; Reviews—read comments about the site; Web Links—search the list of quality links; and Help/About—find tips and tricks for site navigation.

For me, subtle details pave the way for this award-winning mention. Stuff that earned the points: great descriptions next to links, searchable menus, and well-thought-out hints to save you time.

Fee or Free: Free.

The Humor Collective

http://tacair-press.com/humor.shtml

e-mail: none available

RATING

✢

BRIEFING:

Oddball laughs
worthy enough
to share with
fellow aviators.

As the site name implies, it's a "collection." The text table of jokes, jibes, and snippets expands your humor horizon to many topics besides aviation. But, aviation is a component too. We're assured that the "collective" is continually growing and the entries steer clear of distasteful. The good news, along with the good jokes, is that the "last updated" date appears to be timely—eluding to a non-stale compilation of funnies.

Hidden in the table-style grid of clickable titles, Aircraft Radio Calls, Aircraft Maintenance Write-Ups, and Uppity Captain will ring true for aviation enthusiasts. The wit's fresh and funny. Specifically, a series of Aircraft Radio Calls take the form of tower and pilot interchange. For example, the tower warns, "you have traffic at 10 o'clock, 6 miles." And the pilot responds, "give us another hint, we have digital watches." Maintenance Write-Ups take the form of a listed discrepancy and the corresponding corrective action, such as: Discrepancy— "evidence of hydraulic leak on right main landing gear;" Corrective Action—"evidence removed."

You get the idea. The jokes come fast and furious, demanding at least an occasional visit to lift your spirit.

Fee or Free: Free.

Bookmarkable Listings

Aviation Adventure Stories
http://www.bushwings.com/stories.html
e-mail: none provided
Over 20 individual adventure stories by bush pilot
Ron Fox.

World Airshow News
http://www.worldairshownews.com
e-mail: weinman@mailbag.com
Printed trade magazine offers many articles online.

Avialantic
http://www.avialantic.com
e-mail: fpierce@avialantic.com
Resources supporting mid-Atlantic area museums.

Boeing 727
http://www.msd.org/727.htm
e-mail: discover@msd.org
Virtual tour of the Boeing 727.

Luc's Photo Hangar
http://www.bayarea.net/~hanger
e-mail: hanger@bayarea.net
Pictorial view of World War II aviation history.

Air Pix Aviation Photos
http://www.airpixphoto.com
e-mail: airpixav@bigfoot.com
Collection of aviation photos and related for-sale products.

Greg's Aircraft Spotter's Guide
http://www.geocities.com/CapeCanaveral/1273/spotting.html
e-mail: greg20@ix.netcom.com
Brief descriptions and photos identify commercial aircraft.

Miss America Air Racing
http://www.missa.com
e-mail: webmaster@missa.com
Get news, event info, aircraft stats, and photo gallery access.

Aviation Employment

AvCrew.Com

http://www.avcrew.com
e-mail: info@avcrew.com

Yet another crew employment site takes the active with this outstanding online service. Succinct, searchable, and simple to navigate, AvCrew delivers on its mission: "to present more employment opportunities to pilots and give employers a qualified applicant pool, faster than traditional methods."

Employers searching the skies for left, as well as right seat applicants will find a growing collection of pilot resumes, positions wanted, and classifieds. Faster than you can say FlightSaftey trained, a search for qualified corporate pilots begins and ends with AvCrew. Employers can post jobs for free (at review time), create a custom online application (fee-related), or have AvCrew conduct a custom-tailored, confidential search for qualified candidates. Site resources equally cater to pilots and employers. Pilots searching for dream assignments need only scan the current positions list and click into more detailed description. "New" tags, date posted, date updated, and previous positions (filled or closed), ease you into a stress-free search. Really. With no distractions from ad banners, giant pictures, or audio gismos, AvCrew gives you easy viewing for position searching.

Fee or Free: Mostly free. Some services have nominal fees.

To summarize, many nominal fee extras combine with quality free stuff to create a solid source for aviation employment. Whether you go fee or free, fly with AvCrew.

Aero Jobs

http://www.aerojobs.com

e-mail: info@spacejobs.com

BRIEFING:

A heavy hitter in the aero jobs arena sparkles with content.

A spin-off from the successful endeavor Space Jobs, Aero Jobs teams up with its space-related counterparts to serve up aeronautics career opportunities. It's clear they're serious about this aero jobs mission. Just look at the 8,300 subscriber base which is sure to grow after this review.

Site design and organization are your first clue into the success of Aero Jobs. Menus are easy to find. Three simple options move you into the site (advertise, subscribe, or search), and page layout aesthetics fall into the "very good" category. Not until you've moved into the satisfying smorgasbord of employment opportunities in the career section is your visiting experience complete. Here you'll uncover a healthy array of possibilities. Tap into the most recent opportunities; search by country: Australia, Canada, France, U.K., and U.S.A.; or get a list of all organizations. Curious about the companies represented here? Ever hear of AlliedSignal, Boeing, Honeywell Inc., Pratt & Whitney, Raytheon, or Lockheed Martin? I thought so. There's many more big names as well.

If you're a job seeker, subscribing is the way to go. You'll get e-mail opportunities delivered straight to your computer. It's especially handy with Aero Jobs' keyword delivery system that allows you to filter and modify your subscription to suit your needs.

Fee or Free:
Subscription to get e-mail is free. Ad placements are fee-related.

Pilotsearch.com

http://www.pilotsearch.com

e-mail: president@pilotsearch.com

BRIEFING:

Pilot job postings and more make a Web debut.

Relatively new on the cyber scene at review time, Pilotsearch.com throws its hat into the online aviation career ring. They've joined the fray with pilot job listings, resumes online, aircraft for sale, airline directory, listings for sale, and aviation links.

At first glance, it would seem the emphasis here is on job listings—there's quite a few. Update status is displayed by date and hour (so you know it's current!). And, each pilot listing describes the open position thoroughly with: requirements, responsibilities, area of operations, company name, and contact info. Most have phone, e-mail, and Web address.

Site design appears to be a work-in-progress (I hope), and other content offerings (resumes, aircraft for sale, and links) rank among the "moderate to thin" variety. Always the optimist, I'm holding out for strong, content-rich growth at Pilotsearch.com. There's always room for a young career-oriented upstart!

Fee or Free:
Resume and aircraft listings are fee-related.

Aviation Employment.com

http://www.aviationemployment.com

e-mail: info@aviationemployment.com

RATING

+ + +

BRIEFING:

Worldwide aviation employment opportunities on an online silver platter.

For years Employment Publications Inc. has been doing one thing well: printed aviation/aerospace employment guides. Today they continue with printed excellence in the form of *Pilot Employment News* and *Aviation Maintenance & Engineering Journal*. Now they've expanded their successful single employment vision to the Web world. Sure it's a natural transition, but a satisfying compilation of page elements isn't so natural. If fact, it's elusive to most digital dabblers. But, Aviation Employment.com has managed to rise above the mediocrity with their clean, inviting, and easy to use online resource.

Your eight menu options that follow you to each page are: Job Listings (an alphabetized laundry list of positions by title); Companies Listed; Printed Magazines; Submit Your Resume; List Your Company; Schools & Training (list of schools and training programs coming soon as of review time); About Us (get to know the company behind the coding); and a Home Page return.

As you'd expect from pros, there's many job listings to review, so a well-designed search engine is fueled and at the ready. Just identify your requirements and qualifications to find the matches. Narrow selection by state, your current educational level, type of aviation job you seek, full and/or part time positions, permanent and/or temporary, and salary requirements.

Fee or Free: Free to browse, but fees apply to those wanting to post jobs.

Air Base

http://www.airforce.com

e-mail: online form

BRIEFING:

Fancy online Air Force recruiter informs and invigorates potential members.

Straight out of a virtual dogfight scene from your favorite flight simulator game, Air Base cranks up your adrenaline a notch with a heads-up display interface that's second to none. The Air Force recruitment info housed in this online hangar presents itself in a compelling, almost electric way.

Just before you think this site's all sizzle and no beef, don your flight suit an take a ride. It's packed with details and overviews concerning an Air Force career. Yes, it's a pixilated pitch. But, if you're contemplating Air Force possibilities, research is merely a click or two away. Here's the lineup: The Training Center invites you to take command of the FighterJet simulator to test your skills. The Hangar lines up a full array of USAF aircraft—complete with specs and pictures. The Education Center promotes the wealth of training and education opportunities available to USAF members. The Career Center, Hot Jobs, The Base Hospital, Life on the Base, Special Tactics, and Info Center round out a full flight line of informational resources.

Fee or Free: Free.

Fltops.com

http://www.fltops.com

e-mail: webmaster@fltops.com

RATING

BRIEFING:

Working behind the scenes, Fltops.com is your personal airline crew job informant officer.

Quietly discussed in cockpits, pilot lounges, and personnel offices industrywide are hints, tips, tricks, and essentials for landing a flight officer position with a major carrier. Fltops.com owners and editors behind the pages are active pilots with major carriers and continually provide the "Internet-based intelligence" helpful in your pro pilot quest.

Just a look at the intro page, and you'll agree you've stumbled upon a major resource. Jumping out at you are scrolling banners of breaking industry news, top stories, and updates. Get up to the minute insight on topics like: new hourly pay rates for crew members; benefits comparisons among the "big six" airlines; and contact info on the "big 13."

It should be clearly noted that everything on the site isn't free. In fact, Fltops.com is primarily fee-oriented for the good stuff. Become a "crew member" and receive quality industry intelligence. Even if you're just dabbling in Fltops.com's resources, be sure to scan the free section available to all: FlightLine news, airline financial updates, fleet profiles, and a special report for older pilots.

Fee or Free:
Some info is free; more detailed stuff requires fee-related membership.

Aviation Employee Placement Service (AEPS)

http://www.aeps.com

e-mail: aeps@aeps.com

RATING

✝ ✝ ✝

BRIEFING:

Get yourself in front of over 2,800 aviation companies with a few clicks of the mouse.

Solely text-based and unconcerned with visual niceties, The AEPS still soars with their worthwhile, well-organized employee site. Billed as the "online job connection," AEPS offers an award-winning selection of resources built upon its main menu of: New Visitors and Inactive Members Page, Aviation Companies (for employers), Free E-mail Job Alerts, and Other Info.

Once an active member, you are invited to partake in a long list of menu options including: Renew Your Membership, Member Aviation Companies (over 2,800 at time of review), Update or Add Your E-mail (keep e-mail current to receive The Aviation World Reports, job alerts, etc. automatically), Update Your Qualifications (all updates are free), View Your Qualifications, Conduct a Sample Data Search, Aviation Info Exchange, AEPS Newsletter, AEPS Feedback, and of course the Jobs Page.

As always, job postings and data bank searching are free for all employers.

Fee or Free: Free.

Air, Inc.—The Airline Pilot Career Specialists

http://www.airapps.com

e-mail: airinfo@airapps.com

BRIEFING:

Plan a thorough career course here before you go wheels up.

Fee or Free: Some free stuff. Membership career services and magazine subscription are fee-oriented.

For airline career seekers Air Inc.'s lofty online resources span the industry to give you a jumbo-sized heads-up. Climb aboard an unrivaled career guide for pilots.

Without so much as a mouse click, the latest airline industry tidbits are ready for the reading in the Public Information column. Once you've caught the latest hirings and articles, a linked list of topics are close at hand: career seminars, airline forums, job fairs, FAQs, sample magazine & newsletter, and membership info.

Once you've committed to membership, the jetway pulls up to religiously updated Hot Air News; Rumours: Fact or Fiction; detailed airline information and address directory online; latest issue of Airline Pilot Careers Magazine; and Newsletter. Where you'll probably spend the most time is in the Resource Center. Read countless articles broken down by category: Airline Pilot Center, Military Pilot Center, Low-Time Pilot Center, and Student Pilot Center.

Nifty articles and industry news help propel Air, Inc.'s Web wonder nautical miles past the rest.

Aviation Jobs Online

http://www.aviationjobsonline.com

e-mail: info@aviationjobsonline.com

RATING

BRIEFING:

Award-winning seeker site. Yes it's fee-oriented, but they do all the grueling work.

Searching for that dream job sometimes requires as many allies as one can muster. Sign up with Aviation Jobs Online and you'll instantly have the beginnings of a powerful job search—24 hours a day, seven days a week.

Self-proclaimed as "the only site on the Internet that maintains a current airline directory which includes minimum qualifications," Aviation Jobs Online is your complete employment source. Although site navigation leaves a bit to be desired (plan on lots of scrolling), informative topics abound. There are free and member-ship-only areas, special offers and contests, a Book Store, AvJobs Business Directory, Aviation News Now, free job posting for employees, and more.

After you get through the hard sell areas, you'll find that these folks are serious about aviation jobs with their resourceful personnel service. They'll help with re-sumes, finding articles on specific companies, and help to prepare you for the job interview.

Automatic e-mail updates, over 2000 links, Zip Code Weather, and Electronic Post Office round out the site's cool creations.

Fee or Free: Fee-related. Many fee options are available—see site for details.

Find A Pilot

http://www.findapilot.com

e-mail: webmaster@findapilot.com

RATING

+ + +

BRIEFING:

Meet the no-frills, yet focused employment matchmakers at Find A Pilot.

Fee or Free: Fee-oriented services available.

With a few years of success under its Web belt, Find A Pilot takes the active with its own cyber-version of online employment exchanges. The site seems to avoid any gratuitous visual pleasantries—skipping right to the meat of the matter. It's all about jobs and aviation pros. Period. No dreary news. No QuickTime flybys or audio oddities. Serious aero hunters will appreciate the fluff-free focus. It's refreshing.

A similar text-based menu springs up everywhere, giving even frantic job searchers easy maneuverability. The occupation-only offerings for position shopping pilots include a jobs listing area, where employers are invited to post free listings, and fee-oriented services of resume posting. Personal "home page resumes" include your choice of background colors or wallpaper, multiple category listings, user defined links, and free unlimited updates!

Employers shopping for new recruits will enjoy free position posting and handy pilot searching tools. View the resume database (although a tad thin as of review time, watch for a quick increase in volume) alphabetically or sort by job type. Listings are categorized into: airline, avionics tech, cockpit crew, corporate, flight instructor, ground crew, helicopter, management, mechanic, reservation/ticket agent, seaplane and others.

Airline Employment Assistance Corps (AEAC)

http://www.aeac.net

e-mail: info@aeac.com

RATING

BRIEFING:

A resourceful fee-oriented aviation career counselor. You'll find (or fill) that long-awaited aviation position with help from the AEAC people.

You've hung out long enough down at your local airport. Face it, you'll need to get a little more serious if you're going to find an aviation job. But, hold on to your headset, the Airline Employment Assistance Corps is your new online resource. Although the name would imply airline only, there's room here for any career in aviation.

This lofty employment service provides a long list of helpful categories: worldwide classified ads; resume resources (post your own here, or get resume help from pros); an industry look at opportunities (titles, salary ranges, education requirements, and employers); airport careers; aviation and maintenance careers; air traffic controllers; aviation safety inspectors; flight attendant careers; government aviation careers; pilots and flight engineers; salary relocation calculator; and a host of aviation-related links.

Because this is a professionally maintained employment site, a membership fee is required. If you're really an aviation job seeker, the value here is obvious.

Fee or Free:
Some free areas, but membership gives you access to everything.

Aviation/Aerospace Jobs Page
(NationJob Network)

http://www.nationjob.com/aviation

e-mail: njsales@nationjob.com

RATING

+ + + + +

BRIEFING:

Looking for aviation employment? This FREE, professional service does the job.

Offered up by the huge employment resource, NationJob Network, aviation opportunities abound here. Access an endless sea of jobs one of two ways: either click on home page logo icons for some big name industry leaders (Boeing, Learjet, Raytheon Aircraft, Cessna, The Nordam Group, Thomson Saginaw, etc.), or search through jobs listed here by location, position type, salary, keyword, and more. Simply click on an appealing job in the lineup. From there, you gain access to a company profile as well as an enlightening job description. Most likely you'll be overwhelmed by the variety of categories. Positions range from flight test engineers to buyers, and from A&P service mechanics to vice presidents of operation.

Even if you're not thrilled with the arduous task of sifting through these nationwide listings, just ask "P.J. Scout" to do it for you automatically. This convenient little feature makes employment hunting effortless with an e-mail notification service. Simply enter your job preferences and e-mail address. "P.J. Scout" will search the furthest reaches of the Web and find jobs that match your parameters. He reports to your e-mail weekly. It's free, confidential, and cool.

Fee or Free: Free.

Bookmarkable Listings

FAA Aviation Education—Resource Library
http://www.faa.gov/education/resource.htm#career
e-mail: julie.a.seltsam@faa.dot.gov
Downloadable documents with insightful employment info.

Av Canada
http://www.syz.com/avcanada
e-mail: avcanada@syz.com
International aviation employment services.

Corporate Pilot
http://www.corporatepilot.com
e-mail: contact_us@corporatepilot.com
Matching corporate aviation flight departments with pilots
and mechanics.

AeroTrek
http://www.fivesticks.com/aerotrek
e-mail: aerotrek@ix.netcom.com
Contact information database of over 5,500 operators from
major airlines to small freight companies.

Corporate Aviation Resume Exchange
http://scendtek.com/care
e-mail: sti@scendtek.com
Employment bulletin board of resumes for corporate aviation
professionals.

Universal Pilot Application Service
http://www.upas.com/
e-mail: Webmaster@upas.com
Extensive pilot database offers exposure to position-seeking
pilots and qualified pilot info to employers.

Airline Pilot Job Update
http://www.flyingjobs.com
e-mail: info@allatps.com
Promo site for the monthly airline hiring newsletter, *Airline
Pilot Job Update.*

Index

G

Glider 110, 204, 318
Global Positioning System (GPS) 56, 169, 179, 217, 249, 268, 278, 279

H

Helicopter 56, 61, 66, 73, 93, 103, 115, 187, 215, 237, 248, 250, 290, 297, 303, 335
Homebuilt 179, 209, 224, 240, 245

M

Meteorology 48, 57, 125, 130, 138, 184, 189
Mooney 253, 261

N

Navigation 58, 84, 116, 167, 183, 184, 197, 287, 308
Navy 98, 115, 293

P

Piper 261, 285

R

Radio-controlled 61, 66, 92

S

Safety 12, 34, 63, 87, 101, 102, 107, 108, 143, 144, 162, 163, 165, 172, 193, 195, 199, 201, 209, 212, 216, 219, 221, 226, 229, 235, 242, 245, 293, 309, 336
Soaring 56, 103, 107, 204, 318
Space 165, 210, 212, 230, 239, 242, 243, 244, 245, 305, 309, 327

U

U.S. Air Force 75, 89, 115, 236, 330

W

Women in aviation 65, 70, 81, 85, 86, 187, 309

About the Author

Merging his eight-year private pilot experience with almost twelve years of corporate marketing management, John Merry owns Specialized Marketing Agency—an aviation marketing company, offering online promotion, Web design, and traditional marketing consultation.

In addition to authoring two prior editions of this book, Mr. Merry has written many Web-related aviation articles for such publications as *Plane & Pilot* magazine, *Inflight USA*, and *Plane & Pilot News*. Memberships include the Pilots International Association and Aviation Owners and Pilots Association.